RACIST ANIMAL CRACKERS
ON STEROIDS

22 Plus Years of Cruel & Unusual Punishment BOOK 1

Published By: Roy Snell

TABLE OF CONTENTS

INTRODUCTION

This collection of 24 letters spans over twenty years, with the first in 2002 to present, documenting a deeply personal and painful journey through terrorism, discrimination, intimidation, professional roadblocks, complex sabotage, racism, community terrorism and at times physical violence to brutal violence. It is not a recounting of events, but a reality of what happens when the Management gives the orders, knowing police have Qualified Immunity, leaving the police to stand on "HEY", I am just following orders, take it up with the Management, and The Management don't have to see the vandalism of my life, and the Police don't have to feel guilty about maiming and vandalizing my life, when their just following orders. At the end of the day, both have plausible deniability. All you need to understand is that an order was given. It's a proxy war that was signed by the Management and carried out by Satan, Satan's Sympathizers and Coons to achieve its goal by any means necessary. Race soldiers go where their directed. My story begins in an academic setting, where Animal Crackers prejudices seeped into interactions with peers and professors, leading to experiences that undermined both my education, self-worth and safety.

What began as isolated incidents in academic settings, soon grew into a relentless series of conflicts to eventually community terrorism, following me from classrooms to workplaces, everywhere in society. In restaurants, offices of all kinds, landlords, tenants, grocery stores, laundromat, stores malls and several workplaces. I encountered relentless harassment from nasty threats to outright aggression. There were tons of day's incidents after incidents where employee and supervisors engaged in acts meant to intimidate, silence, or even harm me. Animal Cracker violence, whether verbal, emotional, vicious sabotage, or physical, was compounded by a system that consistently were the real perpetrators, by being active participants in my oppression. Each job brought new confrontations, and each new workplace seemed to echo the same bitter truths, that individuals would go to great lengths to enforce the boundaries of Animal Crackerism, no matter the cost to my soul. My countless appeals for fairness and justice brought great laughter, and blaming me for everything, I fought not only for my own soul, but also for the hope that exposing these truths might spark change. This collection of letters is an indictment of the pervasive unapologetic Animal Cracker injustices that persist in society, and the mental strength required to endure Satan.

Each letter serves as a record of my resolve to stand against forces determined to break my spine, from a failed system that was supposed to protect you. My story is also one of resilience amidst a concerted effort to silence me, a true testament to the enduring struggle for justice in the face of overwhelming community terrorism. But despite the overwhelming forces against me, this book is a testament to my relentless hope. In the face of intimidation, systemic terrorism, racism and isolation, I continued to document my truths. Spoiler Alert, after 8 years of terrorism, I retaliated by telling on the police manufacturing drugs on the biggest level. They were swimming in corruption but are allowed to lie and set you up. This is what happens when you let devils be the validators of truth and injustice, you get injustice.

"A-Shift" Redneck...the Beast Within

English 101-184: College Writing

May 16, 1999

I hope that I didn't have to look at his face for too long. I hoped that he had called in. I stopped to look at my watch. The time was 6:45 a.m., and it was about time for the Beast to make his presence through the solid, steel doors of Parlec.

I started working for my employer three months ago. Parlec, Route 31F in Fairport, located in the middle of the country, is one of the world's leading manufacturers of building toolholders. The company is known to train their employees to be great machinists fast and well, like Navy SEALs training for World War Three. That's why I chose to work there. I have had bad luck in the past with companies downsizing and insufficient training. I was going to bite the bullet and enroll in an apprentice program for half the pay just to get the experience I needed to excel. Working for Parlec is like being in an apprentice program with decent pay. The only thing that wasn't appealing about my position was that I would have to work the C shift. Working the C shift isn't all that bad. It's adapting to the time change on the weekends that's hard to get used to.

Upon my arrival at Parlec, I was warned by co-workers about whom to stay away from, whom to trust, whom not to say too much around, and whom not to listen to, etc. I let negative advice go in one ear and out the other and give everyone a fair shake in life, like a high school football coach scouting his team to see who has made the final cut. I listen to co-workers bad mouth other co-workers and I tell myself that there are three sides to a story – their side, the other person's side, and the truth. What's the truth, I ask myself. I would have to find out as time takes its toll.

In general, Parlec is a great place to work. All the negatives that I have heard turned out to be false. I believe that it is the negativity in a person's life that makes them feel the way they do. There was one truth to what I heard and saw with my own eyes. It was the legacy of the Beast that roamed Parlec. The Beast has a reputation for being an A-hole, working people to the extreme, being one-sided and fabricating stories, or just plain lying to upper management to get people out the door and fired. That's what he's trying to do to me. The Beast uses the company's black and white logbook (located in all the workstations) to write down things about me. Most things he wrote about didn't need to be in there. He complained about how I didn't clean up my area well, how my set-ups weren't good enough, how I should have changed the tooling, how there wasn't enough oil in the machine to his liking, how my product wasn't good, and he tried hard to find something wrong, so the product could be rejected by the quality control department. He would write things in the logbook so sincerely that if read slowly enough, one could tell that he was crying when he wrote it.

I remember the first time I saw the Beast. I was working at my workstation, just finishing up a great night when all of a sudden, I got this cold tingling feeling down my spine that sent shock waves throughout my entire body like lightning hitting an electrical outlet. I turned around to see why I was so disturbed. I could never have prepared myself for what I was about to see.

There was the Beast himself. There stood before my very eyes a big, tall pile of human carcass. His face stuck out like a sore thumb. One could see that when he smiled, his face cracked and peeled, like that of a baby chicken hatching from their eggshell. With his eyes, small and beady, you knew you weren't looking at a man, but that of a coward. His forehead was wide and sloped out, like that of Robocop. His ears were long and pointy, like that of Spock from Star Trek.

As the days passed, I deliberately ignored the Beast, but his presence was so strong it would ooze through the air, find its way to my workstation, and linger throughout the establishment. I soon watched him with the curiosity of a child at the circus. At first, I noticed the way he dragged hard on his Marlboro pack of cigarettes. Then he would roll up the pack in his T-shirt sleeve. I saw a long dog chain extending from his front pocket to his back pocket, holding his wallet. I observed that he wore his Wrangler jeans so tight that one could see a gap of sunlight between his legs when he walked. Today, the Beast and I are still in conflict. He still lies in the logbook and craves authority like a dog in the basement waiting to be let out so he can eat. One could tell that he must have been a neglected, battered child growing up – getting nothing for Christmas, having no friends, only cornfields and his pet frog.

PREJUDICE STINKS

English 101-184: College Writing

May 17, 1999

My perception of prejudice falls into three categories: physical, ethnic/cultural, and social. Prejudice to me is unfair and wrong. When a person is prejudiced, he or she is making preconceived notions about people based on outward signs such as looks. When you are prejudiced, you are missing out on possible opportunities and what life has to offer. When you meet or see someone, you first notice his or her skin color and skin tone. I am an African American with a medium complexion. Within my race, we have dark-skinned and lighter-skinned complexions. My observations and experience have led me to believe that if I were dark-skinned, I would get treated a little more unfairly than if I were light-skinned, not only by those in my race but also outside my race. Spanish people have the same problem. When a Spanish person is white in skin color, they are treated better than other Spanish that are dark. Look at Spain, for instance, the Spaniards don't like the Spanish people from Puerto Rico. And why? Because Spaniards are mostly all white-skinned versus the Spanish people in Puerto Rico who are light, medium-dark, and dark in color. After a person is evaluated on their skin color, the focus of attention is on the person's physical attributes. People immediately judge a person on whether they are fat or skinny. Men always look at a woman's curves, breasts, and buttocks when they get a chance when she isn't looking. The same holds true for women, except they are slyer about it. In society, a person is judged by their shape. If a person is too skinny, they are not totally accepted, yet they are not shunned as with the obese person. The media, such as advertisements and television, reinforce that thinking and mindset of a person. After focusing their attention on a person's shape, people start judging the person's other physical characteristics, such as height and facial attributes. In society, there is a double standard for men and women. For men, if you are short, you don't fit in. With a woman, if you're short, it's not looked upon too closely. For women, if you're too tall, you'd better be model material, or you're looked upon as unattractive and lanky. For men, if you're tall, it's good because people look at you as a good basketball player and/or powerful man. People look at every tiny, little detail about a person's appearance. Even how big or small a person's nose is up for scrutiny. People even look at a person's nostrils. They look to see if any hair is coming out of them. They look at how wide, high, or pointy the nose is. They even see if you have any boogers. They look to see if they can see how high the slope is of your nose when you turn to the side. They repeat the same process when it comes to the ears, but instead of looking for nasal mucus, they look for dried caked-up wax in the ear. And if you have big ears with hair growing out of them, forget about it because you have been labeled as the person with the big dumbo ears and that you don't take care of yourself. You're judged repeatedly. People won't tell you their real opinion on how they perceive you, instead, they come on as your friend. They even judge you by the facial hairs on your face. Whether your beard is well-trimmed or bushy, or if you have a Goatee. People look at people with Goatees as a bad boy, versus the man with no hair on his face as a nice, clean-cut guy.

After you get past the physical attributes comes the ethnicity culture of a person's deep prejudice within. You're judged by the clothes you wear. No matter what you wear, someone will criticize you, whether it is to themselves or others. If you are a man and wear your pants too tight, you're perceived to be "gay." If you're a woman, you're perceived to be "easy." If you wear your pants too loose, you're perceived to be a gangster or "wannabe" gangster. When women wear their pants too loose, the perception is that she doesn't care of herself and she's grungy. When women wear short, tight skirts, she's perceived to be a whore. When women wear long dresses, she's perceived to be a lady. A whore can be a nurse, doctor, dentist, astrologist, astronaut, psychologist, biologist, chemist, policewoman, lifeguard, babysitter, and definitely the girl next door. I wish people would get it through their heads that whores come in all shapes and sizes. Just because she wears a short skirt doesn't make her a whore. Just because she is a professional doesn't disqualify her from being a whore.

Education is another area where people are judged. Those with no high school or just a high school diploma will be looked upon more negatively in the job market to social situations. Some women will only date professional or "white collar" men. Some "blue collar" jobs may pay wages similar to the "white collar" ones, yet the perception is that you are valued less as a person because you don't have that "white collar" position. Even where you live and what kind of house you live in is taken into consideration. In our city, the east side of the city is perceived to have more affluent people than the west side. The bigger, better home you live in, the more important you are considered. With wealth and possessions comes more acceptance and influence with people. The more "toys" (e.g., fancy cars, computer systems, stereo systems, jewels, furniture, etc.) you have, you are perceived as successful and, therefore, more worthy of being accepted. It is as though unless you have these things, you're a nobody.

All of these things add to the prejudices people have against one another. All the outward things that aren't important in the long run. What matters is what's inside a person. Their values, morals, personality, and ethics are far more important than any of these outward signs that people seem to value as being all-important. Looks will fade with age, money comes and goes; it's what is inside the person that stays and grows.

If You Look at The Obvious, You Will Fail to See the Evidence.

2002

First letter to MCC that I gave to four professors, and the next day MCC introduced me to the Sheriff's Department

How can one day everything be Yankee Doodle Dandy, and the next, Dark Friday? Why would a person wake up at 3 am to study CNC programming for the past year, and all of a sudden, don't want anything to do with the trade the next day?

How could a person be a loyal servant one day, and have dark thoughts the next day? Rather than looking for the answer, people look at me reacting. I wonder if it's true when one says actions speak louder than words, I guess that depends on who is talking and who is reacting. If you look at the obvious, you would fail to see the evidence. Let's get to the nuts and bolts of things!

So what happened? It's a long story, so I'll start from the beginning. Brian is a racist. When I used to work in the computer lab last September, he used to always look me straight in the eyes with no emotion. Why was that, especially since we hadn't been formally introduced? Pretty much the whole semester was like this back in September. Why didn't I say anything then? It didn't affect me, and I have dealt with lots of people like him in my lifetime. I just ignored him. What can you possibly say to a person like that? Nothing, that's what. So the semester last September went without a problem, and why, he wasn't in any of my classes and the only time I would see him was in the computer lab where I focused all my attention on my programming homework. So where did all the problems come from, or should I say start? As soon as I started working on the ProtoTrak M2 controller in Pat's lab, Brian would give me the same old funny looks and would sometimes lean on my machine when he saw that I was having all the problems in the world with the controller. Stop and think for a second, if you knew that a person was having difficulty learning calculus, why would you lean on that person's table, staring them in the eyes and half smiling at them especially when you and that person haven't even been formally introduced, let alone not even had one conversation? Why would you do this? So what did I do? I told you guys what happened and for the most part, at first, you thought it was funny. Then as time went on, when I told you guys what he was doing, you guys became irritated, in fact, I was even bothering some of you. All my life, I was a person who reacted rather than respond. So for the first time in my life, I was responding rather than reacting. Where did it get me? NOWHERE! I wonder if I had done something like that to one of the students, what would have happened to me? Can you imagine me doing something like this to a young white woman; all hell would have broken loose? So I saw you guys getting annoyed by telling you what he did next, so I didn't say too many more things about this. At least, I tried not to.

So where does Darwin come into play? Easy, when he saw that I gave you guys something, he wanted that something too. So he would hang around my machine, answer my questions and even show me some things on the Proto Trak. Mind you, he was very anxious to show me things for like two days. As soon as I gave him something, he was gone in the wind. Okay, sometimes he would come over to my machine to show me some things, but I had to go and haunt him, and when he came over, he didn't stay for long. Before I gave him something, he was at my machine before I was. He was like a little kid in the playground having fun. So I thought that would continue, but as you guys know, it quickly faded away. Like I said before, he was missing in action after he got what he wanted. So what happened next? I told person "A", I'll just call him person "A", I told person "A" that I wasn't getting the help that I thought I was supposed to be getting and the very next day, Darwin had the meanest face I had ever seen on a teacher's face when we came into eye contact. He even, no lie, yelled half words at me across the room, looking mean as all hell. I know that I told one of the teachers that he swore at me, but if you saw his body language, you would've said the same thing. I could tell my girlfriend that I love her, but if my body language and facial expression are mean as I'm yelling mean things and a low tone, do you actually think my girlfriend would believe me if I told her that I love her? I think not. So what did I do next? I went over to Darwin and asked for his help, and no lie, he waved his hand at me and told me to get away from him. I was devastated. Never in my life had a teacher done this to me. I would've told you guys this way before now, but I didn't because of two reasons. First and foremost, I wanted to learn the Proto Trak at all costs. I felt that if I had said something I would be looked at as the one who was causing problems and you guys wouldn't allow me to enter the lab off my regular schedule. Two, all of you guys get along very well. I didn't want to break the bond you guys had. So, all the yelling and mean faces carried on for about 2–3 days. I couldn't take it any longer, so I walked up to Darwin when he was working on the manual lathe one day and asked him what I had done wrong. He tried to downplay the whole thing by saying he was having a bad day and that I didn't do anything wrong and that he was too focused on other things and not to pay him any attention. So I said, to defuse the whole thing, that sometimes I say things that I don't really mean and that I'm just frustrated with the Proto Trak. I thought that would be the end, but I thought wrong. Every single time I went up to Darwin when Pat was there, and trust me, I made sure Pat was there, I would ask Darwin a programming question, and as soon as Pat left, and I mean as soon as Pat left, Darwin would wave his hand toward my face and told me to get away. How do you think I felt when he was doing this? How can anyone have a can-do attitude when teachers are blowing you off like you're a nobody, a piece of scum, and the dirt under their feet? What effect do you think that had on my overall well-being? Make of that what you will, but everything I just wrote is 1000% true. And what does Darwin do to cover things up? He spins, mingles, tangles, twists, and turns the truth until nothing is there, in the end, what do you know, it's all my fault. Why don't you have Darwin read this and ask him if it is true? Why you're at it, ask him how many times he put his hands in my face to tell me to get away from him. Pat, don't you think it's condescending for Darwin to be nice to me in your face, but as soon as you turn to leave, Darwin looks mean as hell waving his hand in my face? If he was condescending to you with me, what's the probability of him being condescending to you again?

Wait, it gets better. Brian, like I said before, is a racist. Darwin was having a tough time learning the ProtoTrak lathe. So Brian would show Darwin things on the lathe increasing Darwin's career and out of loyalty for Brian, Darwin teamed up with Brian. I know that they would deny that last statement, but it's true. In fact, one time on a Monday, when I was supposed to be in class, from 1:00-3:50 I was at my machine, struggling once again and Brian was over at the lathe helping Darwin, then all of a sudden, Brian looked around Darwin's shoulder and gave me one of those big smiles. Darwin pretended that nothing was happening. Then Brian walked over to where I was, and another teacher was right there, and Brian gave me another big smile. Both teachers to this day haven't said one thing to me around Brian. If he is there, these teachers go out of their way not to say or even look my way. Later on that day, Brian said, out loud indirectly to me, to the other two teachers that he erase all the programs that he created so that other people wouldn't copy his programs. The other teacher, not Darwin, laughed out loud and agreed with Brian. I'll just call this teacher the mystery teacher. Trust me, he knows who he is, because the next day he came into the lab to talk to me about something that wasn't important.

Either he felt guilt for what he did, or he came in there to throw me off, as in big guy, I am on your side. Whatever! To the mystery teacher, I never told anyone your name, just do what Darwin does and distract attention off yourself. I never would've brought this whole thing up, but everyone thinks I am delusional and a class-A liar. I don't want you to get in trouble, trust me, I don't. I am just setting the record straight once and for all. In one sense, you really didn't do anything wrong, but you made me feel really bad for a long time. If things were reversed, how would you have felt? Talking about a stab in the back. I just want to ask you 2 things. One, what type of message do you think you sent to Brian when you showed agreement by laughing and have never said a word around me when he was around, let alone making any type of eye contact with me when Brian was around? Do you know you influenced his racist beliefs and perceptions? Two, do I really look and sound that stupid for you to think that everything you were doing went over my head? I know Brian is increasing your career as well, but to increase your career at the expense of another is like climbing the ladder and stepping on other people's backs to get there. Well done.

So why I'm I so mad? Because those guys have gotten away with murder, and when I finally came to you teachers to tell you exactly what happened, you didn't believe me. And why is that, because I'm off balance when I'm at The Applied Tech that I can't think straight. How can a person think straight when that person has been mentally abused? Can you actually think right if you're mad 24-7? Let's get it straight once and for all, I am not the perpetrator, I am the victim. And what did those guys do to turn the tables? They destroyed my credibility so that no one would listen to me. It's like what I like to call a diversion tactic. Those guys have assassinated my character by distorting the truth until nothing was there. I thought one day that someone would say, "aha", but that "aha" never came. Darwin has deluded people into thinking everything was okay when it wasn't. How could you teachers be so blind to the facts? All Darwin and whoever else was on the bandwagon did was demonize me. It's not hard to do around there, especially since the way I pronounce my words, I'm opinionated, and I told you guys at the wrong time. It's bad timing because I told you guys that I wanted to tell you the whole truth by setting up a meeting. Like I said, bad timing, because you guys think that I'm mad just because of Brian. WRONG! Brian was the last straw. After I gave him what I gave him, he told me that I would be kissing his ass. To me, that was the most racist thing that was ever said to me under the current circumstances. That was just the last straw. Everyone has a breaking point, and that was mine. I even waited two days afterward, trying to make eye contact with Brian in my classes that we both take, he didn't even look at me. He actually wanted me to kiss his ass. The only time he would say anything to me or even look at me was in the lab around you, Pat. Brian would smile as if to say, everything's a-okay, but it wasn't. Condescending just like his buddy Darwin and the mystery teacher. Those guys should run for office one day, at least they would be in good company.

Dear Darwin, I love how you twisted, melted down, and evaporated the truth by demonizing me to the teachers and students. Very clever. I know what you told them. You told them what I said about the dollar bill and the Masons. It's irrelevant that you don't believe it because some teachers go as far as to say everyone should know. Anyway, I love how you can have limited skills and still get a job at the college and live off of other teacher's and student's knowledge. I don't know how you did it, but hey, stranger things have happened. I wonder how you feel watching all the material I presented and demonizing me in return. Keep up the good job, because history has shown that one can go to the top with that value system you have embedded in yourself. I know where I went wrong with you. I told you that I knew this and that, this about the computer and that about this, and you hated that. Like most. I could say $5+5=9$, and a person like you would say, that's incorrect, try again. If I told you that $a2 +b2=c2$, you would have a fit. By the way, why did you walk up to Brian when both of us were at the ProtoTrak Lathe shook his hand, and asked what was going on. I wonder why you did that? Don't you see Brian every day? Were you trying to send me indirect messages? Or maybe you were just in a good mood that day. That and what Brian did was the last straw!

Whatever happened to the student-teacher-confidentiality? Brian knows just about everything I have ever said to you teachers in general. Why is that? If I can't confide in an authority figure like a teacher, then who can I? I know some of the things I have said have been hard to take in. I didn't intend to play with one's value system, because God knows that it's the hardest thing to change in a person. I am truly sorry for this. I was just in amazement and wanted to know what a bright mind thought, that's all.

So how is my semester going? Not good. I can't

think clearly when I am mad 24-7. Can you imagine taking a test when you found out that your wife had been cheating on you with your brother all the while you were at work? That's how I feel 24-7. Then to not have you guys believe me, just adds to the stressed-out dark thoughts. Let me say once in for all, I wouldn't say anything about you know what. It's not about that, it's never been about that. IT'S ABOUT RESPECT! This is supposed to be an institution, not a vigilante against me. I am being ostracized for what other people have done. I know you teachers think that I have bitten the hand that has fed them by giving me that scholarship, but in return, I can say the same thing. One day I hope to pay you guys back for the scholarship to prove to you guys that it wasn't about that. If it's the last thing that I do, I will pay you back.

So what is my point to all of this? Those guys got away with murder, period. Brian is a racist, and some of the teachers influenced his behavior. Can you imagine me as a teacher doing something like this and getting away with it? If I were a teacher and gave just one mean look to a student, my ass would have gotten tossed out the door before someone could say ready set bye, bye. What say you? There is no statute on murder in this country, and there shouldn't be a statute on teachers behaving in the way they did towards me! Just like murderers, if they kill once, they kill again, and why? They feel a surge of power once they kill. It's like a high!

ROCON MANUFACTURING

December 29, 2004

Dear Mr. Paul:

I would like to let you know that I feel that I was terminated unjustifiably. I am writing this to you to give you the facts that happened, since there was no real investigation. Before I explain what happened in detail, I would like to go back in time to when I first started working for your company. I am talking about the altercation I got in with James. I never to this day knew that things would escalate the way they did. A couple of days before our altercation, Mike, James' uncle, came up to me and said that he was going to get a bunch of his friends to come up to the job dressed up as Klan men and scare me to death. As soon as the words finished from his mouth, I said out loud, "CHARLIE." As I was walking toward Charlie, Mike followed close behind me. I informed Charlie that Mike had just told me that he was going to get a bunch of his friends all dressed up as Klan men to scare me. Mike tried to put some honey on the situation by saying he was just joking around with me. Charlie said in almost a soft tone to Mike, "Don't say things like that anymore, and that it wasn't nice." In my opinion, Charlie should have been firmer with him. He should have said something like, "We don't play that around here and if you say something like that again I'll guarantee that you won't work here anymore." And the next day he should have written him up. Mike is the kind of person who listens to Michael Savage and takes the dark things that Savage says to fuel his hate against you. By Charlie not being firm with Mike, the situation gave Mike the opening he craved. Mike literally transformed James with all the hateful perceptions Savage is spitting. Every single day, before the altercation, Mike and his new first-round draft pick James would ask me why black people do this, that, wear this, that, listen to this, that, drive this, that, and everything under the sun. So I told those guys that I didn't want to be a part of their little investigation and the next couple of days, Mike came up to me when I was working on 18, and said the Klan statement to me. And a couple of days after that, I was in the lunchroom taking my break, Mike and James were sitting together when James called me a fat fuck across the table. Your daughter had just entered the room, so I got up and left. I left for two reasons - one, your daughter just came in there and two, I didn't want to get double-teamed in such a tight confined place like in the lunchroom with all the chairs and utensils up there. After the break, I went up to him when no one else was around, and I said to him that I was a man before I was an employee and to watch what he said to me. At that point, James pushed me so hard that you would think a car had fallen on him. We then started fighting and when Charlie touched me on the shoulder I stopped IMMEDIATELY. All the other employees who witnessed this verified this. Before that fight, it has been at least 5 years since my last fight. Mike was a flaming racist who motivated his nephew into his little world of hate. You guys even admitted it to me. Over the phone and in the office, Bruce asked me did I think James was racist. I said no, but Mike on the other hand is. He agreed with me. I have one question, suppose Charlie would have been firmer with Mike and written him up, do you think James and I would have had an altercation? Loud and nasty, that's the only way it sticks. By Charlie not being firm with Mike, Mike thought in his mind that he had permission and the right to do what he wanted. Mike's mind is like rain beading down on a roof, looking for a crack to get into the interior to destroy and collapse your ceiling.

So what happened this time? Take my hand and walk with me. There are things I should have learned in school but didn't know that most of the guys know. They don't respect me for that and put their intelligence in front of mine openly and indirectly. A man dies once; a coward dies a thousand times. How many times do you think I have died around there? Anyway, six months ago, I had problems with Jeff that almost led to an altercation. He and another employee were going to double-team me in the parking lot, but nothing ever came of it. People thought Jeff and the other guy were scaredy-cats. That fact has never left Jeff. So Jeff under your noses got two of his friends a job there, John and Jarred. I let Jarred borrow a music CD. The next day, he came to work without saying a word to me all day. I knew something was wrong, so I didn't bother asking. I figure he just wanted to be alone in his thoughts that night. So I didn't entertain his thoughts and crowd his space. That night, when I went out to my car, I saw the CD that I let Jarred borrow stuffed tightly in my driver-side window. I didn't know what to think, but the way the CD was left so tightly in my window, I knew that Jarred had a problem with me. The next day Friday, December 17th I walked up to Jarred and asked him if we were still cool and why he left the CD in my window like that, marring the surface and destroying the CD. He said we could talk about this outside on break if I had a problem. Just when he was saying this, Jeff was walking by. I waved Jeff over and when he approached, I said, "I didn't know that I had beef with you guys." Jeff said something like, "Now isn't the time to talk about this" while Jarred stood there looking at me intimidatingly, nodding his head. I just left. The only thing I had on my mind was taking my finals, so I could finish out my degree. I had to change the rougher inserts on 18, so I walked towards the direction of the tool crib and noticed that Jeff and Jarred were in my path. Jeff was working on the machine by the water fountain and Jarred was there talking to him. I said to myself, "Let me try this again." I said to Jeff and Jarred, "Look, man, I don't have a problem with you guys or anyone in this company." Jeff said that he and the other guy weren't going to double-team me six months ago to fuck off and to get the fuck out of his face and leave his work area. Jeff has never talked to me like this before. Now that Jeff has two of his friends working there, he has something like an S on his chest. So I said fuck you too. That's when Jarred looked around, turned to the side, and reached into his pocket. I backed away and asked him if he had that knife. (One day we worked together, and I was trying to rip open a box with my hands, and Jarred pulled out this black sharp, sharp knife that looked like something Crocodile Dundee would have approved of. I asked him why he carried a knife, and he said that he was a little guy). He looked at me very boldly and said no. I got out of there. I went to the tool crib, got my rougher inserts, and went back to 18. About an hour or two later Jeff came back there where I was working to work, I think, on the twins in the corner. So this put us both a lot closer together. I didn't say anything to him, and he didn't say anything to me. The problem was, that Jarred came back there to talk to Jeff about a hundred times, bypassing my machine and slowly looking at me intimidatingly. Look at my production output on Friday the 17th, low huh? I didn't know if Jarred was going to stick me with that knife he had in his pocket, so I would look around, load a part, look around, unload a part, look around, stone the part, look around, deburr the part, look around and check the part all night long. At lunchtime, I had two employees escort me outside because I wanted them to see what was going on, and I didn't know if they had called their buddies. Just about everyone was in their car parked looking to see if something would happen. There were people out there waiting in their cars that never take a break in their cars, mind you, it was very, very cold out that night. One employee said it was too cold, so he went back in. The other employee said he had to get his coat. I followed him into the building because his coat was at the other end of the building. Just when he got his coat, Jeff was at the other end of the building with both his hands in his jacket looking at me as in, here we are, what's up? The employee that I was with who went in for his jacket said, "Hey, look at how Jeff is staring and looking at you." Then Jeff disappeared. I waited for about two minutes to stall for time and when I and the other employee got outside I got in my car without warming it up and took off to go and get Chinese food. I kept replaying over and over in my mind how important it was for me to take my finals that following Monday. After lunch, Jarred would walk by my machine more frequently and when our eyes hit he would half smile, intimidating stare me down. I think there were 5 or 6 employees that left at 1 am. I left around 1:30 and when I went out to my car, there was spit all over my windshield. All those guys clocked out at the same time. Do you mean to tell me that no one saw anything, especially since my car was parked in front of the building in the middle? I just left, went home, took a shower, and tried to block it out of my mind by studying for an hour then went on to bed.

On Monday, December 20, I thought about what was going to happen to me at work that night when I was supposed to be thinking about my test. I could barely study, but somehow I pulled it together and passed. I arrived home around 5:10 p.m. and when I got in the door, I just sat down in my living room for about 45 minutes thinking about what I was going to do about work. I didn't know what to really do, but something inside me said to call your supervisor idiot. I did. I called Charlie and told him the whole story from start to finish. If you don't believe me, look at your phone records with my telephone number. I called between 6:00 p.m. and 6:30 p.m. and talked for around 10 minutes. In fact, I called two times because the first time no one answered. I hung up and called back, and that's when Charlie picked up. We talked for around 10 minutes and about a half hour later to 45 minutes after I arrived at work. Think for a second, why would a person (regular employee) call work talk for 10 minutes to his supervisor then clock in half an hour/45 minutes later? I think someone is lying to you. Don't you think that if I just called Charlie to tell him that I would be in, that phone call would have lasted under a minute? When I told David Storie that Jarred had a knife, he said, "Why didn't you tell anyone about this before, why are you telling this now?" I said, "I did say something, I called Charlie and told him the whole story and especially about the knife." At that point David Storie,

Bruce Wahl, Keith Denton, and Luccioni turned their heads so fast to look at Charlie, I am surprised they didn't get whiplash. Charlie looked cool as all hell and said that it wasn't true and there wasn't any knife. How convenient. Can you say liar liar pants on fire? So I punched in and went to work. Jarred and I worked in the same cell that night. I did everything possible to not look at him without turning my back on him. I parked in the back parking lot to let them know that I wasn't going to be treated like some battered housewife. Nothing happened that night, I guess they didn't have that knife on them. They even ate their lunch upstairs. I thought that would be the end of it, but Tuesday when I came in, I could tell Jarred had that Crocodile Dundee knife on him because he was back to looking at me, as in, what do you think it's over? I didn't say anything to him at first, and when I went to change my roughers he looked at me up and down with that smirk on his face. I walked over to him and said, "If you have anything to say to me, say it outside." When I came back from changing my tools, Jeff and Jarred looked at me both very seriously nodding their heads and saying "Okay you wait" I said "I have something for that knife too". To tell you the truth, this is embarrassing, but I planned to mace them if they had attacked me with the knife then call the police. I had my cell phone on me the whole time. The way I see it is 3 against one and maybe 4 against one. By the way, if you haven't figured it out, Jarred is ghetto and on the ghetto side of life. I know he is a small fellow, trust me, I know this. Jarred is the kind of person that can hang on the street corner with our city's worst. The average car goes by that street corner and sees Jarred; people think to themselves that those black men on that corner must be pushing Jarred around behind the scenes. Not me. I think to myself, what has Jarred done before, he did something to get the respect of those thugs. Any fights I was every in were with people larger than me. I don't need to fight people I outweigh by a hundred pounds. How can I call myself a man and live off of that esteem? An hour later, Charlie came up to me and said, "I need to talk to you, Jarred, and Jeff." (By the way, Jeff read my letter a while ago and is using my own letter against me to vilify me in his and Jarred's favor to make a case. I didn't see that coming). Upstairs, Jeff and Jarred were lying as if for every lie that they told, they would win what's behind curtain number one. Jarred admitted staring at me all the time. Charlie said that wasn't a bad thing, next. I said, "Jarred, at least admit that you were going to pull out a knife." Jeff, not Jarred, said he was pulling up his pants. Then Jarred jumped in and said, "No one can do anything to me for carrying my knife on the side of my belt," making it sound like a simple Boy Scout fishing knife. Charlie said, next. I said, "Jarred, tell Charlie how you invited me outside." Jarred said, "Oh I didn't mean outside, I meant I'll talk to you later on my break because I have to get some work done". Charlie said, next. That tree clubhouse meeting lasted for no longer than five minutes, with Jarred and Jeff high-fiving each other. And when I came in the next day, Charlie came up to me with termination papers. I tried to talk to David Storie, but he wouldn't let me get a word in.

I'm upset that I was terminated without a full investigation. Remember that I gave your staff the knowledge and how-to's to make most of the machines run a lot faster. I didn't even ask for anything in return, but just not to get laid off when the layoff came around. You have a lot of men around here who are ex-crackheads and ex-junkies, and some are still in practice. Let me just say, that I don't have a problem treating them like a person, a man, and a human being, but they want you to treat them like the Pope. I do have a problem with that. By the way, it's common knowledge that Charlie had a problem in this area in the past. And speaking of drugs, some employees grow marijuana and sell it to people who work there during working hours. One of these employees told me he made over $143,000 last year. I asked him why he worked there, he said, "Dude this job is just a front." As you can see, some of your men don't need a job. I need mine. When I left work, I came home, and it was a car in the ditch on the complex grounds, rather than getting out to help, which I love to help my neighbors out because one never knows when you might need them. I just drove off. Add that to the list of people who think that I am a bad person.

Have you ever seen that commercial by Capital One when the couple pulls out their credit card and Vikings come from everywhere, ram shacking the place? That is exactly how people act around there when you're not firm with them. Charlie has it out for me because I told him that I was aware of the role he played back in September, which he admitted. I was fired because Charlie withheld important evidence. I told him everything on December 20th between the hours of 6:00 p.m. -6:30 p.m., check the phone records. By the way, I will take a lie detector test on ANYTHING I have stated in this letter as well as anything I wrote in the past.

I need another job making $615 to $700 weekly, which is what I was making with you. Please contact one of your many friends and let them know, and you won't hear from me again. What happens in Rochester stays in Rochester.

MONROE COMMUNITY COLLEGE

June 9, 2005

Mr. Richard Ryther
Associate Vice President
Monroe Community College
1000 E. Henrietta Road
Rochester, NY 14623

Dear Mr. Ryther:

The reason for writing this letter is to secure a job so that I can pay off my $20 thousand student loan, cleanse my mind, and rest all the speculation. You wanted me to write you a letter back in September. This is my story with perfume on it. As you will see, I don't have things upside down. So why am I so mad? Because the obvious has happened. I got mugged of my education, which has littered my future with low income and all sorts of problems at work. One can say that my degree is counterfeit, make-believe, and pretend. Practice no study equals experience, study no practice equals theory. In my opinion, if not fact, my field isn't about intelligence, it's all about experience, actually getting your hands dirty and doing tasks. The only thing that is about intellect is programming and the math aspect of things.

Machinist skills were supposed to have been ingrained in me, but were not. All the other students that have my degree are seasoned with this skill. They're like the Delta Force Elite. All students in the United States with my degree belong to this elite machinist group, or at the very least, have a good handle on things. ALL STUDENTS. Those guys are living in or soon to be living in paradise without any fuss. The teachers can't even tell you that I am an okay machinist. Sad, but true. I'm not talking about a Liberal Arts degree. I'm talking about a degree whose main ingredient is machining skills. Like raisin bread, the main ingredient isn't raisins, it's flour. I am a chef who has read over 1,000 cookbooks without baking. How do you think I will get along with the other chefs in the kitchen when I am supposed to be a world-class chef with his papers from France University? Can you at least admit that I will be talked about by other chefs? It's like learning to be a surgeon without operating on a patient. I am like a cigarette without a light. Other machinists look at me without substance. My skills are foolish, and I look incompetent and stupid. That being said, how could I be gentle, calm, peaceful, and relaxed in general? Do you think other machinists would accept me as a member? Or do you think they would cut me from the team by throwing me back in the pile with all the other wannabes? My skills are discredited the first day most times, certainly the first week when I start a new job.

People are always tugging on my shirt sleeve asking me "What do you know," "What is it then," I thought you were supposed to know certain things like the fundamentals of machining and actually performing certain tasks without help, questions, and in a timely fashion. One could make the argument that I forgot, but the first time I ever touched oxygen and acetylene and an Arc welder was in 1992. That's a hard skill to learn. I haven't touched a welder since 1994, but could pick back right up where I almost left off if I had to. Fundamentals included. Not good at Tig and Mig. Even though I did it a couple of times, but that was just for a test. The sad thing about it is, that I never once had a job welding. Let's back up for a second. If the college hired a secretary for your office from the most prestigious university that specializes in typing, you would expect her to be an efficient typist. You wouldn't expect her to type with just her index fingers and forget most of the keyboard placement. You know there will be some kind of dispute and bickering among the other secretaries. Look at a cop, for instance. A cop could read a million books on being a cop, but if that cop does what the book tells him to do without hands-on training from another cop, the likelihood that the cop will be shot is high. After reading this letter, you will see that I'm the cop who has been shot due to the police academy and a lack of hands-on training by officers and sergeants. It's a perfect recipe for disaster.

Call me nuts, but I anticipated and expected to make a decent income, like all my classmates with my degree and people who have just a certificate. I have accomplished really nothing. Why do I have to keep lying to people and explaining why I haven't got this skill? With my skills being the way they are, if a person is nice they aren't as nice as they appear, if they're mean, they're meaner to me, if they're racist, their racist belief has a way of seeping out at times, and sometimes it turns into a flood. Like a baby walking around nude in front of a child molester. Because the child molester has a big appetite and inner cravings, he will attack that baby. Who's at fault? Someone could make the argument that it's the parent's fault, but child molesters are predators. Some could make the argument that I look for and confront racism. That's the farthest thing from the truth. I am only concerned with it when it's directed towards me, and especially by predators. In short, I am missing the main ingredient and EVERYONE knows it. Including every job that I worked for, ask away. Better yet, look at my social security number because some jobs are not on my resume. There aren't any of them that will tell you that

I am a good machinist. What they will tell you is that I am a great operator who makes lots of parts, which basically means that I press the green button more times than the average person. How can I be in harmony and agreement with the rest of the other workers? I used to be in those manuals like I was a mechanic, and where did it get me? Can you say booby-trapped? As a result, I'm perceived to be the village idiot when it comes to machining at work.

What about specific happenings?

1.   My back was turned to people most of the time.
2.   I only trammed the table on the mill once or twice within a semester the whole time I went there.
3.   Never able to grind form tools on the grinder.
4.   I haven't been on a manual lathe since 1997.
5.   I didn't finish all my projects back in 1995 and 1997 but got credit for doing so.
6.   I got an A in all the machining labs that I'm talking about.
7.   All the projects I did and handed in to get credit from the Proto Trak Mill were just profiles, just simple outlines about .020 deep. Altogether I did around ten profiles and spent the rest of the time trying to get used to the controller's math function.
8.   Never did one project in the spring of 2003 that I got credit for (TAM 255 Comp Aided Mfg Lab). It's funny how I received a D rather than an A, huh? Back in the spring of 2002, Mr. Brandon asked me to square a little blue plastic block. It took me half an hour to get started, and I still didn't know what to exactly do. One of the teachers ``Ray" came into the lab and squared it up in less than five minutes. All the while explaining to me what he was doing, but fast, because he was in a hurry and

Mr. Brandon was waiting for the square block so he could use it on an engraving machine in his lab. My point, if they did not know that I was a good machinist, they knew at that point that I wasn't a machinist who knew what to do with the most basic machining operations in the world. So what did they do, they told me that I could come in with the regular class in the summer. That my name wouldn't be on the list, just come in. The problem was it was too late. All I could think about was all the evil things that happened to me that previous semester. So as a result, I didn't go most of the time. One could make the argument that it's all my fault. I needed to regroup, you know, shake it off. I endured enough torture, attacks, and torment for one semester that I could handle, and I had my fill.

9.   There's not one student who could tell you that I'm an okay machinist. If someone tracks down a student who says I am, ask them what I made, and how I did it. Better yet, give them a lie detector test.

10. In 1997, I re-took shop practice. I told one of the teachers that I was excited about taking the class again, and since everyone was new to him, if he would come over to my machine more. He said that he couldn't and that I was going to have to be on my own, that he would come over on occasion, as in sprinkled throughout the semester. Most of the time I got frustrated and left. I already knew what my grade was going to be anyway, since I got an A the last time I took the course.

11. What machinist do you know who used to spend day and night searching for CNC instructional videos? Most machinists couldn't care less about an instructional video. Why? Because they're already making the big bucks doing what I was

trying to learn. The only people who really care are instructors, companies, and beginners. Why would a person who has been in the field for almost 10 years now, search religiously for CNC/machining videos? Don't I have anything else to do, like read emails, play games, and chat online, but videos, something doesn't add up. Think for a second, how could I have all these videos and still complain about my lack of skills in machining? I know, maybe I'm insane. I read somewhere that said the definition of insanity is doing the same thing over and over and expecting different results. So I knew that it was going to be an uphill battle for me, so I did something different by tracking down instructional videos to get the knowledge that I needed. So people can't say I'm insane because I did something different, check!!!

12.   These events that I just wrote about are very specific. As in, do you have that in a size 10? Yes, we do Sir, good, send one to my address. To be completely fair about things, every time I took the lab classes (I'm talking about the main artery) the classes were full. The teachers liked me and all, but really catered to the bright students who were working on the cool projects, and most of the other students knew one another or teamed up together to become one as in a group. A group that I wasn't welcome in. Trust me, I wanted to work with them, but it seemed like they were always too busy and working on the next project. Somehow, I got lost in the fog.

Most of the time I have to flat-out lie to companies to get my foot into the door. My rationale, once they see my work habits, good attendance, and have been to school they won't fire me. But, when things get slow, owners have to cut costs somewhere. So what do you think will happen? They let go of their less skilled workers. And since everything in this field is based on supply and demand, you can see where I fit in. I interview with companies, and they take me around their shops. I show and explain to them the CNC controllers (from my instructional videos) and for the most part they are impressed. But when they ask me simple things about machining, I usually get it wrong. Their eyes get all wide, they turn their heads to the side and make believe that I was nervous and assume that I know it anyway. I get hired and laid off or get a big pay cut. And when I get a job that requires them to train me, it's almost as though they give you enough to get you by. Like a fish swimming around in their fishbowl with half an ounce of water in the bowl, which is really insufficient and really empty. And other people it seems to have sufficient and abundant training which is really full. Once they show me things, I am efficient at doing the task. When I try to figure things out on the machining side of things, I fumble the ball too many times. Like trying to balance myself on a log that's in the water. And as a result, they end up disqualifying me and cutting me from the team. In other words, I am unfit to be a machinist. Chucked once again into that famous pile. When I was in school on the Proto Trak Mill, 99.9% of the time I had my back facing people, because I was involved with learning the controllers. I did what I thought was the right direction to take in learning the controllers. I ignored the machining aspect of things because I just mirrored myself into the image of what I thought other high-paying machinists did. If you go to just about any CNC machine shop that has manual mills and lathes, most of the time these machines are not used. So why would I want to be practicing on the manual equipment? So I practiced all my time on the Proto Trak Mill without any interference. No one told me that you need to be working on the manuals more. All the guys at work concentrate most of their time pressing buttons on the controller, so why wouldn't I do that very same thing, especially if no one told you so? If a two-year-old walked across the street in front of oncoming traffic, who's at fault? I didn't know and didn't understand. I was just imitating and modeling myself after a high-paying machinist. I even, no lie, chewed chewing tobacco for three years. When in Rome, do as they do, right?

When referring to people, such as a group, I think the word "all" needs to be omitted from the dictionary. That being said, I know for a fact that all companies aren't racist. I know people like to label me with that. But, that's not how my mind communicates. Since I have only talked a few times with the owners, 95% of the time you don't even know they are in the building. So to actually call a company racist, you have to talk with the owner and see if he is racist. And since most of the time I never see them, how can I think that all companies are racist? Now if you were to ask me about their employees, I would say most, not all the companies I worked for, have or had one of them. I worked for this one company called Chase Machine. I only worked there for two weeks. I was doing very well running production, and getting along with other people. One morning, the owner's son arrived at the same time I did at my machine. We noticed that the night crew had left the machine out of order. The owner's son was really mad and told me to "get a broom and sweep this floor, boy". I left and called his father and told him what had happened. A year and a half later the owner's son was working at Lexington Machine where I was working. That told me right then and there that the owner took care of business by either firing or not allowing his son to work for him. Even if it was for a short period, the owner eventually took care of business. One day at Applied Tech, the owner and his other son (who is not at all racist) came into the CNC lab, looking for people to recruit. The owner remembered me; he just looked at me and said he was sorry. So you never could say all. I don't hold any animosity toward any company, even Rocon. Even though the owner led me to believe that he would be giving me unemployment, but didn't. I was planning on taking computer classes, so I could leave the field. I waited for two months and then at the last minute, I was told that my case was being litigated. I lost. It's water under the bridge. The fact remains that my credit score was 684 out of a possible 700 and now suffers big time and before things get back to normal, my score would be around 200. It's a good thing that my car is paid off. Anyway, there is this one company I have a dislike for, XLI Machine. When I worked there, the supervisor was straight-up racist to me. He would show this other black guy things on purpose in front of me and trust me, he showed him things that he'll probably never have any chance at using. Not to mention that most of the time I didn't operate a machine, but instead cleaned brackets, and counted golf balls. When he laid off the whole second shift, I was with him in his office [paperwork stuff] and told him that I wish I never had applied here. I said that because of his supervisor's attitude towards me. I didn't know Peter [owner of XLI Machine] had a mean streak in him, because he told the teachers what happened under my nose and people took what he said seriously. I saw it all over their faces at times. When I told one of the teachers what happened to me in the lab with Darwin and Brian, he said, "Oh yeah, what happened at XLI then, Roy?" I told him what happened, he looked at me and was embarrassed. He told me he understood. And Peter, talking about starting rumors, by Peter doing what he did, it's like setting up a million dominoes that took you a long time to construct, and before the competition starts the next day Peter sneaks in the middle of the night, knocking down the dominoes like some kind of cat burglar. How do you think teachers took this? Peter has influence with the teachers, trust me.

Can I say one thing? The whole thing about the secret society was way overblown. Darwin must have used my own words against me in that if you look at the obvious letter. Now, that was hitting below the belt. Even though at the time I was learning about them, I wasn't like some Jehovah's Witness shoving pamphlets in his face and trying to get him to read them. The whole thing was about me reading them programming and operating manuals and remembering what they said better than him. For instance, on one occasion he and other teachers were around the Proto Trak Lathe, and he couldn't figure out how to use the offset when programming I told him in detail word for word almost what the manual said from memory. He and other teachers looked at me funny and said I was right. It's things like that that caused Darwin to react the way he did. So in my last letter when I said things like, I could say 5+5=9 and a person like you would say that's incorrect, try again, that's what I meant. He probably felt that I had embarrassed him and I thought I was supposed to be in school. I never once met a math teacher who got upset with you when you gave the right answer. It's unheard of. I said the whole thing about the secret society; because I knew Darwin would demonize me, he didn't need any help because I demonized myself by writing that part.

So how can a person like me end up in prison? Easy, because it's not about what you know, it's about what you can prove. Anyway, I was living with a friend of mine on Dewey Avenue. My parents had just kicked me out of the house at the time. My friend and I didn't have transportation. We recently met some guys who came by to pick us up on Dewey Avenue and my friend and I at the time were fascinated because those guys were the first guys, we met who used weapons. We just thought that it was cool at the time. We said, those guys are the real deal. We went to the beach and when we got out of the car, we walked across the street and noticed a large group of boys standing around. We walked over to them and I noticed that a couple of them were from Greece, Arcadia, and were in this little gang that went around spraying people with mace and beating them up. It seems like most of them were five feet. At the time I was very popular, I had a big reputation for getting into fights. I didn't want to let people see me with them, and since the beach had around 10,000 people there, it was easy to be seen with them. So I walked away, and every two steps I took I knew someone, and I stopped and talked to just about all of them. My friend had left with that group of kids from Greece, Arcadia, and the guys who picked us up on Dewey Avenue. After I was done talking, I went looking for my friend, so I headed for the pier. As I was walking on the pier by myself looking for my friend through the crowd of people ahead of me, I noticed my friend kicking and punching one of my friend's brothers. I ran up and stopped the fight and most of the group wanted to fight my friend's brother whose name is John Romanski. Bottom line, the whole group would have torn him apart if it wasn't for me. I saw my friend, Mike Romanski, and when his eyes met mine, they were all watery, and he said, "If it wasn't for you, my brother would have gotten killed. My brother told me everything." I think he even asked me if there was anything he could do. I just told him to tell his brother when he got to court to testify, to tell people exactly what happened. He said not to worry. Later on in the trial, John Romanski downplayed everything, and it made it look and sound like all I really did was pick up a cigarette butt that I placed there in the first place. John Romanski told me himself that, "if it wasn't for me, it would have been him lying there on the pier". Anyway, my friend Jim was very angry with me for breaking up the fight. He said I was going soft, I was always breaking up his fights, so I got mad and walked over to some stranger and I just bumped him hard with my shoulder. Jim kicked him in the chest or chin and within a split second, there was a stampede. The bottom line is I didn't punch, kick, slap, spit, or bite anyone. After the fight, everyone ran down the pier, and guess who was right next to me running down to my side smiling and laughing like woody-woody pecker? It was the prosecution's head witness. The prosecution emphasized how he was taking criminal justice at MCC. I don't know how far he went with it. My friend Jim, who is no longer living, was always mad about how Steve got off so clean and was able to testify for the prosecution with the highest honor. Jim said [and I didn't know this until everything was all over] that Steve hit that guy when the guy was on the ground lots of times. I told my lawyer only what I saw, and that Steve was running on the side of me off the pier, laughing and smiling. That's all my friend talked about. I know this is speculation because I didn't see it. I only saw him smiling and laughing as he ran off the pier. This is the guy who sealed my coffin on my second trial. My only crime, I told this one hot blonde that I was friends with that I did it, but I truly didn't. She called me and asked if I did it. I figured since she liked bad boys, I said yes. Why not tell her that I did it? Who knows, I might get lucky, right? You should see a picture of her, you'll understand. I would like to tell you that things shouldn't have gotten that far. I turned myself into the police. The detective, who interviewed me, grilled me like no tomorrow, shoving pictures in my face one by one, confusing me. I could only identify three pictures out of around 20. He had me almost in tears, and then he looked at me and said you really didn't do it, and that my only problem was that I knew too many people. He actually told me that he was sorry, but he guarantees that I will hang for it". I told my lawyer this on my second trial; she called him right in front of me. After she got off the phone, she said that she totally believed me. The detective met us outside the courtroom, she talked to him and came back and told me that it would be too hard to prove. See, see, it's not about what you know; it's about what you can prove.

So what happened in prison, I had almost 20/20 vision at the time. An inmate who wasn't supposed to be anywhere around knives like in the kitchen where we worked together at the time threw heavy-duty liquid detergent bleach straight in my eyes, causing me permanent eye damage where I must wear glasses. The prison knew, and every time I sent out mail to file a notice of intent, they would throw it away, and before I knew what they were doing, it was too late for me to sue. If Mike Tyson was at a Buffalo Bills football game and a huge fight broke out in the stands, how many people from Rochester would come back saying that they saw Tyson punch, kick, slap, and bite a person in the stands? That's what happened to me because of my reputation back then.

1.   I didn't do it.
2.   That detective [not the police department] knew I didn't do it.
3.   At my trial everyone in the courtroom knew that something was funny because everyone told a different story and not the same story. It was almost comical. What sealed my conviction was

Steve and the pretty blonde and a lot of negative perceptions. Thank God I didn't get the death penalty.

I just want a regular life. I can't wait for prosperity to come in cans. So I wouldn't have to worry about it anymore, because I'd be shopping for it daily. I have bared the intolerable and still came up short. If stress takes years off your life, how many years do you think it has taken from me? I am related to stress now! My wish is to walk down the street smiling and meaning it in Rochester. Why should I have to go through roadblocks, underground tunnels, tight security, motion sensors, and 1000 firewalls just to have a good education and a decent income? Sorry for listening to loud rap music on campus. I wanted all of you guys to know that I was angry about what was going on. How can a person play the violin one day, and drums the next day? I felt what those guys felt when I listened to that music. Funny thing, I haven't listened to much music in the last couple of years before all the events happened to me.

I could write a book on CNC, but I lack the main ingredient which is machining, and because of that I'm target practice for all. I'm like an omelet without the egg. I decided that this field was the only thing for me. So I bought all these expensive tools and an 800-dollar toolbox that I can't use. I had insight into a future that came with a lot of hope. My hope, at least in this field, has been dismantled by school and work. Lots of men in my field can't read, including the ones that make the big bucks, even supervisors. The average machinist thinks that just because they can close their eyes and throw a penny behind them and that penny lands on top of a needle [that's 15-foot high] they have a right to ride around mentally in a limousine running over piles of wannabes. This field isn't about intelligence, it's all about actually doing tasks on the machine. Practice no study equals experience, study, no practice equals theory.

In closing, the purpose of this letter is to give you an idea of where I am coming from. I'm only asking for the school's assistance in helping me secure a job so that I can pay my student loans and have a prosperous life in Rochester. I don't want to live in poverty. Wherever you lead I'll follow. This is as far as I want to go with this letter but will take a lie detector test on all or parts of this letter. What happens in Rochester stays in Rochester.
Sincerely,

Roy Snell
Enclosure: Resume

BROADCAST EMAIL

Following the letter sent to Assistant Vice President, I sent the following email to various local officials and media requesting help.

June 9, 2005

I need your help. My career, cash flow, and personal and social life have been burned down like the churches of Alabama due to these hate crimes. All students who have my degree and have been in the field for ten years could work just about anywhere in the world with the skills they have learned in school, like electricians and plumbers. Their skilled craftsmen get paid at least a base pay of $14 an hour and up. They go on to become supervisors, plant managers, and the owner of shops. I am not talking about your average degree. I am talking about a skilled trade craftsman degree. Here are letters I have written to the college summing everything up. You have all but one. All the college has done is give me the middle finger and send the police after me. I don't know where to turn. One time I sent out over 150 resumes and not one machine shop hired me. It's like I am blacklisted or something. If a company closed down, it wouldn't matter to most of my classmates, because they're skilled tradesmen and I am not. They could get a job just about anywhere in the world, like electricians and plumbers. Because I have addressed the conditions at school and work by writing letters and trying to sue, I am in poverty and about to get evicted from my apartment as a result. Can you help me, please? I could explain anything in my past, for I am a good person. Please help! I don't have anywhere to go. Why should I have to apply for welfare?

P.S.

The reason why I have taken this to heart is because I have been demoralized, humiliated, and degraded, which has deteriorated my soul in the workplace and now on the streets. Not to mention, being paid the same as a dispensable employee. I wrote a letter while I was still in school; I could see if I was out of school for five years, then started writing letters. I would love to take an MRI lie detector test. Everything I worked so hard for has been wiped out. I had a legitimate complaint when I tried to sue, and obstruction of justice to the rescue!!!!!

2024 UPDATE

I quote myself from the above letter. "I know this is speculation because I didn't see it" end quote. I used the word <u>speculation</u> wrong, all wrong. Why would I be guessing after my friend clearly told me what he saw Steve do. After not seeing my friend Jim for like 3 years, we met at the Mall, and the first thing he said to me after we hugged it out, was that Steve, the prosecution's head witness hit that guy when the guy was on the ground lots of times. Why would that be the first thing one of your best friends tell you after not seeing you for like 3 years? That's all Jim talked about was how Steve got off clean and was the prosecution's head witness. I knew Steve, but Jim knew him a lot longer than me.

DISCREDIT VS THE TRUTH,
WHAT DO YOU THINK?

February 9, 2006

Anytime someone talks about a heavy issue, there is always going to be someone taking offense and taking a swipe at you. I am at a point of no return by writing this letter. By crossing the line of scrimmage, I know it's a matter of time before I get tackled. This letter did not have to be written. I have been at the negotiation table all this time with the college, and they have just made paper airplanes to throw them across the table at me, not to mention sucking my credit like a leech, killed my cash flow that has left me down on four flat tires, running me up the flagpole and destroying my social and personal life. The college could have pressed the remote to change the channel at any time, but they are satisfied with the channel it's on already. Why would you change the channel if everyone is enjoying the show?

Does the truth really matter anymore, or are people going to let the college and police department throw my life away? Punching below the belt just isn't okay; it's rewarded in this community. No one is supposed to know my personal business, and now this whole thing has spread like the AIDS virus. And why are the good people of this community silent? Because they'll get laid down and bent back like I have. They should be screaming at the top of their lungs, but when your credibility has been hammered away and under attack and made into a demon like mine, they'll look stupid doing so. And when your enemy speaks out against you after being demonized, he's just perceived as crying wolf. Boohoo, he's crying again. These guys know how to play the game and navigate their way through lies and deception like pilots. They don't want to see the truth even if they have a magnifying glass. The greatest trick the devil ever did was convincing the world that he didn't exist. The Beast is alive and well.

Looking at the three stooge's personality traits, there are three different personalities in men according to Men's Health. Curly is the kind of guy who takes a pie and smashes it in his own face to make people laugh. Therefore, you can't pick on him because he picks on himself. Larry is the kind of guy that will kick a bum off your lawn, out of the two he is the best worker and by far the best one to marry. He never wants to be the President, Vice President, or the Supervisor at his job. He doesn't want to deal with the hassle and tell people what to do, that's not how he gets his energy. Moe is the kind of guy who tries to slap Curly and Larry around, that's how he gets his energy. Moe is a born manipulator who has a big ego and tries to exploit the Curly's and Larry's of the world at every opportunity when he gets a chance. That being said, I am 100% Larry from head to toe. I get along with other Larry's, Curly's, and sometimes Moe's. In high school, I got along with Moe's because they saw me or heard about me beating down other Moe's'who tried to exploit me or my friends Larry's and Curly's.

How do my rights get violated and accepted by this community, by painting a picture of me being a demon and tricking the community into thinking that I am an unlikable person. They have shifted the blame game over to me. It's a cheap distraction tactic that has power, deception, and a slipper bluff written all over it. The college and police have manufactured ways of breaking down my credibility piece by piece. At first, they said, are you mentally okay; as in, are you seeing things. Now they are saying are you mentally okay and by the way, people don't like you, Mr. Snell. Since it's wartime, everyone can relate to someone or something they hate or dislike. People are on high alert with their emotions and anger. That part about people not liking me is a very powerful tool that will slip back and forth through the backdoor of one's mind when a person meets or hears about me. That one line is enough to control the average person's perception of me. Don't let that cheap trick control your perception as well. Think about it for a minute, who do you believe, me the average Joe, little ant, or a bunch of condescending professional liars? That one phrase "people don't like you, Mr. Snell " resonates in people's heads big time. Like if I told you not to think about the color "RED" and you better not be thinking about the color "RED" I am warning you, you better not be thinking about that color, what do you think you're going to be thinking about? Oh, come on, all they are doing is recycling the truth and spitting out straight-up lies. They act like they don't know what's going on. This isn't a game or a sport, this is my life. They are getting carried away. This is the work of a Moe, and it has his signature all over it.

Speaking of Moe, I know where and whom the police got their information from when the college said "People don't like you, Mr. Snell ". I won't say this Moe's name, Moe doesn't know that I know, but trust me on this; once this letter reaches you, the police will let Moe read my letter. TRUST ME. This Moe has the mentality of kill your parents, screw your friends, and have a nice day just to fulfill Moe's childhood fantasy of becoming a cop. Not to mention that Moe took the police test lots of times and failed. At least that's what Moe told me. This Moe I am talking about is a bouncer at the dance clubs who know most cops around town. Moe hangs in the street more than traffic lights do. Most of Moe's friends that Moe hangs out with are bouncers too. Not to say that they are bad people, but most have King Kong personalities, just like Moe and Moe's around the world. To tell you the truth, I get along with most of them because they know my history and that I am a good boxer. I don't get along with all the Moe's, because Moe is a born manipulator and always looking for an opening, but always respects someone that can fight. Back to the Moe who told police that or the police made him say that. If the police have all their money on this Moe, and think that he's a franchise star quarterback, let him start the game coach! I know something they don't know. Let's just say, if I should die today, I am in good standing with God. God will take no revenge on me whatsoever. As far as "Moe" goes, by God's law He has to take revenge. Use your imagination. By the way, I haven't got caught in a lie yet, because I speak reality.

At first, they said, are you mentally okay; as in, are you seeing things. How is this for seeing things; not unless my eyes and ears are lying too. The college put out an All-Points Bulletin on me. I don't know the exact date, but it was between these dates – August 20th to September 1st, 2004. What sparked these events was the previous semester I had emailed a lot of media news networks my letter "If you look at the obvious, you would fail to see the evidence". I wouldn't have emailed a single person if the college had done the right thing. I proved without a shadow of a doubt that two teachers and one student were straight-up racist to me that affected my education big time at the college. They didn't want to do anything about it, because it was a sore subject, I have a record, I didn't spell everything right, and my grammar wasn't on point. So what to all of that, because if I looked anything like Natalee Holloway it wouldn't have been an issue, no one would have said squat. Anyway, the college didn't want me to attend there because of all my emailing that lasted only two days the previous semester. So when I registered for my final class, statistics 160, to complete my degree to satisfy my requirements, they put out an A.P.B on me. At the time, I was working at Rocon, which is only three miles away from my apartment. Between August 20th to September 1st, 2004, I don't remember the exact day, but the college does, I left for work one day and, no lie, there were 30 cops on my path from the time I left my apartment until I arrived at work which is only a three-mile radius. Outside my door where I live until I arrived at work. As I passed the cops I looked them in the eyes, which I never do, and all looked straight in my eyes. It seemed like sweat was pouring from some of the cop's foreheads. That's not a good sign, wouldn't you think??? Trouble with the police is something I don't want, like a liver infection. I did a perception check, just to see if my perception was correct. So at 10 p.m. I took my lunch break and went back to my apartment for dinner, and the same thing happened to me. From the time I left work until I got out of my car to go into my apartment, 30 cops again were in that three-mile radius. As I left my apartment this time, a cop was in the parking lot at first with his lights on, and then he turned them off and followed me out onto the streets of Rochester. 30 cops were in that three-mile radius again, but this time when I turned onto my employer's street to go back to work, a cop speeded up behind me to show me that he meant business. I don't have to tell you how scared I was. The next day at 10 a.m. I called the college, terrified as all hell, and asked to speak to Mr. Ryther. My first words to him were to tell him that I wanted to send a message out to Rochester, and that message was, "What happens in Rochester stays in Rochester". I also told him that I wouldn't sue the college if he would only call the wolves off of me, please, please, please. He denied everything except his name. We talked things out over the phone, and he said that I could come to his office when I was through writing another letter for him to sum everything up. I thought everything was all right for me to come on campus and that he would be expecting me. The next day I arrived at campus and told the college security who was parked in front of the building I was there to see Mr. Ryther. He told me to park in the parking lot C, I think. I did, and when I got out of my car to head towards the direction of the building, an undercover with dark shades on walked very, very fast toward my direction and behind me with a long skinny box held tightly to his body. I could almost feel his breath on the back of my neck. I thought he was going to blow out my candles right there in broad daylight. I thought for sure he was going to pull out that thing and blow my ribs out and have me leaking like I was a cooked pop tart. At one point, I stood dead still because he ran up on me like a track star or something. There wasn't any reason for him to react that way. I had on tight jeans and a T-shirt. I want to live to be 200 years old. There is no killer in my blood, I can't even stand the sight of blood. If I ever take a lie detector test, which I will in a heartbeat, ask me if I like the sight of blood! I am a Larry, remember? You don't know how many times my mind has pressed rewind to replay that episode over and over again and again. The problem is, I have tried to erase it, but it finds its way back home. I thought and felt he was going to pop me like a pimple and blow off one of my limbs. These systematically abusive cops have a real taste for blood and can't stop even if they wanted to, like that of a cannibal. For anyone who doesn't believe me, you got to be kidding me. So I walked in to see Mr. Ryther, and I was so overwhelmed and shaken up by the whole experience, wouldn't you be too? When I walked into his office, I broke down and the sensitive side came out of me. I told him not to kill me, that I was just telling the truth, and that my rights had been violated enough to last a lifetime. At first, he downplayed everything, shifting the blame game on me. Are you mentally okay, Mr. Snell? I told him that he could have the plate and fork, just call off the wolves. I knew I was being recorded, because he kept shaking his head up and down, as to say, okay, okay, okay, but without saying the word okay. By right, I should have sued the pants off the college without any interference whatsoever from the police department. The police department messed everything up for me to sue. Isn't that obstruction of justice? Now, the college has had time to sit around in some think tank and come up with roadblocks and twists that they know everyone could dance to. Look how long it's been. What's better, to have three professional liars, or a thousand professional liars that are handpicked, trained, and manufactured for retail?

That wasn't the only time I almost got popped on campus. I used to take out math statistics instructional videos from the math lab at the college. The videos have to be returned by 8 a.m. the next day that you took them out, or you can't take out videos anymore. I had called the previous day begging the person on the phone if I could bring my videos in the next day because I only had to be on campus twice a week, he said yes and that he would hook me up. Every time you enter the math lab, you have to sign in with the computer that's in the lab. When I arrived the next day at the math lab, I saw the guy who hooked me up behind the counter, so I went up to him to thank him and forgot to sign in with the computer. Now my normal routine when I am on campus, and especially early like that day because I had to study for a test, is to get a cappuccino from the cafeteria. So I got situated at a desk in the math lab and headed for the cafeteria to get my cappuccino. I didn't have on a jacket or anything that would cause suspicion. I didn't notice anything strange when I headed to the cafeteria, but when I was coming back from the cafeteria, I noticed this undercover with black shades on walking towards me really fast, just like the running man out in the parking lot, with a small box on his shoulder. As we passed each other in the hallway, I looked at him to say what I did, he just kept going in the opposite direction, but I could feel the wind hit my face as we passed each other. By the way, the hall was empty or almost empty in that section of the hall. I barely got any studying accomplished, and when it was time for me to go to class, I went to sign off the computer and I noticed that I never signed in. I knew at that point my perception was right on point. I just wanted cappuccino to wake me up, and you mean to tell me I almost got some lead in my face for doing so? I am not pulling your leg on any of this. As you can see, the big bad wolves don't give a damn about my rights. They have rained on me like windshield wipers. And that same cop who wanted to pop me outside the building that day I talked with Mr. Ryther. Shortly after the episode, I went to Walmart Super Center in Gates. I was walking towards the entrance of the store in the front by the stop sign. The cop was sitting in this black pickup truck with this blond woman, both wearing shades, and as I walked in front of his truck by the stop sign he revved up his engine and moved toward me a little. I looked at him to say this is enough, I had it. That cop and his blonde partner got out of the black pickup fast and followed me into Walmart. I knew I was safe being around a lot of people. I went down this one lane to get a gold outlet plate for my apartment and as I turned around I noticed one of them dashed out of my view. I wonder if they had their guns out, only Walmart security and Walmart security cameras know the answer to this question. Cops have been all over me like white on rice. Isn't this a form of extortion?? I feel like I am a community inmate who lives in a concentration camp of fear.

When I first emailed my letters, my phone was ringing off the hook like crazy. I didn't answer it; because I knew it was the college, I had my fill. About a half hour later I was downstairs watching T.V. sitting on the couch, I looked up through the glass doors off the deck and noticed a Caucasian man in his late 20s or early 30s walking fast looking through the house trying to see where I was at in the back of the house. The problem was I lived out in a country-like setting and the only thing back there were trees and grass. I know that look on a cop's face when he's busy at work looking for something. It definitely wasn't the neighbors. Or maybe that was the boogie man. I even remember the first time I got approached by the police on the street. I'll never forget, because it was the first time I wore my brand new white jacket. My white jacket is sort of bulky, and I didn't want to get it dirty with my seat belt, so I thought I could go undetected by not wearing a seatbelt and as soon as my tires touched the town line a cop came around the bend in the opposite direction and looked in my car at me like the Incredible Hulk. He spun his car around like the dukes of hazards with his lights on and sped up behind me, traveling around 150mph. When he came to my car, still looking like the Incredible Hulk, he lowered his head, looked all in my eyes, and asked to see my driver's license. The cop knew for sure who I was. He didn't come out and tell me not to send letters, he just stared at me and said he knew and to calm down. I have had so much contact with the police over this whole ordeal, it's enough to make the average person throw up. Like Christmas Eve and the day before, I am talking about 6 weeks ago. I went to the mall to do my shopping, first stop, was JCPenney. As I was going in the store, I noticed around two cop cars outside. Every single place I went in that store I would see a cop looking at me pretending that he was looking for something. Or if I didn't see a uniform, I would hear a radio or a walkie-talkie going off everywhere I went. Then, when I entered the mall to do more shopping, I would come in eye contact with the police walking in the opposite direction looking like the Incredible Hulk at me walking tall chest out in arms swinging to the side. Mall security would come out of nowhere behind the shadows like some kind of night stalker. EVERY SINGLE PLACE I WENT IN THE MALL. The next day I went back because I wasn't done shopping, and what do you know, same thing. After I finished shopping and left the mall. There was a cop two lanes from where I was parked looking in the direction of my car. I got in my car, backed up, and pulled beside him to ask him what I did. He denied the police pressure. I told him that he was one of the officers intimidating me just 15 minutes earlier; he denied it, and then I said, it's not about what you know, it's about what you can prove. I knew that he was recording me because he would shake his head when I told him that I knew too many people in Greece to be fighting with them. And then he said it. He said not to email my letters, as in, take one for the team. This will be so easy to prove me wrong on because he recorded me the whole time. Make me eat my words, not unless the tape is missing in action. Like I said before, he was one of the officers intimidating me. At the time, I was talking with someone I had gone to college with and was having the same problems I was having at work. I told him that the police were pressuring me right then and to look around, he saw it too. He even asked me what I did. I took his phone number. Give me a lie detector test, him and his girlfriend or sister, and ask us all if we have seen or heard from one another since that day. Then ask him and his girlfriend or sister what they saw that day, with the police putting pressure on me and all. It just so happens to be that the cop I was talking to in his car, almost bumped into that guy I was talking to from school. That's why I remembered the cop's face. The guy from school had his back turned to the cop, then that cop stared at me walking slowly with his chest out, arms to the side passing me and the guy from school. That cop's shoulder was only an inch or two away from me and the guy's shoulder from school as he passed us. That's when the guy from school said, "What did you do". I will only give someone from out of town the guy from school's name and number. Let the lie detector test fly. I told "Moe the bouncer" at the bar about all the police and mall security guard pressure, and he said I was just seeing things. I asked him if he remembered a time that I lied to him, and he said no, but that I was still seeing things. Then I told him about the part when the cop told me not to email my letters anymore. "Moe the bouncer" got mad and said, "what was the officer's name"? As in, I can't believe the guy slipped like that, he knows better than that, he's messing everything up. It happened exactly like I just wrote it. By the way, did I mention, "Moe the bouncer" has one police sticker on his car and another on his wife's car? Did I mention that "Moe the bouncer" also carries a gun on the side of him when he's working at night outside the dance club? Only if you knew what I knew, laughs out loud. If "Moe the bouncer" had those police stickers on his car before all the police started messing with me, I didn't know about it. I know for a fact he didn't have a gun, at least not a legit one, before police hired him to try to kill my character. I understand how this thing works. The cops could easily tell every scumbag, hood, and creep on the street that owes them a favor who I am and promise to hook them up if they take care of me. I hope you're extra aware that the police are talking on the streets about me around the dance club area where I used to hang out. I used to love it there. Now I have to walk around in shame because I know that look in a bouncer's eyes when something is wrong. At first, all the bouncers were treating me well and wanted me to become a bouncer. When they saw it wasn't going to happen, they were okay with it and still treated me fine. "Larry's don't enjoy telling people what to do, so I wouldn't have made a good bouncer anyway". I remembered a couple of times I was parked on the street and traffic was heavy, and they stopped traffic just so I didn't have to wait. I don't know what was said or what happened, but I know something is not right, starting with their eyes. Not all, of course, but the chosen ones. One thing that I did learn from prison was to spot trouble, and if you think that you can get a one-on-one with a bouncer, you must believe in Santa Claus too. I shouldn't even be thinking about one on one. I should be thinking about where me and my wife will go on our next vacation. Of course, I can't prove this as well, but my perception is on point, and I am very, very mad about this. They probably even told them about the time when I was in Mr. Ryther's office and the sensitive side came out of me, at the very least they told them that. This was definitely one of the last straws, because not only do I have to fear the police now, I have to fear the unknown when I go out on the weekends. If I can't be happy, I want to at least be around people that are. I am not about to be some patient with tubes coming out of my neck and chest over this thing just because I am telling the truth about EVERYTHING. That being said, it's time for me to leave this city before I can't leave without someone pushing my wheelchair from behind or placing me in a box like a pair of boots.

I didn't know the police could do anything that they wanted to do with the Monroe County Library computer system, too. I have been a member of the library system for a while. Since I am living in poverty living 1 ½ miles away from the library now, why wouldn't I want to go to the library and take out free books and free videos? I pay taxes too, right? Every week I would go there around the same time so that they could see that I wasn't up to anything. I would take out the maximum number of videos that were allowed and return them on time. I guess they didn't like me going there, because one day I got a call and it said that I had books overdue. I thought it was a mistake, so I called the library, and they said it wasn't a mistake. They said that I took out this one Charlotte Web children video and that every day it's late. I would have to pay two dollars a day late fee, which was already a week late. They also said I had 3 or 4 books out, which was also late. I forgot the names of the books, but one was about diabetes. First, I don't have children and second, I don't have diabetes. I know, it's the computer's fault!!! By the way, the police know that they have done me wrong, so they have sent me this not-for-profit organization honorary member card, that says if I give them a 25-dollar contribution they would send me a police window decal. First, they have terrified me, destroyed my lawsuit, kicked me out of the library, put me in poverty, and now they want me to pay them 25 dollars not to bother me anymore, is that what they're saying? I won't tell you how I really feel, it's unprofessional!

I didn't know the police could steal mail too. I got fired from Rocon. I wrote a letter explaining what happened and after a while the person on the phone from N.Y. State Labor Dept. told me that the decision would be in the mail. I called her back almost a month later, and she knew that something was wrong right then and there. She said that she could get in trouble for telling me what she was going to tell me, that she had sent out my decision three weeks ago, and that I only had thirty days from that date three weeks ago to appeal.

Talk about being corrupt and abusing your power. I told you, the greatest trick the devil ever did was convincing the world that he didn't exist! If that's not evil, what is? By the way, my letter hits home so much that Rocon hired a lawyer to change the company policy. Their policy now is, that if anyone passes letters around, you can be terminated, effective Oct. 1st, 2004 Policy 3.09. I bumped into a guy who used to work for Rocon, and he told me that the supervisor told him that the company wanted me out of there because of all the problems I was causing the college. I will only tell someone from out of town his name because I don't have his number. One of the biggest reasons I lost with the NYS Dept. Of Labor is the lady who asked me on the phone why I was in a certain location by the guy I had a problem with. It's really a trick question because to fully understand you would need to take a picture of the place and see where I was working. A picture could have proven everything. I wonder if Rocon told them to ask me that question.

If that wasn't evil, this is. They want to see me homeless; because I had a headlock on my credit score "of 684" and these guys have cleaned my clock and left my credit down for the count. Now I am the king of the peanut butter & jelly sandwiches and late fees. The first thing that went was my cell phone. I don't even have a debit card, let alone a credit card anymore. I used to take my car and have it washed just about every week. I haven't washed my car in over a year. I am always paying my car insurance late. My electricity and phone have been shut off and by the time you receive this letter, my phone will probably be off again. I haven't had internet service for about a year, and if you know me, I am always talking about the computer. Talk about a pipe dream. I have been late on my rent at least 6 times. I claim 7 and 8 on my W2's to try to make up. I am going to be in trouble with the I.R.S. If you gross 15 thousand and are used to living well, what would you do? Last year, before they started their Shock and Awe champion on my cash flow, I made over 35 thousand. Look at all the years I have been working and tell me that everything is okay. I can't remotely remember the last time I made 15 thousand. Problem is, I am a college graduate. They're still dashing through my credit by slicing and dicing away at it. I feel trapped like a little mouse because they have killed my credit and taken my wallet out of my pockets. I am hungry as ever, and they have the nerve to walk around popping their collars and flossing in front of me. They won't be satisfied until they hear me saying, would you like regular or unleaded, would you like fries with your order, for 99 cents more you can get! Basically, they said open your mouth and swallow this hate, by the way, deal with it! I had big dreams about what I was going to be doing in life with my credit. I am 35, no children; I was saving myself until after graduation so that I could start a family and provide for them by buying a home and making a good income. I had everything planned out years ago, I am talking about my long-term goal here. My career was finished even before it took flight. All the wrongdoers, excuse me, evildoers can say "It wasn't me". Hey Tom, was it you? No! Let's ask Billy, It wasn't me. Hey John, did you have anything to do with this? I most certainly didn't! Let's ask, get my point? The truth is all I have left now. I have sacrificed everything to get to the point where I am. And these butchers have slaughtered and suffocated everything I worked so hard for by dismantling my credit through my cash flow. They have cleverly thrown the book at me to put me in poverty, I can't defend myself. I am only one person, help! The only thing I could say is, uncle, as they get an erection and hooowwwwwwlllll like a wolf to victory. It's like they don't have a conscience. My rights have been completely thrown out the window. No child left behind, yeah right! In Rochester, they don't only tie your ankles to the fence while they run around the track, they also bury you from the neck down, on your mark, get set, go. Then "They" run around the track and have the nerve to call you slow so they can feel like a beast.

Once again, the only thing in my field that's about intelligence is the programming and the math aspect of things, it's all about experience, If you've never seen a basketball before, and person "A" has not only been around basketballs but had and has the opportunity of throwing that basketball a trillion times, not to mention that Michael Jordan and Kobe Bryant trained him, of course he's going to be better at throwing the basketball in the hoop better than person "B", it's simple mathematics. Not only is the ball going to go in more frequently than person "B", it's going to go in with finesse. If you take 100 white men behind curtain #1 100 black men behind curtain #2 100 Spanish men behind curtain #3 and 100 Asian men behind curtain # 4 and give them a trillion tries at machining, especially if they get trained by the Michael Jordan and Kobe Bryant's of the world, of course, they're going to be better at performing the job better than person "B". Please tell me what basketball has to do with intelligence. By the way, I think basketball is a boring sport and never watch it! I would rather be playing with computers. I don't have all the answers and I know there are different forms of intelligence too, but given enough tries, that part of your brain will have time to strengthen the muscles that it needs to, and after a while, your subconscious mind will take the driver seat. I am saying everyone can do the job, but there will be people learning the job faster than others, but everyone can do the job that is physically capable, and make the big bucks like most people in my field. Look at an auto mechanic. We all know mechanics or heard about mechanics that could take apart an engine and put it back together again quickly but can't read a coloring book. This is cut and dry, Class dismissed!

If there was a white man, "The Great White Hope" Heavyweight Championship of the World] that came on the scene in the boxing world with an undefeated record of 100-0 knocking out every single black heavyweight man that moved and round one, black people would want to see another black man step up to the plate and win. That being said, people in my field don't want to see a black Babe Ruth. The only thing the average person has on me in my field is 1-machining that I didn't learn from school, 2-experience that I didn't learn at work, and 3-machining that I didn't learn in school. Just look at what happened to me at "AGI" to prove my point. My supervisor, who I thought was the nicest supervisor I ever had, being in this field. Everything was just fine at first. Even though he was 5 or 6 years older than me, he knew people that he really respected who told him I was something like a Mike Tyson in school and that they couldn't do anything with me either. That alone was powerful male bonding. He even bought me a cup of coffee and introduced me to his brother when he came by the shop.

When I started there, he said tons and tons of people don't know anything about machining glass and that most have failed. He said not to worry, because he wants me there and that I basically have a job just as long as he works there. He told me and the owner go out for drinks and not to worry about anything, because they listen to everything I say, welcome aboard my man. The supervisor and the other guy who was training me said most people fail at waxing the parts to the fixtures because if not done right, they will fall off the machine during machining. To this day, I have waxed everything right, and not one has ever fallen off the machine. I waited about a month before I attempted to hit a home run for the team. Why wouldn't I want to hit a home run, isn't that how you get paid more? They had this one CNC machine that they didn't know how to program whatsoever. They tried and tried. I was on the machine for just 5 minutes moving around the X, Y, and Z axes. My supervisor and the other guy came over to me laughing, saying, I told you couldn't program it. I asked him if I could work on the machine later. He said only on my break time. He and the other guy would work on it when they wanted to. I said okay. Break time came, and I had 2 programs completed within half an hour and 6 more programs for a total of 8 the next night. My supervisor and the other guy walked around for two days sad looking and quiet, and told me not to touch the machine. Other people around the shop were pleased with what I did. A different department of course. The company hired a guy from the outside to show them how to run the machine, without asking me anything whatsoever. The guy from the outside company said that the machine wasn't all that complicated and that a monkey could program it if he could. My supervisor and the other guy said repeatedly to me n"a monkey can do it", at least 10 times to me. That was the start of the end because I got offended and showed them at least 10 different sequences on the CNC machines that have been there for a while that they trained me on, that make the set-up time A LOT faster. My supervisor had a nervous breakdown. He worked me to death. So I got offended again, and I told him about my philosophy on how all the cycle times could be reduced big time. He said not to say anything, not one word. He kept working me to deaf, so I did say something to someone he's intimidated by. Bottom line, the cycle time was 13 minutes, and because of my philosophy, the cycle time is 9 minutes now. This is just one job, most cycle times he programs can be reduced like no tomorrow. He hates me for this and preys on me by working me like a slave. By saving the company thousands upon thousands of dollars, this is what I get back in return. Since I worked there, the only time that I messed up was when I dropped one part that weighed less than an ounce on one occasion and another part that weighed about the same on another occasion. Those guys messed up all the time. They messed up 2,5,10 and 20 thousand-dollar jobs within the blink of an eye. I am not about to have my supervisor have a mental orgasm on my account. Let that pervert go and climax on someone else. It's things like this that have plagued my future in this field. My supervisor wouldn't have responded that way, "maybe" if I had learned to machine in college like all my classmates. By the way, my supervisor was a soft core "Moe ". What's the difference, between being raped by Pee Wee Herman or being raped by Mike Tyson? So, I put my two weeks in, and they had the nerve to tell me to leave now, bye, bye nice knowing ya!

The college wanted me to fill out this one survey that I didn't fill out like the rest of the other students that graduated. They must have known that I was having trouble at work. And they probably figured that if I was having trouble at work, there was no way Mr. Snell was going to fill out that survey for us. So this one company called me and asked me to come in for an interview. I did, and I called the college and told them that I would fill out this one survey if I got that job. I was also under the impression that they were going to be paying for me to take all these computer courses that I wanted like no tomorrow and paying for me to attend another college, so

I could get my degree in computers. He said he'd talk to me later about it, and I thought I was going to be making around 11 to 12 bucks an hour and working 70-plus hours a week. I was looking at the job only short term, just so I could pay off my bills fast, because the Shock and Awe campaign has left my cash flow in ruins. I filled out that paperwork for my college giving them an A+ on everything, I even lied when it asked me where I had worked in the last year, and I said "AJL". The problem was, I hadn't even started working there. Everything I wrote on that survey was a lie, and the college knew. I just wanted to be done with it all. The company "AJL " called me in to tell me what I was going to be making and what shift. At the time, I wanted to get away from my present supervisor at the time. I went to "AJL " and they told me that I would be making 10 an hour non-negotiable. I ended up caving in and said yes. I called my college the next day and told them everything that happened to me at "AGI". I asked him about me learning computers, about paying for me to attend another college and also asked him why I can't have a better job, because after all the things that happened to me in school and work, I should be able to work for the Post Office, Xerox, Kodak or even City Hall. He knew that the survey was in the mail and told me that was all they were going to do for me. I asked him if I could take my letter up with City Hall, he said go right ahead. I went to City Hall, dropped off my letter, and left. The first day I worked at "AJL " everything was fine and the next day I think, I only think that they knew that I went to City Hall. I started working there on a Monday, and the next Monday after lunch the foreman came up to me and said he needed to see me in his office. He said things weren't working out and that my supervisor would escort me out of the building. I am sure the police will get their cheap laughs in on that one. This was definitely the last straw; because I didn't do anything wrong and everyone knows that I am the poorest man alive. It's not hard to trick me; I just wanted to get on with my life. My college tricked me by filling out that survey. This isn't the same thing as getting tricked when you click on a pop-up ad. I have been ready to work with them from the beginning, and this is how they repaid me by giving me a $ 10-an-hour job. Is this what I invested my life and money in? I GUARANTEE that Darwin "the teacher I got fired" is making really good money, because the college had the nerve to put his picture on the front of their catalog with Darwin smiling from ear to ear. I gave them that "If you look at the obvious, you would fail to see the evidence" letter back in 2002. His picture is on the front of the catalog for the 2004-2005 school year. Putting his picture on the front of their catalog just confirms their racist position on this matter and, at the very least, also confirms "The General" who is really running things behind the scenes feelings on this matter. Doesn't the "General" have to approve and make the final decision? I know it was the clumsy secretary! If a professor from Florida sends a hundred thousand dollars to a terrorist group, what is he really saying? It's a battle between rational and irrational thought. It's insane! Don't you at least find this wishy-washy? Darwin could have all the chips in the world, and he's still garbage. I saw the cover by accident myself. Like I said, I gave them my first letter back in 2002, so there is no way that it's an honest mistake. For those who do think it's a simple mistake, it's because you have a counterfeit sense of self. You're being dishonest with yourself, which really means you're hollow. Who wants to believe in something evil, I know I don't because I want to have happy thoughts like everyone, or almost everyone. I used to believe in Santa Claus when I was younger, but I don't anymore because I am all grown up now and able to tell the difference between make-believe and the truth.

Bottom line, the only reason why I brought up the prison thing was because of all the police pressure, I honestly thought they were going to kill me and find some way of blaming it all on me by discrediting and undermining my life. I respect the law, even though it doesn't respect me. I let the prison thing go a long time ago because I knew there was no way of winning when it came to a bunch of hungry wolves, but it was essential that I told them the truth because I thought they were treating me on the same line as a terrorist suspect. To prove I was a happy-go-lucky person, just look at all my NYS driver's license pictures and look at how happy I have always been, including the time I got released from prison. I don't want a head-on collision with the police department, which really runs this city, so I am asking for an out-of-town escort, one could call me a coward, but cowards live longer! There are snakes in the water and wolves in the woods and I don't want to be a moving target. For anybody that thinks I did do it, shut your mouth, because you weren't there.

I am so disgusted that I didn't go to my graduation; I haven't hung up my diploma. The only thing I have done with my degree is make copies, so I could fax companies it along with my resume. If I was smart, I would try to sell my degree on eBay. There has to be someone out there I could sell it to. I am so furious, because that isn't what I asked for, that isn't what I wanted, that isn't what I needed and it obviously didn't work.

At this stage of my life, as you can see, I am an angry person. That being said, how can I be generative, silly, carefree, joyful, and relaxed in general? Instead, I feel choked up, quiet, awkward, and pissed off. This whole episode in my life has made me act out of character. I still haven't lost touch with reality and my feelings, because I love people too much, animals too much, and living too much, it's embedded in me. I haven't really gone around my family; for fear that they will start messing with them to get to me. So I basically go over there on the holidays for the most part. The problem is, my family only lives a mile away from me. You mean to tell me that I have to move away from my family to get peace? Well, that's no different from me getting separated from my family like the people of Katrina.

To prove I am not a "Moe". In my last letter, when I said I got lost in the fog, I was downplaying the teacher's role in all of this. How can I possibly get lost in the fog when I am the only black student in the class? I said that part because I don't want them to get in any more trouble than they have to. I am no monster. Like I said before, they catered to the bright students, because they were getting knowledge from them as well. I guess you can say I have officially flipped-flopped. Can't you feel me? A "Moe" would have said that in his first letter, but with a lot more force. I am a Larry, remember? And another thing, the one teacher Mr. Brandon said that he would teach me anything that I wanted, except machining. He knew the whole time that I didn't know squat about machining, but was in a power struggle with the other teachers. He taught the CNC part of the school. Ask the other teachers how much he taught me, because I learned 95% of the stuff through manuals and instructional videos, let the lie detectors fly. Looking back on it all, Mr. Brandon knew but wanted to see some of the other teachers fall on their faces. He didn't really hang out with the other teachers, though. I mean, they weren't at his desk all the time, and he wasn't at theirs either. The other teachers were always together. I could have easily not given any of my letters to the college, I could have written the letters and sent them out of state a long time ago. This should prove I wanted to work with them from the start and that I am no "Moe".

To live in fear, poverty and be demonized is not my idea of the American dream. How can I raise the glass and toast to be an American? How can people sit there and let these cannibals throw me out the window like that? This is a hate crime and rational people know it. Think for a second, why would I write the words, "What happens in Rochester stays in Rochester"?

What part of the Constitution allows these people to get away with this? How can people protect evil, hooligans, and a bunch of rough-riding wolves? It doesn't matter what side of the coin you're on, democrat, republican, this is a hate crime against humanity and you know it! What happened to me is no honest mistake. The only head that has rolled over this whole ordeal is mine. The college has even suggested to me on more than one occasion to leave town. Who would have thought, that going to college would put you in poverty and almost killed! My cash flow and credit have taken a pounding. My money situation was so bad, that on Tuesday, January 24th, 2006 I had to go to welfare, so my lights wouldn't be shut off, talk about degrading. The brakes on my car are rubbing together; you can hear me coming around the corner. I haven't paid my rent and my landlord is looking at me funny because my car hasn't moved in a while. You see, that's what they want, to break my will, break my spirit, break my back. I'll huff, and I'll puff, and I'll blow your house down! This is all I have, it's just me and they know it. Who are you going to believe, the little guy who just wanted a sandwich? That couldn't get a crumb or a bunch of manufactured professional liars? This deserves a firm response. Do you think they're making the world a richer place to live for people? This whole thing is broken, and I can't fix it by myself, I need help and fast. No one is going to bang bang on me and come up with a lie saying, you should have been here, Mr. Snell went crazy on us, so we had to take him down. Sorry! They already know my recipe, so if anything happens to me, you know it's murder. I am not apologizing for anything that I have written, not unless my life is threatened again. This is how they are running the business in the rotten apple of New York, in the Shitty Black Flower City.

People have killed and jumped off the buildings for a lot less. Who would have thought, that going to college would make you want to escape reality, have you in the poor house and almost killed? Racism is one thing, but having an all-out blitz is another.

Can you help me rebuild my life, because this "Shock and Awe" campaign has cleaned my clock and left me on four flat tires? I have to leave town if not this state with a hundred bucks to my name. I am used to living well, just look at my apartment and all the clothes I wear. I don't have to work in this industry. They could have my toolbox, but if one of them Fortune 500 companies wants me to work for them, I would. I just want a good-paying job, no matter what I am doing. I want my credit score back. I think I deserve it and God knows I have put in all the work. I LOVE computers. I don't know a lot about them, but since everything in the world is on them and 95% of people don't know anything about them, I know this is the way for me. Beat me up with them.

Letter to U.S. Dept. of Education

May 15, 2006

Mr. Randolph E. Wills
Office for Civil Rights
32 Old Slip, 26th Floor
New York, New York 10005

RE: Case No. 02-06-2051

"The discredited little ant vs. the seasoned character assassins, licensed, experienced professional liars. The calls for justice"

Dear Mr. Wills:

If you give a man a fish, he'll eat for a day, but if you teach a man to fish, he'll eat for a lifetime. I overpaid for my fishing license and still have to beg for fish. Plain and simple, the teachers didn't do their job and because of that I can't do mine, and no law should protect them. They have watered down and manipulated the facts long enough, and it's time for them to own up and come clean, etc. They're using the system as a doormat making the system into a laughingstock and smashing a pie in the face of what everything America stands for by being bullies and abusing their power, unlimited resources, authority, and it should not be tolerated. What an insult to the education system. An injustice here is an injustice everywhere. What doesn't kill you makes you stronger; by your ruling, you're making their superegos stronger. When will it end? This wild recklessness needs to be confronted because they have lost focus on what this country stands for.

The factual information was incomplete: At first, they said I was jealous of Brian. I said I don't know of any black man who is jealous of another white man. We think the fight is fixed and that white man is supposed to have it all anyway. Then they said the teachers were worried about me that they didn't know where this was all coming from and that I should talk it out with them. Once everything was proven wrong, they said, "The teachers don't like you" Can you say flippity flop, floppy flop flop? This is also on tape. When Mr. Ryther told me that they fired Darwin, I said, I bet you didn't fire him for what he did. He said what difference does it make. At the time, I didn't have an answer, because I couldn't believe how cold of a response I had gotten. If a child molester rapes a little boy, wouldn't you want the courts to convict him for child molesting and not a speeding ticket so he could molest again? No remorse whatsoever! To solve a problem; you have to understand the problem. Fifty percent of the solution is finding out the problem. I detailed the problem, and all that has happened is a cover-up. I have connected the dots and taken a snapshot of hell, and they have thrown my life in the street like empty cans and vomit because of it. I am not big on letting racism, bigots, and freeloaders throw my career in a dumpster and not saying anything about it.

The mystery teacher in my letter entitled, "If You Look At The Obvious" was the tooling and machining coordinator. He is the first face that you see when entering the program; before you even meet a teacher or see a machine. He speaks for and represents the college and is the first line of defense. He lied just like I said he would in my look at the obvious letter. The college thought it was another teacher and when I found out that that teacher had got in trouble, I told them who the real mystery teacher was. I think 3 to 4 months went by before I told them. The mystery teacher knew the whole time that I was talking about him. He was going to let his colleague take the fall. On the day when he knew that I was going to be telling on him, the mystery teacher, Bob Lash, knew that I was in class and where I was sitting. He looked through the door window, put up his hands and begged me not to tell, something like sign language. Mr. Ryther asked me who the mystery teacher was and why I thought he was prejudiced. I told him if little Johnny was being picked on by little Billy and someone of authority saw what was going on and laughed and turned their back to ignore it, then the authority figure was just as guilty. He agreed with me. This is also on tape, word for word. Doesn't that say a lot about their character and who they are as an institution by having the coordinator act this way? It's kind of like the child molesters on Dateline showing up to rape little boys and when they're caught in the act they lie and end up saying this is the first time something like this has happened and that it's the 8-year-old fault. You can't be good and evil at the same time, it's one or the other. As you can see, they don't have any table manners and they need a timeout.

Proof that I had chemistry and the teachers liked me.

I used to work in the computer lab at The Applied Tech for a full semester totally free. I never received one dime, but what I did receive were instructional videos that the school had purchased from Master Task worth about $5,000 I think. They let me copy them right in the computer lab because they wouldn't let me take them home. Since I had to be there all the time, I learned how to manually program on my own. Mr. Brandon even said openly that I was the best student in my programming class. They made a deal with me that I had to be in the lab only two days a week. The teacher Pat had his daughter work there the other 3 days. She quit without notice, and they couldn't find anyone at the time, so I said I'd come in 5 days a week and that they still wouldn't have to pay me. I just wanted to copy the videos, so I could start putting some real food on the table. I didn't know Brian then, but he would always look at me in the lab without emotion, something like a blank stare.

I know if I get caught in one lie, all my letters will be disregarded and will face prosecution and another round of witch-hunts.

Brian is a computer hacker and hands down is better than all the teachers combined at machining and CNC programming. The only teacher who knew CNC was Mr. Brandon. Brian taught the rest of the teachers everything about CNC programming on just about all their machines. The teachers would lick, suck, and feast on his brain at every opportunity they got. The teachers had the mindset of give me, give me, give me when it comes to bright students. They tried to hog as much new skills and info as possible and when I came along knowing nothing "Not now", "what do you want", "Haven't you got it yet", and shortly afterward, "I have to help someone else" then they're back feasting on the brighter students again. What a bunch of freeloading selfish greedy leaches. Mr. Brandon is very smart when it comes to CNC, and Brian was even teaching him the machines. Brian was their meal ticket. For some reason, Brian wasn't great when it came to tests, because he would always have to leave before the test started. One teacher even took the same class Brian had to take "English 101" so that he could coach Brian as "payment back for all the things Brian taught him" so that Brian could pass. I believe this is why they thought he was the mystery teacher. One of the teachers gave Brian the original Mill Write software that's worth, "this is what Brian told me" $75,000 and Brian hacked it to pieces. Brian gave me a copy of it when things started hitting the fan, so I would stay quiet. I have been looking for that Mill Write CD all this time, and this is the real reason why this letter is so close to the deadline. When I find it, I'll send it FedEx style. I tried to tell Mr. Ryther about this and the videos once over the phone and once in his office and both times he let out a hard "SHHHHHHH". Common sense told me that he already knew differently about the videos. I knew I touched a nerve, so I left it alone. This is the only proof that I have of Brian hacking for the teachers. I opened up the CD, and it has his name on all the folders and one with an EXE.file extension. You should show no mercy on them on that alone, the law is on your side. They think not getting caught in a lie is the same thing as telling the truth. Let's see if they could lie their way around this one. How could I make something like this up? Brian had the green light to do what he wanted to do as a result. It was not my intelligence, lack of getting along with people, will, or determination that caused this. It was racism, bigotry, selfishness, and greed that caused me not to get the education I overpaid for and worked so hard to get. They even had Darwin trained this one black kid who was in the lab after my letters came out. That's no different from having a 10% off sale on jewelry; it still costs too much.

If someone won the Lottery and was mad and acted mad, wouldn't you say that was crazy? If evil, bad things happened to you, and you acted like you were happy all the time, wouldn't that be crazy? I can't bring my A-game when it comes to being happy, because of all the evil events that happened. It's like saying to a diabetic, pump some more insulin. They expect me to walk away and jump rope while the other students are living like Caesars being hand-fed grapes.

I believe the determination was incorrect because: if you put enough pressure on anyone, you can get what you want. If a Judge lets a child molester go and that child molester sodomizes and kills little children, whose fault is it? The Judge, most will say, but child molesters are predators. The police department played Judge and Jury and forced me to put my tail between my legs and throw the towel in the ring. The college knows the law, and loopholes, and was stalling for time because they know more tricks than the Globetrotters. My only crime is not knowing how the law works. People now could say I should have done this, and I should have done that. I was worried about my life period, point-blank. What was I supposed to do? What would you have done? Now they're hiding behind their lawyer with their crimes.

The analysis of the facts was incorrect because four police departments came after me. Need I say anymore? If they come after me again, I am just going to punt the ball away, because they don't play. Thinking things through, I can't fault the police, because they were just following orders from their superiors.

The legal standard was not applied correctly because the last time the police messed with me was on Christmas Eve and any time that they thought I was going to be emailing my letters over the net. Since this was about school, it was well within the 180-day time frame. If I got a bunch of goons together to put pressure on a teacher to give me a better grade, and the courts found this fact out 5 years from now, do you think the prosecution will let me slide? Absolutely not! It would be a witch hunt. Equal justice for all.

I have always been in Special Ed since the first grade. I know after I got in trouble and sent up the river for something I didn't do, I knew much of that had to do with me not being educated. I knew that education was the key to success and staying out of trouble, so I hung up my gloves and stopped hanging around people who would lead me down that road again. You have to be focused when trying to better yourself. I had a thirst, hunger, and a craving for learning. It's not how you start, it's how you finish. I went to college because I wanted to become a better person. I didn't want a job anymore, because a job pays the bills. I wanted a career that had room for advancement and ended up owing $20,000 without a career and begging for fish. They have lowered my expectations and dreams to Plan E rather than Plan A.

I don't have bipolar disorder. The doctor's medical interpretation was incorrect, and they're translating it to be what they want it to be. I went to the doctor a long time ago seeking help, because I was slurring all my words. I even had an operation on my nasal passage, because I wasn't getting any air through, really. I took Ripped Fuel, which is a weight loss pill. The main ingredient is Ephedra, and it caused me not to sleep, lose a lot of weight, slur my words, and have or increase my VCD "Vocal Cord Dysfunction". I couldn't really breathe to save my life. "I have always stuttered my whole life since I was born, but I couldn't get my words out at times and when I did, I would slur them and people drew back from me all around. The only thing that's keeping me breathing right is the breathing exercises I do every day.

They want you to think I am chemically unbalanced.

Evil people make good people look bad. I have been demonized to the point where my character has been made into an Ork like one of the things on Lord of the Rings. It's not that kind of party. They're running a ruthless smear campaign with people not liking me, and it's time that I address and confront this perception to these evildoing professional buffoons. It's almost like giving someone the AIDS virus and getting away with it. They have a knack for it. Their strategy is to divide and conquer. They have to say something, right? First of all, I got along and befriended all the black men working in the machine shops that I worked for. There was only one black man who said something about me after I left Rocon. I don't know what was said, because I wasn't there. I even got along with my crackhead supervisor the whole time I was employed there. I got close to him, and it turned out that he was pumping me for information so that he could go back and tell the owner, and the owner would in turn tell MCC. He would even let me take long breaks. When I found out what he was up to, our relationship of being cool was over. Every company that I worked at I was always tight with the brothers, even though some called me white boy jokingly, I got along with all the brothers. I got along with most of the people at Rocon too, but they have it set up there that the veteran workers could murder without prosecution on the newer workers, and at the time I wasn't going for that. Why don't you ask all the brothers at "AGI"if they liked the kid? Ask the black men at Parlec if they liked the kid. Ask the black men at Lexington if they liked the kid. Ask Chris King who was my group leader at Lexington and his super smart best friend in QA if they liked the kid. Ask Beebe, Maloney, and Mike, at Gillette Machine on the Horizontal Mills, if they liked the kid.

Ask Mike Mitchell "the owner of Mitchell Machine " who at the time was my supervisor" at Rogers Tool and Die and ask Dick Wagger who was my group leader at the time also at Rogers. Ask Roman in the die shop with all the other people in the die shop at Erdle Perforating. Also, ask Storm the head supervisor at Erdle if they liked the kid. Ask all the teachers who taught me on the main campus at MCC before all the letters, did they like me. One teacher who always went out of his way to say hi to me looked at me mean as all hell after I sent letters out. Since I went to prison for something I didn't do and being uneducated made matters worse, I have turned into something like a rude intellectual and brought new concepts to the table and teachers like that, but only if you're right. Not only did I get along with the teachers very well, but I also got along with 99.99% of the students on the main campus, and especially the rude intellectuals. Ask the Liberians at MCC if they like the kid. I used to practically live there, especially on Saturdays, open to close rain or shine. Ask the Principal and Vice Principal of Hilton High School when I went to school there if they liked me. I was friends with all the blacks, not a problem. If you were to look at the 1988, 1989, and 1990 yearbooks, I got along and befriended about 90% of them. Look at the JV and Varsity football pictures, I was friends with most of the guys. John Reynolds "who owns Charlotte Tavern", Craig Reynolds "who worked on Wall Street" Andy Wegman of the Wegmans family, Mike Romanski, Tim Slater, and Kevin Rule, and many more. If you saw John, you saw me. By the way, I had one of the biggest parties ever in Rochester back then at my parent's house, and people especially liked that there were just about more girls there than guys. The only people I didn't get along with were the pig farmers, toilet mouth trailer trash, meatheads, and headbangers. One dirtbag smashed this girl Lisa's head into the locker because I was friends with her, and he hated blacks, I guess you know what I did to him. Ask the people from Gates High School and the same year, do they know and like me. Sean Bower, Jerry Price, Andy Sawchuck, Inzo, Mike Giordano who is now a doctor, and many more. Ask the people from Spencerport like Mark Dirisio, Steve Rahr, Mike Lacotta, Elvis, Joe Lipresti, Sean Fagon, Matt Cookinham, and many more. Ask the people from Greece Athena like Paul Manning, Jim Kotay, George State once owner of the Prince's Restaurants, Lou and Joe Polizzi "owner of the Diplomat Party House, Jose, Jason Palvensi, Rick Secore, Bendgy, and many more. Ask Pete Tufo, Pat Fraser, Eddie Long, Anthony Richi, Steve Hay, Steve Mills, or anyone on the football team at Greece Olympia in the same year if they like the kid. Ask Kevin McGinnity "Who owns McGinnity's on West Ridge Rd", the last class of 89 at Cardinal Mooney High School does he like the kid, Bevoloko, Bird, Scott Hyless, and many more. Ask the people of Greece Arcadia like Joe, Tammy, Mike Alberty, Art Gamberdino, Arron, Freddy Kotay, Boner, and many more. Ask the Turkish people from East Ridge High like 2-by, Hagin, and just about all the Turkish people. Ask the people at the Summit Federal Credit Union if they like me. My very best friends back then were Matt Cookinham, John Dettman, and John Reynolds. Ask them or anyone about how big my party was and all the friends I had. Also, ask John Reynolds if he thinks I committed that crime on the Pier. He saw me across the street at Abbott's just after it happened. Ask him what he saw and what I said. Ask John Dettman and Matt Cookinham if I am good at names. People have always come up to me saying that they know me and that we were friends, and I honestly didn't remember them. When I go to the Charlotte Tavern, it happens all the time.

Crimes they have committed:

1. Breach of contract, because they didn't fulfill the agreement by teaching me.
2. Obstruction of justice, because they sent the police after me, knowing that I was trying to find a lawyer so that I could sue them. They wanted to silence me. Now I am in poverty, because of it.
3. Conspiracy to commit violence, I almost got shot, ran over, jumped etc., etc.
4. Violating the Constitution, they're guilty of violating the 4th Amendment, "right to privacy" because they have told everyone about me. Every job I go to, people want to litigate my letter out to me by referring to exact events in my letter. I get more auditions than American Idol. And whatever Amendment I missed.
5. Stalking. I have been followed more than a GPS could handle. My sense of traveling in the rain is gone forever because that is the best time to kill someone.
6. Confidentiality, because the teachers told "Darwin" that I was in prison. It happened I think in 1996 and there wasn't one student around then to read about it in the papers like they claim.
7. Forgery, because they changed my grades. I had a 3.064 GPA to 2.8 GPA. I then received an F then my GPA went up to 3.020. The media made them change it back.
8. Reckless endangerment because they had the police "punk" me lots of times and I thought I was a moving target.
9. Impeding an investigation, because they have stood in the way of justice that caused me to have an untimely claim.

10. Perjury or predicted perjury, because I know they're going to lie when we go to court.

11. Defamation of character, because they have turned my name into mud by demonizing me and telling everyone my most personal secrets. When I do have money, I am a good tipper at the bars. Some bartenders used to be happy when I came around, and now they look mean and don't want to take my tips. They have burned the concept of people hating my guts in people's minds.

12. Misconduct and unethical practices, because they allowed events to happen in

1. school and turned their back to the facts.

13. Excessive force, because I almost got shot outside school, in school, Walmart, and any other place I didn't know about.

14. Endangering the welfare of a child, because someone asked my 13-year-old niece at the time in school about me. My point is, how do they even know that we were related because we have different last names?

15. Falsifying records, because I got an A in all the machining courses I took.

16. Insubordinate to life, because they don't want to see people bettering themselves.

17. Putting me in poverty and leaving my accounts, cash flow, gas tank, and future jobs on "E".

Sincerely,

Roy Snell

March 8, 2007

Dear Mrs. Jarvie:

If computer skills were survival, from what I learned at Computer Confidence, I would be in a casket. I have a lot of things to say. First, I was in Maria's office and told her that her course was a gimmick and a loophole in the system. She stood up and said threateningly, "that I already made a fool out of M.C.C and that if I said anything about her company, I was not the only one who knew people." Threateningly is the keyword. Maria's course isn't for a beginner. Did you know that one of the prerequisites of her course says that one of the requirements is for students to have at least 6 months of experience? She knew that I had zero experience. Any computer technician in the world could tell you that I am sharp when it comes to following and understanding directions because I passed the hardware part of the A+ exam without ever building a computer. BOCES students told me that's what they did most of the day from Monday to Friday. The only operating system that I know is Windows XP. The only operating system that I worked on in school was Windows XP. The A+ operating system test could be on any one of the operating systems. On the A+ exam I took, the exam was based on Windows 2000 and Windows NT. A lot of the differences in the operating system are the paths it takes to get somewhere. Here is a sample question so you can fully understand where I'm coming from.

In Windows 98, where would

you optimize virtual memory?

A. Settings/Control Panel/
Virtual Memory Manager.
B. Settings/Control Panel/
System/Device Manager.
C. Settings/Control Panel/
System./Performance
D. Settings/Control Panel/
System/Advanced.

I had over 900 questions and answers that I paid for and that I memorized for the test, but when it came to paths on an operating system that I never worked on before, all I could do was guess. Please tell me how I was supposed to remember these paths when I never had any hands-on experience with Windows 98. Most of the questions on the A+ exam that I took were like that. That being said, how could I make a first down, let alone a touchdown?

The whole time I was there I read and reread the 950-page A+ book. When I had a question, 99.9% of the time they told me to Google it. They didn't even know what chapter I was on pretty much the whole time I was there.

To fully understand what you're doing, a person has to break something or mess something up. A person learns through their mistakes, right? I never messed anything up or broke anything the whole time I was there. How could I break anything when I did not have anything to break?

Maria is a shark, and her idea of Computer Confidence is wasting valuable Departmental resources. It's a disgrace to learning. These sharks should not get fed, and I think you guys need to adopt a new slogan. "No hands-on, hands off," as in hands-off Department resources. Let's just say I did pass the test. What now? If I had gotten hired at a computer shop, what could I have brought to the party? Do you need any help lifting that computer? Do you want me to shovel the sidewalk? Want me to sweep the floor? If the students at BOCES did not pass the test, they still would be very handy around any computer shop and, at the very least, work on the side fixing other people's computers. If my computer breaks down, I would have to pay to get it fixed.

I am putting my life in your hands, Mrs. Jarvie, with this. I don't feel safe in this city, so I have been locked up in my apartment since I started writing letters over a year ago. Trust me; I am not doing anything wrong. It's the same everywhere I go; I get followed or when I arrive at the supermarket for instance, security is on point and there are people in the parking lot waiting in their cars or trucks for me. One could make the argument that they're casing the scene. This is more than just creepy to me. How would you feel? I can't go here, there, or around the corner. How would you feel? So I lock myself up because I don't know what to do!? Maybe it is what I said in one of my letters about Moe the bouncer. I trust you with this, Mrs. Jarvie. You know what he did? He killed at least 2, 3, and maybe more people before. It was a long time ago. It did not happen here. So if the police are following me because of this, it's cool with me, but to tell every Tom, Dick, and Harry about me is not cool. Moe is too close with some of the police and knows some of Rochester's worst people on the street with guns, trust me on this! If you only knew! Wouldn't you be locked up too? This is a classic example of divide and destroy. That MRI test is sounding good!

At my job, I run 7 and 8 machines. If I go somewhere else in the field, the only experience that I will take with me is knowing how to juggle 7 and 8 machines. I like the fact that they have a lot of minorities there, and I am not starving like I was a year ago. People with my degree and who have been in the field for 11 years are making 5 and 6 bucks more than me without being just an operator. If I get laid off, I am back to square one, where my classmates could work anywhere in the world.

I am sorry it took me this long to write this letter. This has weighed me down for a very long time. Rest assured, now that I am back to writing letters, I am going to write you a longer letter explaining in detail everything that happened at Computer Confidence. You will have it in a week; I promise this time.

Sincerely,

Roy Snell

August 10, 2008

Proof That Computer Confidence Is Full of Fluffy Feces!

Computer Confidence isn't for beginners, since ring around the roses. The course is more like a trick than a treat. It's almost like Marie has found a way to get away with as little as possible legally. I didn't know that getting a decent education in Rochester would be so difficult. I thought all you had to bring to the party was your brain and the desire and willingness to learn. I wasn't qualified to take the course since I had no experience and the course outline said "You need 6 months or more experience to take the course". Get 10 people together who have been reading their whole lives and don't know the first thing about computers and have them sit at a desk reading a 950-page A+ computer book (without ever building a computer and loading an operating system once with help) and see if they could honestly pass both parts of the test. When I told people with computer experience that I passed the hardware part of the test without ever building a computer, they said wow! Matt had 10 years of hardcore experience building and fixing computers, and he only passed by a few points. Taking a course there is the same as buying expensive bottled water that's from the kitchen sink.

It's a teacher's job to teach, and not say "Google it". I went through 4 teachers and all had that mindset. There is no other explanation but to point the finger at how the course is run and set up. I think I would have been better off buying a cheap recycled computer and practicing on it, and then taking the test when I was ready. It's just one problem with that, you paid computer confidence to teach me. Computer Confidence is a place where you sign in, read a 950-page book to yourself, "Google it", have coffee/cookies then sign out.

I know Marie is an experienced businesswoman, but she used her experience to get away with the bare minimum. If she could, she would warehouse students in warehouse-like boxes, and crates with only a desk and a computer book. I don't care what the law says, but that's fraud in my book because she is raping the taxpayers. I think the Republicans are right when it comes to spending too much on education, from my personal experience. Schools and institutions should be held accountable and or the people who approved that law that allows schools and institutions to get away with slick scams that set people up in a no-lose situation. She has got herself one hell of a deal.

I bet NO ONE in history has ever sued BOCES for not teaching them right. BOCES A+ course costs $5,000 with all the hands-on experience you could handle from I think 9 am to 4 pm Monday to Friday. Repetition is the mother of learning, right? Computer Confidence is a whopping $6,000 with no hands-on experience from 8 am to 12 pm, but you could stay at your computer till 4 pm if you don't bother the teacher because that is when the teacher has to get his work done. Check BOCES's student overall attendance compared to Computer Confidence's overall attendance. Look at all the times students left at noon at the two schools. Trust me, if you're learning something that you want to learn, you don't think about time unless you have to be somewhere. Most people at Computer Confidence can't wait till noon or sooner, because all they're doing is reading and rereading a 950-page book that they could read anywhere. When I argued with her about me not learning how to build computers, she said that Computer Confidence was mainly here to help people pass the A+ Computer Test, as in Computer Confidence is a testing center. Make sure you ask me this question under an MRI lie detector test too! I told her about BOCES charging $5000 with all the hands-on skills, and her charging $6000 with no skills, and she ran "Game", Jedi mind trick by saying "BOCES students have to wait until the classes are full or just about full before you can take their course, you can take my course at any time because we cater to our student's needs". BOCES students used to laugh and say to me "I don't know how you do it man, I wish I could learn like that, I learn by doing things hands-on, but if that's how you learn that's cool because not everyone learns the same way. I said that's how I learn best, too. They laughed and said you got robbed. Ask the BOCES students who went there when I went there. I don't remember their names, but one guy was an African American and taught kung fu somewhere.

Marie is a shark and the kind of person who will shoot herself in the arm, then call 9-1-1 and say that you did it, just to save face. Reminds me of another institution that I know. I know I told you that I told Marie about M.C.C. and I did. But the real reason why I told her is because she would look at me really funny, as in, are you going to wig out? She had an unsafe air about her, so I wanted to put things at ease. That's the real reason why I told her. I completely understand the fear on someone's face. What was behind that was someone telling her everything about me and my letters behind my back. I couldn't have Marie being scared of me the whole time I was there, so

I told her about M.C.C. Tell her that you would make this thing go away if she told you the truth, who told her about me and M.C.C? As a matter of fact, give her an MRI lie detector test because she is very good at manipulating. About a week later or even that same week, "Matt" called you and told you that the course was a joke. What difference does it make who called you, me or Matt? Proof that it was an act of retaliation! Since she knew about me and the college, she thought I was the one who called you to complain. That was the beginning of the end because she targeted me for destruction. As in, he is trying to cause trouble here like he did to the college, and I will not allow that to happen. You came in to talk to me one day at Computer Confidence and asked me if I was using obscenity language around women. Remember? I said no and when I got back to the class the male teacher wanted to know really bad why you came there. I told him, and he got really mad and said, "Marie is sneaky, and she stands outside the classroom door listening to me that he had caught her lots of times." He told me if she starts anything to let him know and gave me his email address. The day before or earlier that week in the lab me, the black ex-BOCES student, and the male teacher were talking about politics and I used a couple of swear words. We were the only ones in the room and trust me, the teacher and the student didn't get offended. So I was uncomfortable with the lady teacher fill-in saleswoman, and she knew that something was wrong and told me that I did not say anything whatsoever out of the way to her or around her, that was all Marie's doing. By the way, I have only emailed that teacher once.

Marie called herself throwing me a bone by letting me sit in on her overpriced top-of-the-line corporate class for 4 days, with two stipulations. One, I could not talk to the other corporate student with 10 years of hardcore work experience about anything that happened there or my feelings towards Computer Confidence, and two, I was just there to sit in. The first day, Marie got into a fight with the real teacher who was supposed to teach the course, so he left and squealed out of the parking lot with his truck. So Marie let her fill in saleswoman teacher teach the course. All she did was read from the book word for word. When I tried to stop her most of the time to explain what she just had read, she told me that I was there to only sit in and listen and that the course was for corporate students. So that means that if he knew something or a certain section of the book, we would skip that part or section. There was something wrong with the networking system, so when it came to doing the Operating System practices in the book, the sales lady would jerry-rig a way to do it. Not by the book but through her experience. The book would say do this first and that second, and most of the keys she pressed were not in the book but were shortcuts only an experienced person would know that had networking issues. I still, to this day, don't know what they did because it was always different. That was the only hands-on experience I received. She told me to take the book home and practice all these DOS commands on my computer because of the networking issues. I said what happens if I mess something up? She said don't you know anyone who can fix it?

I am an innocent student. I hired no teacher, I didn't write any textbook, and I don't have any say on what I am being taught. I am like a broken curl bar that doesn't hold any weight. The sole responsibility is the institution, and in this case, it's Computer Confidence. I can't learn if I am not taught. They get paid to teach, not high jack funds legally. Matt had a problem with the teacher not standing up in front of the room teaching from the book. I didn't, because I was used to teaching myself out of a book anyway. I had a problem with not getting any hands-on experience building a computer and hands-on experience working with the different operating systems and practicing the examples in the book where you get your experience. The test isn't about knowledge, it's all about the trial and errors you've seen and felt when you were practicing, which equals experience. Education isn't just about knowledge, it's about action, putting to use what you learn. Education is useless without action. Especially computers and CNC machining. Going to Computer Confidence is like studying or memorizing the names of the white pages of the telephone book, useless. If you don't do anything with your knowledge it's useless. I didn't pass the Operating System part of the test, because of my lack of experience and not my lack of ability. I understand what I read, but without practicing what the book says, it is useless. The test was mostly about experience and not knowledge. As a beginner, just reading and rereading a 950-page computer book is useless without action. One of the books that was purchased we didn't even open once. It was the "A+ Complete Lab Manual 220-301 & 220-302 by Sybex " where you get your hands-on experience with Operating Systems like Windows 98 and Windows 2000 to pass the test. The only Operating System software I ever used there was Windows XP and remember that the network system was screwed-up. How could I blow past my expectations like that?

The computers Marie had for students to practice on, so-called build computers, were stacked up in the corner and splattered across a table missing pieces. This component didn't go with that and that didn't go with this, etc., etc. All the teachers said the only thing Marie had was a pile of junk for computers and one teacher even said "If Marie thinks that I am going to bring in anything from my private stash at home, am not". Then, when I would say I was upset that I took this course here, the teacher would say" why are you mad, you don't have to pay for it out of your pocket". One day, they had all the pieces to build a computer, so Matt built the computer while I watched and one of the students complained about the noise Matt was making building the computer (not me and him talking) but the sound of parts going together. So Maria said, we couldn't do it anymore and besides Matt had short-circuited one of the few motherboards. She ran "Game", Jedi mind tricks by saying, that she would talk to the owner and see if Matt and I could go in the basement to work on computers, but every time I brought up the subject, she stalled for time by saying she hadn't talked with the owner yet or the owner hasn't gotten back to her yet. That slick jive-talking lady Marie is guilty of deception, swindling, and defrauding.

I understand what I read, and that test was about not remembering what you read, but about hands-on experience. Either you did it and remembered how you did it; or never saw it, never practiced it, and when it's time to take the test, try to guess how it was done. It's like learning to swim without getting into the water. I passed the hardware part of the test with a practice test that I downloaded from the net. I made better use of my time studying at home. I would study for 50 minutes, then rest for 10 minutes for 2 weeks before I took that test. I shouldn't have had to rely so heavily on studying so hard on the practice test, because I should have relied on the hands-on experience that I got from practicing with computers. Studying with the A+ practice test without any hands-on experience is like flat-out cheating and won't get you any closer to being competent. One could pass the A+ hardware test if they had an updated version of the practice test without ever seeing a computer because the practice test has a lot of the same questions and answers that the real test has, provided that the test is updated. Just reading the A+ 950-page book without ever building a computer and practicing what the book says and passing both tests is next to impossible. I called this one computer school and asked the person on the phone if it was possible to pass the test by just reading the book without any prior experience, he said he couldn't do it and that it wasn't realistic and that one needs to practice. When I studied for the Operating System part of the test, I studied the practice exam for 50 minutes on and 10 minutes off for most of the day. I had a timer and everything. I am at my best when I wake up and when I work out. I probably took like 50 naps and did hundreds of push-ups and still fell short of passing the test. Not because of my ability, but because of my lack of experience. The Operating System part of the test is all about experience, and it could be on any of the Operating Systems like Windows 95,98, ME,2000, XP, and so on. For the most part, all operating systems place files and folders in different places all over the system. The test that I took asked me the driving directions (so to speak) on how would you get here, how would you get there, and what folder would you find if you were here. The only way to answer these questions is from the experience you received from practicing, and since I have only worked with Windows XP, a child could see I didn't get my practice on! There are a lot of places on the net where one can purchase the actual A+exam, but it has to be the current version and up to date to get the exact test for that day. The test I purchased wasn't the same as when I took the test. When I have to rely on cheating (practice exam) to pass a test that I should have practiced with hands-on experience that is paid for, something is wrong, you think?

I read my first book from start to finish when I was 21 and a half years old. Reading is having a deep understanding of what you're reading. Tell any computer professional that I have never installed an Operating System twice, and see what they say about me passing the Operating System part of the test. Did you know I have never installed an Operating System twice the whole time I was there?

That fill-in saleswoman wanted to be the head teacher there so badly, she tried to use her body like one of the sluts trying to climb the corporate ladder. One day when I was leaving for the day, she bent down in a sluttish way out of the eyesight of the other teacher that was in the room. I looked at her and the other teacher looked at me like he was looking for something, like a reaction from me, I guess. So that she could say "did you see it too". I am good at describing things, but I would have to show you what she exactly did. Then, when I was in the corporate class, she would cross and uncross her legs wearing a dress lots of times. One day she did it like 10 times in a row where one could almost see up her dress. Something like Sharon Stone. I guess she wanted me to say something to her out-of-the-way so that she could get me in trouble, I guess! What do you think? Haven't I had a lot of time to think about this? If I were smart, I wouldn't even put this paragraph in here, but it's staying because I want people to know about ALL the pressure that was applied on me out of retaliation that has left me in my apartment not knowing what to do! Explain to her exactly what an MRI lie detector test is, and tell her that your boss has all the cool, high-paying jobs that she could have if she takes an MRI lie detector test and passes. The kid is undefeated when it comes to telling the truth. I haven't gotten caught in one lie yet, and why would I blow my perfect record on some leather-face slut? That's unacceptable!

That saleslady admitted to me that Marie's course wasn't set up to teach hands-on and especially from a beginner's standpoint. At least the M.C.C. tooling and machining course was set up for beginners, they're just practicing racism! I played my position, and it's not my fault that the coach was more interested in filling the stands rather than winning. If I had passed the test, I would have eventually been booed, benched, and fired at my computer job as an incompetent employee the first week after I had thrown interceptions and fumbled the ball enough times.

Marie and the teachers encouraged me to lie about the times that I was there. Rather than being there for two hours, I put down 5 and 6 hours. When I stopped lying on the sign-in sign-out sheet, they got mad. I did this because Marie kept running "Game", Jedi mind tricks on me by telling me that they were going to teach me how to build computers down the basement. I just wanted to learn at all costs.

Marie said Greg "ex-teacher" used to let students stay way past their scheduled dates and that she wasn't going to be doing that anymore. This is Reason talking and not me, why would anybody have to stay past their scheduled date if they're getting taught right? Why do people not show up for class all the time? Unless they had an illness or something?

I tried to put my foot down by buying all the computer components to build a computer from scratch and forcing them to show me how to put it together, but she was nasty about it and wrote a letter to you. I ended up having one of my classmate's "Matt" with lots of experience build the computer at his home. Marie would look at me really mean, especially towards the end of the course. I said look lady I just want to learn how to build computers and my fight is not with you, it's with the college. Marie made me write and sign two different letters saying that I would not sue her and in return she said I could bring in my computer that I already had before the course and the teacher fixed the problem in two seconds because I couldn't get to one of my hard drives and that's it. How could anyone have confidence in Computer Confidence? Mrs. Jarvie, when I emailed you on 3/8/07 and told you that I promised to write you back within a week, I honestly was planning to. A week after I wrote you that letter, I noticed a parking ticket on my windshield outside my apartment on Broezel Street. I read the ticket, and it was from another address. It had my aunt's house address who lives across town off of Warning Road because I was over there the previous night. I even called my aunt to confirm her address and she said yeah and asked why. The next time I got in my car, there were cops everywhere I went. So after I went and got something to eat, I went downtown to pay the parking ticket. I came out to my car one day, and my car was hit. I don't believe in coincidence, especially 3 coincidences because my car has gotten hit 3 different times without me even driving it when it happened since I have been living here. It's very rare that something happens by chance, especially in the heat of the moment. Ask me under an MRI lie detector test did I have anybody hit it and was the car hit before I moved here?

I don't know how you can help me out now because ALL I want now is to leave this country for good. I haven't received a paycheck in 6 months, I can't pay September's rent and I have a little food left. Anyway, you can help me out and I will be greatly appreciated.

Sincerely,

Roy Snell

ROCHESTER, THE NEW
GUANTANAMO BAY

August, 11 2008

Is Rochester the New Guantanamo Bay? Uh, Yeah!!! Racism in Rochester is not just warm, it's sizzling. A city is judged on how they treat people who can't defend themselves, welcome to Rochester where life is blackballed and justice is denied!!! Guilty until proven innocent!!! Sometimes, it's not the pet that's bad, it's the owner who has trained that pet through systematic abuse!!! You can't bargain and negotiate with terrorists who just want to gorilla pimp your life into the ground, just because you blew the whistle on evil. Theodore Roosevelt once said, "If I must choose between righteousness and peace, I choose righteousness". I have no other option, but to choose "Peace". So I want off this soil. I am not an American, I am one of God's children living amongst world citizens because I was born into this world through God and just so happen to live in America living the American nightmare. If I was American, I would be treated like an American and not like the Taliban. I am the casualty, target, victim, prey, and sucker of America. I can't make this any clearer, I don't want to even have children on this soil. Help me pull the rug from under evil. I am held hostage by Satan because I blew the whistle on him and his bag of tricks, and I am being retaliated for it! The police, college, and the machine shops have organized a massive retaliation defamation companion against me, like organized crime, and have given my environment the equivalent of

AIDS, like Dr. Hilary Koprowski. Now I just want out, it's the right thing to do! Truth/Rational Thought vs People that have their Ph.D., Masters, MBA, and black belt in the art of professional lying and experience in deception. Warning, these confederate flag-flying, funky flip-flopping, faceless false prophets, filthy faithless fake plastic Christians, are faker than your favorite actor and if you plan on dealing with these people you better bring a condom. They have put their cigars out all over my body, my life, my career, my banking account, my student loan, my relationships, and my well-being and have denied me of life. They expect me to light their cigar and kiss their ring after the fact. I see through these professional liars like Cinderella's glass slippers, the hard part is letting other people see what I see!!!!

Crimes they have committed:

1. Breach of contract, because the college didn't fulfill the agreement by teaching
    me.
2. Obstruction of justice, because the college sent the police after me, knowing that I was trying to find a lawyer so that I could sue them. They wanted to silence me. Now I am in poverty, because of it.
3. Conspiracy to commit violence, I almost got shot, ran over, jumped etc. etc.
4. Violating the Constitution, the college is guilty of violating the 4th Amendment, "right to privacy" because they have told everyone about me. Every job I go to, people want to litigate my letter out to me by referring to exact events in my letter. I get more auditions than American Idol. And whatever Amendment I missed.
5. Stalking, I have been followed more than a GPS could handle by the police. My sense of traveling

in the rain is gone forever because that is the best time to kill someone.

6.   Confidentiality, because the teachers told "Darwin" that I was in prison. It happened I think in 1996 and there wasn't one student around then to read about it in the papers like they claim.

7.   Forgery, because the college changed my grades. I had a 3.064 GPA to 2.8 GPA. I then received an F then my GPA went up to 3.020. The media made them change it back.

8.   Reckless endangerment, because they had the police "punk" me lots of times and I thought I was a moving target.

9.   Impeding an investigation, because the college had the police stand in the way of justice, which caused me to have an untimely claim.

10. Perjury or predicted perjury, because I know the college is going to lie when we go to court.

11. Defamation of character, because the college, police, and machine shops have turned my name into mud by demonizing me and telling everyone my most personal secrets. When I do have money, I am a good tipper at the bars. Some bartenders used to be happy when I came around, and now they look mean and don't want to take my tips. They have burned the concept of people hating my guts in people's minds.

12. Misconduct and unethical practices, because the college allowed events to
happen in school and turned their back to the facts.

13. Excessive force, because I almost got shot outside school, in school, Walmart, and any other place I didn't know about.

14. Endangering the welfare of a child, because someone asked my 13-year-old niece at the time in school about me. My point is, how do they

even know that we were related because we have different last names?

15.   Falsifying records, because I got an A in all the machining courses I took.

16.   Insubordinate to life, because they don't want to see people bettering

17. themselves.

18. Putting me in poverty and leaving my accounts, cash flow, gas tank, and future jobs on "E".

19.   Evil, because the head detective was an experienced skilled troubleshooter who knew I didn't commit the crime he charged me with that, but sent me to prison. He said, "You really didn't do it, and that my only problem was that I knew too many people and told me that he was sorry, but he guaranteed that I would hang for it". I bet this cop won't take an MRI lie detector for a million dollars, he remembers this event, trust me!

20. Breaking and Entering. My landlord broke into my apartment

21.   Vandalism/Intimidation, my car has gotten hit 3 different times without me even driving it when it happened. I don't believe in coincidence, especially 3 coincidences!

22. Outright Threat, my superintendent threatened me with a gun about two weeks after I moved in.

23. Empty Threat, my neighbor across the street who's very cool with the cops confidently told me "I have a 45 you know" about a month after I moved in. And knows everything about my letters and has told me to watch very carefully where I send my letters, and has said to me "The cops haven't said anything about you in a while to me", when he saw that I wasn't a threat.

24. Black Magic, in prison, I had almost 20/20 vision

at the time. An inmate who wasn't supposed to be anywhere around knives like in the kitchen where we worked together at the time threw heavy-duty liquid detergent bleach straight in my eyes, causing me permanent eye damage where I must wear glasses. The prison knew, and every time I sent out mail to file a notice of intent, they would throw it away, and before I knew what they were doing, it was too late for me to sue. To this day, they didn't even offer to fix my eyes and if they do, they'll make sure something goes wrong during the surgery.

25.   Malicious Prosecution, Concealing Evidence, Falsifying Evidence, and Obstruction of Justice, because the D.A. coached one of the witnesses to her liking and sent me to prison. I would definitely need an MRI lie detector test to prove this, if not, it's like it never happened.

26. Stealing my mail out of the box or at the Post Office, so I couldn't appeal to the NYS Dept. Of Labor.

27.   Falsifying Records on the Monroe County Library computer system so that I would owe money they knew I couldn't pay 27. Rewarding People For Racism, I got a teacher fired for being racist and swatting his han about an inch from my face about 100 times every time I asked him a programming question and the college put up their middle finger to me and put his picture on front of their catalog smiling from ear to ear 1000% proof the college is racist!

28.   Patient Client Privilege/Confidentiality, They bad mouth me to my doctor that now he hates my guts. This doctor once operated on me before, and we have always gotten along. Now he doesn't want anything to do with me.

29. Cruelty, I looked at an apartment in the price range welfare was giving me and I told the caseworker on the phone that the apartment I had visited had lots of holes in the wall, that it looked like rats lived there, and he shouted over the phone "buy a cat then". He knew about me before we even met.

30. Controlled Racism, Black people get to learn a few skills in a year, white people get to learn an unlimited number of things in a year. The only way to "Master" the trade is by learning hundreds of skills and practicing those skills.

31. Justified Racism, because the main people who get laid off when things are slow are the people who aren't skilled enough, with few skills. 500 skills vs 5 skills, who would you lay off? Justified Racism, because they make sure you don't get these valuable life-changing skills.

32. Economic Racism, they only allow a certain number of black people to work in the machine shops.

33. Flat-out Racist, I knew this one professional who worked in the office at MCC who went home at night crying sometimes because she would always hear staff saying racist things about black students and staff all day long in front of her. She had blonde hair and blue eyes, but was really black. I saw something like this on Oprah before. She ended up leaving the college because of the racism within the college.

34. Slavery, because of all the events combined, and forcing me to pay for these sick events.

35. Accomplice/Accessory, Anybody they got to directly or indirectly retaliate against me. Just like it takes more than one person to build a house, it took more than one person to retaliate

on me.

36. Terrorism, they have systematically terrorized me with intense fear, intimidation, and pressure, and putting the squeeze on me that I have been in my apartment basically for over 2 years out of fear. Not to mention hitting my parked car 3 times.

37. Ruined me financially.

They can't deny these charges, because I am the living proof of these facts. If I don't capitalize something, it's on purpose.

Throughout history, whistleblowers have been liked by their abusers before the whistle was blown. I never saw an "Insider" whistleblower that was hated all the time, until they revealed insider secrets by telling the truth. Everyone who tells the truth will be hated, have you seen someone that wasn't? Bingo! Think about it for a minute, what whistleblower do you know that was liked by the people whom he blew the whistle on after the fact? And what company, organization, or person that the whistle was blown on didn't try to demonize the person who blew the whistle? Think about it! I have never seen a whistleblower liked by the people he blew the whistle at after the whistle was blown. I have never seen the people he blew the whistle on not try to demonize, use ruthless tactics, dirty tricks, manipulate, and cause enough reasonable doubt that their evil doings are minimized to hide their dark side. As a whistleblower, I am being retaliated against and my human rights are not protected because I am a whistleblower to unseen evil. I could see if I snitched on someone really important, but I blew the whistle because my human rights were violated, and I did not get what I worked so hard for. They have tried to stick it to me ever since my first letter.

I should be able to say anything I want, especially since they say anything they want on the radio without people pulling out guns and trying to run them over with their cars. Like Satan did to me. How would you feel if you paid a contractor your life savings of 100 thousand dollars to build you a nice house for you and your family, and they did such a bad job that the house isn't even close to being up to code, the City says the house must be demolished and completely rebuilt? You're out your life savings and when you go to sue the Contractor, they have strong ties to the police department and send them after you wherever you went to apply pressure on you to make you drop your lawsuit. It was either surrender or get obliviated. What part don't people understand about that? You drop your lawsuit out of fear of being shot or set up to go to prison for a lifetime. You try to sue again when the pressure dies down, then the Contractor look at their watch and say "Sorry "NIGGA" Your Too Late to Sue, Only If You Had More Time, Congratulations On Your Big Loss". YOU CAN'T BE SERIOUS! The police gave the college time to think and made me have an untimely claim against them, their fingerprints are on everything. They're just going to run "Game" on you, dark manipulation tactics, change the subject, and give you the runaround. If someone held up a gun to your head and demanded your wallet, you would give them your wallet, right? Well, what about if 1,000 men pointed their guns at your head and demanded your wallet? I gave up my wallet because these were officials and WHATEVER they do is official. If there was an all-black college, all-black police department and an all-black business that did this to anyone with blonde hair and blue eyes, they would have been charged with terrorism and the military would have flattened their address. They need to be held accountable for their actions like everyone else. I am outnumbered, and a trillion % conquered! I would be a force to reckon with too if I had all the police departments in my pockets. Of course, they're going to win when they're in a no-lose situation. Or how would you feel if you built a home with your bare hands, then someone burned it down, then ran "Game", dark manipulation tactics to make people think that you were the one that burned your own house down. How would you feel? That's exactly what happened. I didn't realize lying was such an art, and telling the truth was going to bring about much hate.

ETS Staffing

I called E.T.S. one day and asked the guy on the phone if he had something for me. He said yes and to come in so he could talk to me about it. I did, and he looked at me with a cocky smile/laugh and said he wanted me to dig a deep hole with a shovel and that the job paid $8/ hrs. This guy was too excited to tell me about this. This had retaliation written all over it, handed down from the college and the machine shops. I said no, and every time I called his office for a job, he said he didn't have anything. Was that the retaliation thing again? If the coach doesn't want to put me in the game, I'll take my ball and then go to the next team! So I went to work under the table doing demolition because they would not let me get a job anywhere. The police were waiting for me outside in the parking lot on the site and the next thing you know when I left the job they got rid of most of their workers and made everyone else sign up with a Temporary Agency. The last day I worked there, the office people made sure that I got my check from the main guy. He gave me that look," Because of you this is happening".

They tried to set me up at work by recording my voice. I was told to come into the office because E.T.S. wanted to talk to me privately. As I was walking towards the office, I just so happened to turn around and the main boss was waving his hand frantically pointing towards the office, as if to say, get him in the office! I knew for a fact that I was recorded the whole time by their actions. Then he asked me questions like "Do you think all machine shops in Rochester are racist"? That's when I said, "You can never say all when it comes to people". As I left the office, I looked straight into the eyes of the main boss, and he didn't even look my way. I wonder whose idea it was to record me, maybe it was the garbage man. They were in constant communication with the college the whole time I worked there. E.T.S. could never pass an MRI lie detector test on the facts I have laid down.

Pierce Industries

The first day I was there the supervisor was on me like no tomorrow, he asked me to change an insert in the lathe, and I was looking for the right size wrench to change it and two seconds later he said never mind I'll do it. He then went around and told everyone that I didn't know what I was doing. People would walk around and look at me because of this. They put me on something that wasn't part of machining but made me work extra hard at it because of what the supervisor said. They put me back on a CNC lathe after a long wait, and I operated that machine like no tomorrow. I would hear them arguing over the decision to pull me off the machines. I was talking to one of the main guys from Quality Control about a certain machine because they couldn't get the close tolerances they wanted, without scraping every other workpiece that the machine produced. These parts were big and had already gone through other machining stages, and this was the final machining sequence. For one part the machine got right, it scrapped 2 or 3 parts. They were losing thousands and thousands of dollars. I took one look at the print and the program and said I know what the problem is. He asked me to explain. I said the print is in Metric and the program is in English and needs to be written in Metric. I said on a 10" linear axis you can only move the off-set 100,000 times in the inch mode, the tool has 100,000 possible positions. And in the Metric mode, you can move it 254,000 times based on a 10" linear axis; the tool has 254,000 possible positions. He said I was right, but those guys have all the power. He went and told the owner and I completely broke down the Metric System for him, and he said from now on he wants all programs to be in Metric. The supervisor flipped and said he couldn't do it and that if the owner wanted him to leave, he would in front of the owner. They made my life very hard for me after that. They worked me to the bone. The other supervisor who weighed 400 lbs. would come over to my machine, press buttons on the controller, and would block what he was doing on purpose, so I couldn't see what he was doing, so that I couldn't learn anything from him. He saw that I didn't like that and on break time would come outside with another guy to fight me if I had a problem with it. I told ETS Staffing everything and to find me another job, and they told me to put in my 2 weeks. I did, and Pierce Industries said this is your last day. Bye! I got along with everyone who worked there, besides the ones who had inside information about me before I even worked there. Retaliation from start to finish. The owner knows firsthand that I was good at what I did, and so did the whole place. I never said anything about this before, because the owner felt bad about what happened. E.T.S. had a front-row seat to everything that took place and agreed with me on EVERYTHING, even though they were in bed with the college the entire time. Some of the staff has moved out of town that used to work for E.T.S. Call them out of town and ask them to see if I am lying.

Temp Service

I sent my resume to this employment agency, and she sent my resume out to this company in Webster that wasn't a machine shop, but hired people from the machine shops with experience because they did an overall better job learning whatever that company did. He took one look at my resume and called the employment agency back several times. She called me back several times (because I wasn't home) and said to call her at home even over the weekend since it was a Friday. I called her and said I was interested, and she said I was basically hired, that all the guy had to do was check out my references, and that the job paid around $15 and $16 an hour with lots of overtime. She was so excited, he was so excited and when he called someone about me, he told her he wasn't interested anymore. She asked me what I did, who did I piss off because someone is giving me a really bad reference. She said that she had lots more high-paying jobs, but didn't want to waste her time finding me work because the same thing would just keep happening, and she wished me the best of luck.

Landlord

My superintendent told me very firmly two weeks after I moved in, "I have a gun that I keep loaded, I haven't used it before, but I will." What was behind that is Nigga, I know all about what's going on and if you get out of line I'll blow your head clean off, and the law will back me up. Two weeks later, a guy that lives across the street had killed someone in front of the police "and the police backed him up in court so that he would get off" told me "I keep a 45 you know, I don't play. Now in some states, if you turn the door knob and crack open the door, that is Breaking and Entering. Now my lease says "The landlord or his agents shall have the right to inspect said property/apartment at any time with 24 hours notice provided". I came home around 6:15 a.m. from working on 8 machines at work that night. When I got home I took a shower, dried off, laid on my bed naked, and fell asleep like that. At 8 or 9 a.m. my landlord knocked on my door VERY, VERY hard (twice is what I heard) then turned the doorknob and opened up the door and said "Roy, what are you doing in there VERY loud". I even saw half his body in my apartment. He had to have seen me naked. I said out loud to him that I was naked and that I didn't have any clothes on. He slammed the door and said again "What are you doing in there, open up" I said wait until I get my pants on, then I came to the door to let him in with just some pants on, no t-shirt. After I let him into my apartment, he changed his tone and I asked him "what's so important, and he changed the subject and said nothing. I just wanted to tell you that you were going to be getting some new windows or something to that effect. Someone told me that he knew the police well and sat on some sort of community board before or something to that effect. I asked him if it was true, and he said no and left shortly. The next time I saw him, I was outside my building talking with one of my neighbors and gave him a mean look for violating me in my apartment. The next day he was back at my front door with his partner looking meanly into my eyes talking about something off-topic. My eyes hit the ground and I submitted so he would not kick me out, he looked at me very firmly as in "I own this building". By the way, I live in a large studio and when you open up the door my bed is 21 feet straight across from the door. That is Breaking and Entering, plain and simple! My other landlord did the same thing to me before in my last apartment. She unlocked my front door, came into my apartment and yelled out something, I can't exactly remember, so I won't write it. But it was early in the morning too. I will take an MRI lie detector test on this or anything that I write! I went to pay my rent one day and said that I was leaving this country, the person responded with confidence, "Why haven't you applied for a passport yet". How would they know that? My point!

Welfare

They put me in poverty and when I finally went to welfare the counselor, they assigned me looked at me angrily and said "Why can't you keep a job"? I started explaining to him and within a couple of minutes he assigned me to go and see a shrink. Trust me, it was already planned that way before I got there. Of course, everything was fine with the shrink session and all. I was getting evicted from my apartment, which I had a timeline to get out. He told me the wrong figure, welfare will pay for an apartment for me, and when I finally got an apartment that I wanted the owner told me welfare wouldn't pay for it. I called him and told him about the figure, and he told me welfare used to add what they were going to give you for food stamps onto the rent and that I would have to come up with my food, or something like that. I called his supervisor to confirm because I could not reach him on the phone after calling his office lots of times. He was very angry with me for calling his supervisor and when I talked with him about the real figure welfare will pay and a particular apartment (in that price range that I visited) had holes in the walls, which looked like rats lived there, he shouted over the phone "buy a cat then"! Retaliation has its petty torments. I called his supervisor and left a message and told her about the "buy a cat" statement when I went to his office people were quiet because they wanted to hear what was said, and I said firmly you said "by a cat" he admitted to it, but downplayed it a little. Retaliation once again. He knew what was going on before we even met, period! MRI lie detector test, please. They paid for my rent for like two months and gave me food stamps for a year. After all I've been through in this city, that's the same thing as walking over to a bum on the street and offering him a baloney sandwich and when that bum reaches out for it, you drop it on the ground. Giving me welfare was like giving me a Scooby snack. Why should I have to eat that poison?

The Experienced Racist Machine Shops

Welcome to Rochester machine shops, where experience is the new "Master". The machine shops are really the American dream, because you could have worked minimum wage all your life, killed someone, and not know how to read, and if you get a job in the machine shop for 2–3 years with hardcore training by the "Master Machinist" you could earn 20+ dollars a hr with lots of overtime, work just about anywhere in the world and skills you could pass on to your family. I have even seen tons of white crackheads walk around with both hands in their pockets looking down on you because they're skilled and you're not. If you have figured out a way that you can travel under the radar and steal large sums of money from the bank confidently without being detected, why would you stop stealing? And if you knew that someone finally figured out what you were doing, why wouldn't you try to stop that person from telling your secrets? They are supposed not to like me. I am preventing them from scoring touchdowns. I am a black white boy from the suburbs, with 99% of my friends being white. I am just being real.

If me and other black men got together and started talking about white people this, white people that, we're being prejudiced. Now, if me and other black men got together and formed a police department and arrested nothing but white people, we would be racist, right? The machine shops are racist and here is the proof,

Controlled Racism

Being a CNC Machinist requires lots of skills, that can only be achieved through experience and lots of practice, they know that. Ask any older white man who worked or works in the machine shops, how many black men have they seen in their life that could set up and program both CNC mills and CNC lathes and check their work pieces on the C.M.M in Quality Control by themselves? I asked this question to two older white men who have been in the field for 30 /40 years, and both said about 10. How could that be when everyone who's physically capable can learn to "Master" the trade by being taught by Muhammad Ali, Michael Jordan, Joe Montana, and Wayne Gretzky of the world and having a million chances at practicing that skill? I never heard of anyone doing something a million times and not knowing what they're doing! Have you? Look at the T.V. Show Celebrity Circus. Those celebrities didn't know how to perform any of those acts until they were taught by the elite of the field. Blacks get to learn a few things in a year, while Joe-Bob and Bud get to learn unlimited skills in a year. Of course, they're going to pitch a shutout. The only way to "Master" and learn the trade is by learning hundreds of skills. Can you say controlled racism? They're in shape without working out. I put in all the mental work, all the time, the sacrifices, pain, and struggle to make it through college, and the average person in the machine shop without a degree/GED would say "I owe 120 thousand on my home, you only owe 20 thousand, I am worse off than you buddy".

Justified Racism

I don't care if they paid a black person $50,000 a year to work in their shops, the question is, what is that black person doing on a daily basis? The answer, he's cleaning up the place, or just finger button pressing a machine to deaf. Since everything in the field is about supply in demand, he will get laid off when things are slow, due to a lack of skills. Oh, you don't have enough skills/experience, so we're letting you go because things are slow. Justified racism at its finest. Or, I am sorry, we hired Bud today, because Bud had more experience than you, nothing personal. As a result, were the last one hired and the first one fired. Justified racism at its finest, trying to come in the machine shops, and leaving the machine shops!

Economic Racism

Explain the fact that if there are 50 people working in a machine shop, there are only 2 blacks; it has to be the system, right? There are 300 machine shops in Rochester, on average if 50 people are working there, only 2 black people are working there on average. Whatever the formula is, they go by that formula and only allow that number of blacks to enter their shops on average. I know since I started writing letters, this topic has had to come up. I don't put anything past them. So, ask any older white man who's retired or soon to be retiring how many blacks on average the machine shops have when he worked there. If it wasn't for Affirmative Action, black men would not exist in the machine shops. They have exploited the average person's intelligence, with this deceptive racist practice. If you do something for 4/5 years you're dedicated, but if you do it for 25+ years it's a lifestyle! The machine shops have always been racist, that's just the way things are. I didn't know this until I was booby-trapped. The only blacks that know how to machine are the ones that learned it in high school, or another black person taught them on the job while they were on break or something. There is no substitute for experience because you need experience to experience, period. I knew this one guy from Africa who graduated from R.I.T who caught so much hell from his supervisors in the machine shops, that the last time I saw him he was selling clothes for a living at the public market. I know this other guy who's a professional who works for the city of Rochester now, who caught so much hell in the machine shops that he quit too. I told him what happened to me, and he said me too. I am saying, that if you get a black person and a white person to start a job at the same time, in year one the white person will learn on average 50 skills, and that year, the black person will learn 2 to 3 skills and that year, learning to become a machinist that way, is like running in quicksand. Can you imagine doing the same 3 skills over and over again at all the companies you worked for, then the supervisor shouts faster, faster you can do it. After 3 years, the white guy could work anywhere in the world. The black guy is still a disposable employee if he is even lucky enough to be employed at the same company because companies always lay off their least-skilled workers. They never want to see us in the ball game, they want to see us on the sideline admiring and asking for autographs, I know it must tickle! This is more than just shady business practices, this is Racism with the capital R. I always hung out with the in-crowd in school, and the in-crowd always used to pick on and look down on headbangers, rednecks, dirt farmers, pig farmers, dirtbags, bikers, and hillbillies. Now, the in-crowd sticks up for them, you can't be serious!

The Evil Detective

It's the job of a detective to pick the minds of the accused. That detective knew from picking my mind that the lies and perception would overpower the truth. They didn't want to find the truth because there is no benefit and finding the truth, but all the benefits with slick talk. When you turn a person into a piece of property, that is slavery, and Satan put me in prison by choice. If that's not the definition of sick, then I don't know what is. I would love to have someone check out this Creep's record because he was too relaxed and got away too easily with evil. Give my ex-lawyer an MRI lie detector test and ask her when she called that detective and ask him did he say that, what did he say, how did he act and what does she think. Now, say I am lying about that.

The Malicious D.A.

I forcefully plied my friend Jim off of John Romanski and someone from the group immediately started hitting Romanski and I forcefully plied him from Romanski as well, while Jim was still going after Romanski. So, that's two people I forcefully removed from hitting Romanski, all the while shouting at the group "That's my friend's brother you better not touch him". If you know something and don't say something, that's obstruction of justice. John Romanski wanted to tell the court what I had done to break up the fight on the Charlotte Pier on my second trial but told me the D.A. threatened him if he changed his testimony, that he would get charged or something like that. So, she coached him. I know all of this because of John Romanski himself. Isn't that like withholding information, falsifying evidence, lying under oath, and concealing evidence by the prosecution threatening John Romanski to tone down what actually happened, or should I say obstruction of justice? To sum everything up, this is in fact Malicious Prosecution, because I went to prison behind these demon-devilish lies. Do you call that a fair trial when the prosecutor and detective set me up? Give John Romanski an MRI lie detector test and ask him if it is true. Now, say I am lying. Also, give Steve Viccaro, the guy who testified against me that was the prosecution's golden boy, an MRI lie detector test and ask him if he hit that guy lots of times on the ground. He is now a cop, I believe. Sure, an MRI lie detector test won't hold up in court, but it will get to the bottom of things. I bet Steve Viccaro won't take one for a million bucks. One of the biggest reasons this harsh treatment happened to me was because they plastered my name all over the local media. I remember when I got back to my cell from getting sentenced, I saw the words "SNELL SENTENCE" on the TV screen, it wasn't even time for the News. When all that racism happened in school the college was like 'screw you', you went to prison, the Job was like, give me a reason, and the police were like I'll push your scalp back like a tuna can with this thing man. All because the Malicious D.A. and Evil detective trying to make their quota, how could they sleep at night tricking people with their black magic and dark psychology, they should write fiction.

My Record

It's time that I come clean. I just look guilty on paper, and I know I will discredit myself and some people's eyes by what I am going to write. I had one of the biggest house parties (in the top 3 of all time, ask the whole class of Hilton High) back in 1990 in my parent's home when they were on vacation. To make a long story short, when I was outside talking to the police, someone stole all the money I had made from the party and then went into my parent's room and stole their mortgage and wedding rings. My mother kicked me out of the house and then eventually let me back in. I have always worked since I was 9 by shoveling, raking leaves, and mowing lawns. I always had money and I lived in a $120,000/ $140,000 house. All my mother talked about was her wedding rings being stolen. She put so much pressure on me by making me feel guilty. That's all she talked about. She even cried. One of my best friend's father had died, and he was upset. He thought he could never go to college because he had to take care of his family since he was the oldest. He was doing roofing in the city one day in one of the dangerous neighborhoods and noticed that people would buy drugs from this old man in his house. My friend told me that he thought up a way for me to replace my mother's wedding ring and a way for him to go to college. So we pretended like we were the police with walkie-talkies and BB guns and I knocked on his front door and asked him for drugs when he opened the door, we told him that we were the police and entered his house with BB guns drawn. While in the house, my friend found a real gun and dispatched what he found to our friends on the walkie-talkie outside the house, so everything looked real. We also took $62 from the house. Then the next thing you know, we were arrested. No one got hurt or even hit. So I spent 22 days in jail and have a robbery second on my record because of this.

When my friend and I went to court, the whole Courtroom, Police, Bailiff, and Judge busted into tears laughing when they found out what happened. Basically, you had two white guys from the suburb go into the heart of the ghetto and rob a drug house with BB guns and took their real gun from them. I was only 20. All this proves is that I was stupid, because I could have gotten killed, and that my balls were bigger than the ones that Serena and Venus Williams sisters were playing with. Like I said, I always had a job and didn't need to have a bunch of money. I did it because of all the constant pressure my mother put on me about her wedding rings. You know what's sickening about all of this? My mother's wedding rings never got stolen. It was all a lie. Why would you go on vacation with your husband and family and not wear your wedding rings? That's why my mother and I don't get along today because I told a lot of people inside/outside the family about this and about her stealing my social security # when I was in prison, and not my father.

The Internal Affairs

I was told to contact Internal Affairs by my counselor at the time at Rochester Works after I already told her that I contacted the FBI about my letters. So I called them up and the guy was waiting for my call and told me to come to his office in the next couple of days around 1 o'clock. After I thought about it for a while, I called the FBI back again, because I wanted them to see what was going on, and I wanted the police to know I meant business. The guy from internal affairs most certainly knew that I called the FBI back because when we met I saw it all over his face and he was mad about that. We sat down across from one another for not even five minutes, and he said, "Why don't you just leave town on a bus and that they would pay for it". As he was talking I noticed how much he looked like my best friend John Dettman gawking at me from across the table, so I wanted to smile, and before I even got it out he and his partner had stood up looking at me meanly and told me that the meeting was over. Nice subject change. I don't remember all the words that he said in the office while we were sitting down, but I remember when he exploded on me by saying "HIS OWN MOTHER HATES HIS GUTS" VERY VERY LOUD that shook the building. They led me to the front of their office, so I could talk to another guy, and when I was walking through the office with the new Internal Affairs guy where all the Internal Affairs people worked so that I could show him my letters online because he wanted to see it, and that guy that looked like John Dettman showed up from behind a closed door and yelled at the top of his lungs "NOBODY LIKES THIS GUY, HIS OWN MOTHER HATES HIS GUTS, HIS OWN MOTHER HATES HIS GUTS". This whole episode caused my life to be what it is today because when the new guy interviewed me, he asked me to name people I was friends with and knew, and I only gave them two names that they already knew about. What would you do? It's like handing over my combination to my safe,"Were not going to take anything, we just want to have a look inside, trust us", and in the meantime being surrounded by a trillion guns, well here is my combination to my safe, you just want to take a peek right? Why would you give a person the key to your safe if you know that person hated you? So, because I only gave them two names, the police, the college, and the machine shops told everyone that people hate my guts and that their treatment of me was justified. Now I have more issues than Sports Illustrated. So when I spoke with the second guy from Internal Affairs, I just wanted to let them know that I wasn't a dangerous threat and didn't take the meeting too seriously. That one Internal Affair guy who looked like John Dettman just complicated a situation that wasn't all that complicated. As you can see, they're incapable of running an impartial investigation and put me into a no-win situation. And once they have my list of friends, they're just going to hurry up with the cover-up. Police are experts at running "Game", dark psychology by talking people into things, they just made me tell on my mother. Let's say that your high school football coach hates you and tells everyone to hate you. What do you think will happen? What will happen to the teammate that stands up for you? Will the coach start him? In my opinion, John Dettman's look-alike is guilty of coercion and unethical practices, which is a serious breach of moral decency. Especially since he is supposed to defend people who can't defend themselves. He planted the seed and watched it grow. They have installed hate in people's hearts, by polluting my life and stretching the law by saying "People hate you". If that's the case, the law is evil too.

Relationships

I never read a book my whole life until I went to prison. I read tons of books in prison and knew that was the reason why I was there. Once I got my GED, I knew that I would get my degree one day because it felt too good to pass the GED test. When I got out of prison I got sidetracked and started hanging out with some of the most popular people in town and knew that if I kept hanging out with them, I would find my way back to prison, because they always liked to fight and had the money to get out of it. So I stayed to myself and stopped hanging out with my friends and slept with a lot of women. I had a very active sex life. One day, I slept with 5 or 6 different girls at different times of the day. I could have slept with lots of my friend's girlfriends and sisters, but never did. I never had so-called "Game" slick talking psychology to get women to sleep with me. In other words, I wasn't manipulating then, and I am not manipulating now. Some people could sell people the moon; I am not one of those people, because people would see right through me. I had lots of energy, very trustworthy, character, extremely outgoing, looks, and always made women laugh. I wanted my degree so badly that I just dated women that I knew it wouldn't go anywhere, because I had the philosophy "paper before pleasure". So I thought I was doing the right thing, by not settling down and having kids I couldn't afford, by turning my life over to my career through college and work. Thank God I don't have children. Can you imagine your baby crying and your wife telling you that you're a failure? I guess I would have to commit a crime, right? Now that they have put my life in a Supplex, I barely go outside, and my sex life has taken a nosedive, and they're using that against me now by saying. "People hate him so much, he can't even get a girl". I started a little late in life with women because I was very shy when it came to them, even though I was very close friends with them. When I was serious about dating women, they were model material that fell in love with me. Nine and Tens, I have pictures. MRI lie detector, please.

When judging a person's personality, it's best to choose what type of personality you're zeroing in on. If you want to know how excited a person is, the best time to evaluate him is when he is at his best. When you want to see how mad a person could get before they snap, the best time to do this is when they're mad, not happy. Judging a person's personality for happiness when that person is mad and at their worst is like judging a person the second after they've just been ripped off or been in a car accident. All these evil things that have happened to me are like spiking my drink with a Mickey and then judging my performance. Have you ever been around a person who was going through a terrible divorce? Well, I am going through the divorce of my human rights, my safety, my career, and my right to exist as a human being. People get away from negative people because they end up bringing you down. How can I be positive with all this negativity around me? It's like I have to have an election to be a person. Then they want to convince everyone that everyone hates me by the look on my face. My Human Rights isn't even on the radar.

John Steward Killing Spree

John Steward came over to my house one day all excited about moving back to Rochester from another state where he had killed lots of people by being in a violent street gang. I don't know how many people he killed before, and I don't think John knows either, or maybe he does. He told me that he shot and killed people all the time in another state. Imagine someone winning the lottery, that was the excitement on his face when he told me all of this. He even tried to explain the gang signs to me and everything. Like some excited professor on speed. I can't believe his deep love for guns and weapons, it's sick. First of all, I haven't got caught in one lie, because I write reality, that's why I am so convincing. Secondly, if I was going to lie, why would I pick this lie? Does that make any sense? MRI lie detector, please. Ask Kevin Roule, what was the name of Danny who had red hair, limped, and looked like Malachai from the movie "The Children Of The Corn". That guy would most certainly know. A guy named Oscar who tried to give his girlfriend an abortion with a coat hanger that was in the paper a long time ago. That was John Steward's best friend. One day I worked in the mall and Mark DiRisio and Rick from Spencerport came and picked me up with my other friends from Spencerport. John Steward was in the back of his pickup truck with all of us and I said out loud, to the rest of the people in the back truck, "John was in a gang and used to shoot and kill people. Ask Mark DiRisio and Rick if they remember that, and how did John react? Ask John Dettman and Matt Cookinham how long ago I told them that John Steward was in a gang killing people. Ask Tory Weaver, John's best man at his wedding, did John used to be in a gang killing people. I have listened to tons of rap music, and don't know how to do one gang sign. John knows how to do them like a pro and hardly listens to rap music. All the police have to do is shove official papers in his face welcoming him into the police dept, but he must pass an MRL lie detector test saying he never killed more than two people. That the test is not 100% accurate and might show a false positive on one, but not the other, and that they allow their men one screw up and the test process because they know the machine sucks, and that this is a one-time offer. Or something like that. I bet he'll run "Game" dark psychology and weasel his way out of it. Isn't this something, this guy went to another state and went on a killing spree then slid back home like he was in the Major Leagues, looking at the police like an Umpire as he slid past home base. "Am I safe?" Of course, we love you". John Steward was even hired by some of the police to spy on their cheating wives, while the police were at work. And he also hangs out with them too. He is a security guard outside the bars who wear a gun openly that the police gave him. He also works security at Rochester's only amusement park, where lots of families take their kids. I know the name of the gang and the State where he went on his killing spree. I will not talk to the local police about this either. Would you? A message to the police from me. Don't be afraid of people who attacks you, be afraid of friends who flatter you.

Police

I paid John Steward to come and pick me up from my apartment because I wanted to go out but knew that the police would pull me over for drinking, because of all my letters. This was when I first moved into Colonial Manor. So as we arrived at the dance club where he worked at, one of the biggest Club spots in Rochester, he told me that he wanted me to talk to someone and not be scared. When we got out of the car, there was a cop with stripes on the side of his uniform. He told me that no one would ever pull me over, and they knew that I wanted to go out to the clubs, that no one would ever pull me over and shook my hand. A couple of weeks later, someone broke into my car outside the dance club, and I used one of the bouncer's phones to call 9-1-1 and report it. I arrived at the dance club late and was only there for around 1 1/2 hours. They didn't have much of a beer selection, and the selection they did have was pricey. All that to say, I was not drunk. When I got the police report back, it said I was drunk, because every checkbox that the 9-1-1 officer wrote on the report spelled everything wrong like I slurred every single word. They record all the calls from 9-1-1 right? The police knew that I had called them, and since they hate me so much for spilling my beans, wouldn't you think they would have kept a copy of that recorded 9-1-1 conversation? I thought they were trying to repair the damage that they were guilty of, but they had war on their mind, and I was gullible and had peace in my mind. So, I knew that they were trying to set me up from the beginning. I was just happy to be working and getting the red carpet treatment, but it was like giving children Halloween candy with poison in it. I told my counselor at Rochester Works about this when it happened.

I can't go to any of the area Malls without being followed and being looked at mean. I can't go to the Public Market without being followed and getting mean looks by security. If I stop and talk to someone, you best believe plain clothes police / plain clothes security is right there. I went to visit someone in the hospital, and they were waiting for me outside. Imagine trying to see something far away very hard, but close up, and that's the look I get. One time I went to the Public Market and I saw John Reynolds with his family. They must have lost track of me because there were a lot of people there and me and John got off the main walkway with his family to buy flowers. We were off the main walkway I guess for too long, then all of a sudden, security came from all directions looking at me. There was this one guy on one of them gulf carts with shades on that didn't take his eyes off me. John Reynolds saw and admitted that he knew it was for me. The police know where I am at 24-7, and use security guards to do their spying and eavesdropping. Wherever there is a security guard, which is everywhere where I live and in all the stores period, they know me and spy on me. There were times that I went into a new store that I hadn't been to before, and then plainclothes police or security would follow me into that store and wait in line with me and everything. The police went from speeding up behind me out of nowhere (on every block at one point) surrounding my car everywhere I went, to having security follow and spy on me. Now, the police don't mess with me, but they make sure that I know their surroundings and use the security everywhere and anyone else they could get their hands on to spy on me. There were times when I was eating at a buffet in the mall, and noticed this one guy sitting in the booth looking at me mean, without even having a plate of food on his table. I went out with a couple of friends for Christmas at

Daisy Dukes and noticed this one clean-cut guy with blonde hair and blue eyes, looking at me very mean. He had his eyes on me all the time I was there. I can't even go jogging. I have basically been in my apartment since I last emailed letters. I was getting out of shape, so I decided to take me and my iPod jogging only a mile away in the park. I would get followed there and always felt like someone was watching. When I got back to my car from jogging, there was always someone in a car just sitting there looking at me. So I stopped jogging. It seems like if I go somewhere twice, it seems like they're on point when I go there again the next time. I used to go to Barnes and Noble and read books for free, the whole time I was there Mall security was very close by looking over my shoulder and waiting in the parking lot for me. So I stopped going. People are scheming on me like a bunch of bounty hunters. I shouldn't have to have butterflies to just go to my car. I see the N-word embedded on their faces. I can't go here, there, and around the corner. They have cornered the market with their hate and their faces are saying "I'll pay you back someday I promise you wait and see". What makes me think that if I move to another city, the same thing won't happen to me again? Either way you weigh it, this is a silent professional hate job targeted at me by police and their undercover snakes. I came home one night from work around 2 or 3 a.m. and saw two guys in t-shirts standing by their car doors looking mean when they saw me they both hopped in the car extremely fast then watched where I was going and followed me. Besides almost getting shot on campus twice and ran over, this was the scariest thing that happened. At Advance Glass Industries I was mad that my supervisor for working me to death, so they saw it on my face then when I left work to go home, undercover police were in the parking lot waiting for me bent over hiding behind cars and standing across the street in plain sight looking at me. I stood outside and talked with one of my coworkers for almost an hour, and they were still there. Altogether, I saw about 4 undercover cops. I could go into a store or get something to eat and the police would have their headlights on across the street, letting me know that they were there. No matter what time of the day it was. Police are experts at spotting trouble, and so are people who have been to prison. My point, they know that I am not a threat, but still keep stalking, mean faces, trying to get me to fight, and slandering me. If that is not an example of terrorism, I don't know what is. Let it be known, the police aren't messing with me at this second, but that's no difference than me and a violent vicious street gang robbing a corner store for EVERYTHING they have in the store and my father gives back a candy bar to the owner and says, "my son isn't robbing you now, and I don't want to hear anymore about this again".

MCC

Who should you believe, someone who has lied and changed their story lots of times, or someone that has never changed their story? A college that won't teach you right won't treat you right. I have proven liability when I provided proof that Darwin put his funky hand all in my face and the teachers were more concerned with increasing their skills rather than getting paid to teach. BREACH OF CONTRACT, point-blank. MCC is liable and responsible for people retaliating against me. There is no way to put a small army on me without top people in the college knowing, impossible. The college is negligent for not teaching me. Mr. Brandon knew that I didn't know anything about machining and didn't say a word. That's negligence right there. Now say am lying. Brian the student was a billion% hacker and hacked very expensive software for the teachers, and out of loyalty the teachers would turn their backs on racism. The name of one of the software he hacked is called Millwright. If I am lying about that software, you can send me back to Elmira prison, because that place has the most rats out of all the prisons I've been to. Now say I am lying Mr. Brandon, Pat. Dave and the rest of you teachers. You know what I am talking about.

I knew this one professional who worked in the office at the college who went home at night crying sometimes because she would always hear staff saying racist things about black students and staff all day long in front of her. She had blonde hair and blue eyes, but was really black. No one could ever tell that she was really black. I saw something like this on Oprah before. She ended up leaving the college because of the racism within the college. Now say am lying.

These guys are certified liars because Mr. Ryther said to me when I was being recorded "You should have picked a better course to enroll in and that the college had no obligation and responsibility whatsoever to what students enrolled in. Basically, I was the dumbass for taking the course, and it wasn't the college's fault. Watch them try to edit their lies now. Now these guys are trying to style on me by airing commercials on T.V. saying. "I got the best job you never heard of".

I wanted to record one of the teacher's conversations so that I could have it on tape with what we talked about. So I went to Walmart by the college and bought a little recording device, and I was followed there and by the time I went to talk to the teacher he was all nervous and didn't say too much. The same teacher said to me about a week before that, "Roy, Roy leave Rochester now, you don't know these people, leave quick, trust me". This teacher liked me too. Wouldn't you say I am outnumbered just a little? MRI lie detector, please.

Give the secretary at the applied tech a lie detector test and ask her if I ever get along with the teachers before I start spilling my beans. One of the teachers liked me so much he invited me to a picnic that was held on the college grounds that was on a Saturday I think, and even if it wasn't held on a Saturday, it was on a day when there was no school just staff and families. This same teacher gave me a nickname. He called me Art Shell, a former NFL coach because of my last name. Ask Pat's daughter if her father ever liked me.

Ask any machinist in the world if it is possible for someone to have a degree in machining when that person has only trammed the manual mill and manual lathe a few times. Ask any mechanic if it's possible for a person to only use a wrench a few times, but yet have a degree in mechanic technology. Ask any computer technician if is it possible for someone to pass the A+ certification without ever building a computer and only installing an Operating System once and not by themselves. This fact isn't just important, it's the smoking gun. If this isn't an act of breach of contract and corrupted education, I don't know what is. I have anxiety because I don't have a skill that I paid for. If I had that skill, I would eventually get bored, and that means that I would have to get more skills from being bored. Anxiety = lack of skills, bored = new skills.

I know what some of the main people look like, who are behind the scenes and lurk in the shadows. It was the weekend of my birthday and about 3 days before a cop almost blew my brains out just outside the college doors. I told Mr. Ryther that I just wanted to have a good time on the phone that weekend for my birthday. They knew where I would be and knew that John Steward would be picking me up, because I would not drive my car to the clubs, for fear of getting pulled over. It was a Friday night and when the dance clubs opened, 18 and over, no one was there until at least an hour later. Since I was the first one there that didn't work there, because John Steward drove me there and worked outside, I had a seat at the bar. A couple of minutes later, this older couple around 65 to 75 and an 18 and over club came in and sat at the opposite side of the bar and looked at me mean all night long, even when I went to dance on the dance floor. I don't know who it was, but someone behind me gave them a mean look too because the older guy put up his hands to say "Okay, Okay I'll stop", but continued after a short period. They were there until at least 1 am, doing nothing but watching me and occasionally drinking. After the dance club ended at 2 am, I was waiting by John's car when one of the M.C.C. staff members came up to me and asked me if anyone was bothering me. I won't say his name, but ask me under a lie detector test if it's true.

Debt equals slavery, paying my student loan is the same as being forced to pay for a Hummer that you haven't even driven, forced to pay child support to a woman that has 4 kids that you didn't even sleep with, forced to pay for a house that I never even stepped foot in, and forced to pay for an education I never got! They must be eating yellow snow if they think I am going to pay my student loan. They better put me in jail or shoot me in my head, because I am not paying anything! NIGGA!!!

Computer Confidence

I tried to give them away out by letting everything go in my letters over 2 years ago. I told them that I just wanted to learn everything about the computer, and they tried to set me up for the kill with that too. When I said I just wanted to learn computers, what I was doing was submitting by saying that I just wanted to be done with the whole thing and live the rest of my life, but these Sea of Demons couldn't let me be. Me and this one guy started at computer confidence at the same time. I had zero experience and he had tons. The first week of the course, he called my counselor complaining that the course was a fraud and the teacher just sat at a desk not teaching. He told me that he called the next day. The owner of the course thought I had called, and tried to set me up the whole time I attended there. I was talking about politics one day when no one was in the room but men. I was mad about a certain topic and swore once or twice at the most. It was me and two other men in the room. The next day, I think, my counselor came in and told me that she had a complaint by one of the women about me saying inappropriate things around women. That wasn't true. Lie detector, please. So I went back to the class and said nothing. The one teacher wanted to know badly what was going on, and I told him, and he said, "I catch Marie (the owner) all the time spying by the door when you're in here. He gave me his email at that point and said, "if Marie tries anything by setting you up, let me know because I know how she is". I have only emailed this teacher once to tell him that I passed the A+ hardware part of the test. Give him and me an MRI lie detector test. Then this one lady told me the next day, I had nothing to do with that, it was all Marie's doing. That was just the beginning because that same lady would try to flirt with me so that I would say something out of the way to her. She wanted to be the head teacher there so badly, she tried to use her body like one of the sluts trying to climb the corporate ladder. One day when I was leaving for the day, she bent down in a sluttish way out of the eyesight of the other teacher that was in the room. I looked at her and the other teacher looked at me like he was looking for something, like a reaction from me, I guess. So that she could say "did you see it too". I am good at describing things, but I would have to show you what she exactly did. Then, when I was in the corporate class, she would cross and uncross her legs wearing a dress lots of times. One day she did it like 10 times in a row where one could almost see up her dress. Something like Sharon Stone. I knew the whole time what she was doing, but didn't think the other guy knew, let alone remember. You could always ask the other guy. I guess she wanted me to say something to her out-of-the-way so that she could get me in trouble, I guess. What do you think? Haven't I had a lot of time to think about this? If I were smart, I wouldn't even put this paragraph in here, but it's staying because I want people to know about ALL the pressure that was applied to me out of retaliation that has left me in my apartment not knowing what to do. Explain to her exactly what an MRI lie detector test is, and tell her that your boss has all the cool, high-paying jobs that she could have if she takes an MRI lie detector test and passes. The kid is undefeated when it comes to telling the truth. I haven't gotten caught in one lie yet, and why would I blow my perfect record on some leather-face slut? That's unacceptable.

Jasco

The meanest machine shop by far that I worked for. I

bet if you were to ask 10,000 people who worked there before if they're mean, at least 95% would agree. It gets to around 120 degrees there in the summer alone. They had me operating 8 machines with short cycle times and if I didn't get enough parts, my supervisor would look at me mean all night long. One time he yelled out to me "We pay you all this money, I want you to do a better job, I want more from you" Firstly, my base pay was only 12 an hour with 15% more = $13.85 hr., because I worked the C- shift and the word was out that people hated my guts and I couldn't get along with people, so that was the only way I could enter their shop. That was the true reason, because my first week there I started work on a Thursday and worked Friday on the A- Shift training, then started on the C- Shift that Sunday night. People even said they had never seen that before. My supervisor was 5 feet tall, and it was the same as someone telling him "Try to get Roy to hit you", because he would always throw things across the room and yell super loud, so the whole place could hear. One day I called the head supervisor about this, and he said, "I don't think this is working out, and I had to get along with my supervisor. My supervisor told this one guy that I called the head supervisor on him, and then that guy would look at me like he wanted to fight. I would look him straight in the eyes and give him the same look he gave me. People would walk around by my machine and would say, I wouldn't take that. During the last 3 weeks that I worked there, my supervisor threw all these expensive casting parts across the shop because he was mad at his right-hand man. These parts were all around the door that people walked through and sat there all night long, and when the programmer/supervisor came in at 4 am, he stepped over the parts like nothing happened. He knew when he saw the parts who was responsible. Everyone knows how this guy is and how Jasco treats people, but had a special thing for me. I could go on and on, but that was the last straw with me and the machine shops. Other people who have my degree are making 15, 20, 25, and 30+ an hour working 10 to 40+ hours overtime a week. The college outright tells you that you will be making 25+ an hour. I had to operate 8 machines with a base pay of 12/ hr. and got treated less than a human being by someone who belongs in a high chair. If this isn't an act of outright aggression, revenge, payback, and a hostile environment by retaliating against me, then there is no such word as retaliation. I am sick of these people eating my food and licking the plate. Period. I called Jasco at precisely 1:05:16 pm and stayed on the phone for precisely 01:18 on Superbowl Sunday, I have Voice Over IP as a phone service, and if a million people call my house, I could see a readout of it on my computer through the Voice Over IP website at any time. The next day, manpower called and left a message on my voicemail saying that I was fired because I didn't call in and show up for work and not to report to work anymore and to call him back. He called me back, and he yelled into my voicemail "I know you're there Roy, pick up the phone, I know you're there". Either this guy is psychic, or the police told him I was home. You make the call. I just had my ringer off so I could sleep. The last night before I went to work at Jasco, there was a cop outside my house with his headlights on and when I was in his eyesight, he got out of the car fast and slammed the door very hard. Cops are experts at non-verbal communication, and so are people who have been to prison. I haven't worked since then, and I didn't sign up for unemployment, because all they're going to do is run "Game", dark psychology mind tricks and make me the scapegoat once again. I am the king of the Ramen Noodle Soup and baked beans and don't have money to pay my rent, car insurance, internet, electricity, and food, let alone gas money.

One guy at Jasco tried to make me feel good by saying "You're not the only one people don't like, when I was in high school people picked on me all the time, so I hung out with my hacky sack friends that people didn't like either". It turns out that the main people who picked on him were very popular and looked up to me! Al and Steve Viera from Greece Athena.

Email that I sent to Unemployment about Manpower / Jasco

I just want to clear some things up. I emailed letters to just about all the Senators, Governors, Media, etc over the Internet on August 11th, 2008 about the local college, the police dept. and the machine shops because they have retaliated against me and destroyed my environment. One section of my letter explained how I got fired at Manpower because Manpower said I did not call in and show up for work Sunday night February 3rd, 2008 "Super Bowl Sunday". Since I have given specific proof of the EXACT time I called into work, now Manpower is changing their story on how they fired me. They had the heads-up and time to think. Have you ever heard of a company ending your assignment because you didn't call in or show up for work? No, because they fire you. And if they end your assignment because of a lack of attendance, why didn't they write me up for it? Companies keep detailed records of everything, where is the proof? Keep in mind, that I worked for Manpower for like a year and a half. Why would I waste time giving you my username and password to my phone records? Manpower knew that I had hard proof, so now they're telling you that I was relieved of my assignment, and not fired.

All the machine shops that I have worked at since I tried to sue the local college have retaliated against me by working me to the extreme and treating me unfairly. I would work for 3 months at a machine shop, and then I would give them my two weeks' notice and hope that things would be different at the next machine shop, but it wasn't. I have gone 8 months without receiving any paycheck of any kind. I am very good at living below my means and had money saved up, and I have been in my apartment the whole time.

Just to let you know, Jasco has tried to offer people money to be a witness for them and unemployment litigation cases. One time they offered to pay this older guy "named Joe I think" 500 dollars to say that he was around when a former employee told the supervisor that he quit. The problem was, this guy got fired and the older guy "named Joe I think" wasn't anywhere near the scene when it happened. Another time, one of the supervisors confrontationally got nose to nose with another former employee and told him that he was fired, later tried to litigate it by saying that the guy just quit. Check Jasco's track record, as you will see similar complaints.

You can read all my letters under my Blog on Myspace.com by searching for Roy Snell Rochester, N.Y. If you care anything about human rights, my letters will make you angry, if you don't care about human rights, my letters will make you laugh and blush!!! Please do not deny me unemployment before you read my letters. Governor Patterson has asked the State Police to look at my letters. I haven't gotten caught in one single lie and any of my letters, and I have proven tons of lies.

Proof That I Sent to Unemployment About Manpower / Jasco

Here is the solid proof. Go to www.voip.com and log in to diddy9470@yahoo.com for Username and my password is 0zXww7hN. My phone number is 585-563-6061. Now go to Outgoing Calls, press call logs, press "Search Calls" at the top, under "Time Period select in the past year", click search call logs, and go to page 21, February 3rd 585-254-0700. That is Jasco's phone number. I called twice that day, as you can see. Manpower said on the phone to me on Monday, February 4th. "No call, No show is an immediate fire". Their number is 585-227-6008. This is only a 1% sample of my letters. I don't have the money to print the pages out, so go to Myspace.com and search for Roy Snell or Diddy, Rochester N.Y., and read my Blogs about everything that has happened out of retaliation for my trying to sue the College and how I have proven massive discrimination and racism in the Machine Shops. I am undefeated when it comes to telling the truth because I haven't gotten caught in one lie. I need all the help I can get. I have been in my apartment for over 2 years, not knowing what to do. I don't know where to turn. Can you please help?

Divide and Conquer

John Dettman was my best friend. I used to go to this popular bar that the police went to, and they didn't want me going there. I was at the bar with John Dettman and Sean Bauer having a good time when this guy came up to me, play boxing and said, I am just kidding around. Then John Dettman walked by, and I said, go play with that guy. This guy went over to John Dettman and pushed him so hard, it was like a football tackle, and then he went over to his group of friends. I rushed over to him and asked the guy why he had done that and John Dettman, Sean Bauer, and about 5 other men backed me up, all the while the police were smiling from ear to ear. He said because you told me to. I knew the police were watching, so I told John Dettman that I was sorry and that it was my fault. We went outside and John Dettman wanted me to back him up if anyone jumped in the fight when the guy came out. I told John Dettman I was sorry 100 times and that the police were inside and had a thing for me. After about ten minutes, we said our goodbyes and every time I called John Dettman he wouldn't accept my calls. I know his whole family and slept over at his house lots of times. He even came to pick me up from prison. We were like brothers, and I have letters from prisons to prove this. This was an act of retaliation and a plot to get me to commit violence. John Dettman doesn't know anything that has gone on, really. I was trying to tell him, but he wanted to just fight, and I broke the bond by not wanting to back him up. He is going to hate me even more now because his wife is the secretary of my ex-doctor who hates my guts because the college bad mouth me to him and by me writing about him, my ex-doctor might take it out on his secretary because he knows that me and his secretary were cool. I called my doctor's office to see if I could get some Nasonex because it was helping me breathe better. He shouted on the phone "No more Nasonex, no more sprays, no more nothing". And not to basically come to his office anymore, got cute with me, and then hung up the phone on me. He shouted the whole time on the phone. The college made my doctor flip on me like Jack Nicholson in The Shining.

I have been friends with John Reynolds, who owns a bar that the police go to all the time now. We used to be best friends in school and hung out all day, then would go home and talk all night on the phone. He was supposed to testify for me at court, because he saw me seconds after the fight on the pier, and knew for a fact that I didn't have anything to do with it by how I reacted, what I had told him, and how the guys that I was with reacted. He never testified because he was scared. He saw me every day, just about. Just like the cops could get family members to turn on one another, the cops have gotten John Reynolds to turn on me. John is not a manipulating person, either; he's just out for number one. John said to me one night, "Hey Roy, I want you to start coming here more, please". So I said okay. I knew something was funny because John isn't a manipulating person and I saw right through that, but didn't want to believe it. The next time I went to his bar, a half hour later, a guy came in and started talking about CNC machining to me. I told him that I was in that field and didn't want anything to do with it anymore. He told me that he was the new plant manager or something and offered me a job. I declined, and he offered me a job about 100 times, and when he saw that I wouldn't accept, he wanted to fight me. If Donald Trump offered you a job once, and you declined, he would tell you to take a hike. This guy offered me a job 100 times, then wanted to fight me. He even said to this one black guy at the bar, "See, I told you" as in, I told you he wouldn't fight. I am outraged, not a killer. The police didn't want to pull me over after I had a drink in the bar, they just wanted everyone to see that so they could say, we're not bothering him anymore. But they do want violence. If I had gotten into a fight with this guy, the police would have been there to arrest me (knowing that I don't have money for bail) and put me in the jail cell with someone who weighs 400 lbs. Then they would try to prove that I had snapped with violence. That is what they truly want from me, violence, so they could show that I haven't changed because I have been in about 150 (one-on-one) fistfights without ever using a weapon. This was 1000% a setup. About 2 months before that, a guy out of the blue called me the N-word in the bar. I didn't fight and nothing came of it. This guy was about 100 lbs smaller than me, too. I felt this was a set-up and the police were lurking in the dark to arrest me, especially since they always knew where I was. I went from being a lion to a mouse; all because I am scared of their lies, and they have way too much momentum in the courts. I should have sent both those men to the hospital. Darwin Snow's relative came into the bar one night and asked me in a whining tone "How did I write my letters, how do you do it"? He looked just like Darwin Snow and said he worked for the city somewhere. Coincidence? Another time John called me and told me to come down to this Festival that was a mile away where he was selling food as a vendor. As soon as I got there, I was approached by two men asking me all kinds of questions, looking into my eyes hard. It turned out that one of them was the head of security at the public market, and the other was security somewhere else. The head of security from the public market would always watch me from afar. They have tried to get anyone and everyone to help their cause, and now they have gotten my one-time BEST friend. That hurts. He is now cooking for them at private parties all the time. I knew something was wrong because the police would shake John Reynolds's hand and then give him their card in front of me. Well, this is my retaliation. John Reynolds is guilty of statutory rape because he used to have sex with a 13 and 16-year-old when he was 21 or 20. To make things worse, he was really good friends with the girl's brother. He also does tons of cocaine and used to sell a boatload of marijuana in college which almost got him kicked out, he told me that he used to copy another student's homework then paid them with marijuana and slept with call girls all the time. MRI lie detector, please.

Vocal Cord Dysfunction

I wanted to lose weight and have lots of energy because I was working long hours and attending school. So I went to GNC and told them what I wanted, and that money wasn't an object. They told me Ripped Fuel was the best for what I wanted. So I started losing tons of weight and worked one day at my job 18 hours straight without even being tired, then went home and worked out. Ripped Fuel put my system into overdrive and caused me not to sleep and slur my words. I could only exhale for like 10 seconds before I ran out of breath. This is the most embarrassing thing to discuss in this whole letter. When you see someone not talking right, people automatically assume it's mental, well so did I. So I went and got an MRI to check and see if everything was alright. They said everything was fine. I wasn't satisfied because I was still slurring my words, so I went and talked with this one doctor who knew I was in prison, and he wrote down that I was bipolar. I didn't know what that was but told me medication could help. So I did what they told me to do, all the while still taking the Ripped Fuel. I talked with this other doctor, and he flat-out told me that I didn't need the pills, but if I wanted, he would still give them to me. MRI lie detector, please. I told them about the Ripped Fuel, and they said everything was okay and that I could still take them. If one were to look up Ripped Fuel side effects online, and look at everything that I told the doctor, a child could see it was the Ripped Fuel. The main ingredient is Ephedrine, and my system can't handle it. I took Ripped Fuel for a long time, and when I stopped taking it, I could talk a lot better. I started taking it again to lose weight and what do you know, the slurring thing was back in my life. As you can see, the doctor's medical interpretation was way off, and they translated it to be what they wanted it to be. I didn't know rational thought and paranoid delusions go hand in hand, and even in the same sentence.

Last thing

If you caught a person and one lie, that should raise a red flag, and if you caught a person and lots of lies, that shows a plot. How many red flags does one have to hold up? One should have said red flag, red flag, red flag. I live off truth; they live off lies, lying for a living. They go off of opinions and perceptions, I go off of facts. Why should liars who have experience at lying be perceived as smart and clever, when they're just better liars by manipulating? What about the truth? I have proven motives why they have lied, cheated, manipulated, violated half the constitution, broke about a hundred laws to justify their racism, breach of contract, harsh treatment, violence, slandering, obstruction of justice, police brutality, malicious prosecution, conspiracy to commit murder, defamation of character, slavery, stalking, confidentiality, forgery, reckless endangerment, excessive force, vandalism, intimidation, endangering the welfare of a child, cruelty, falsifying records, controlled racism, justified racism, economic racism, etc. etc. etc., then they turned the table by running "Game", their dark psychology program to create reasonable doubt, as in, you can see how this could happen to a person like Mr. Snell. They are committed to these lies now. They would rather sell their soul and shoot me in the head than admit any wrongdoings, mass racism, and mass discrimination. I completely understand, and I want OUT and off this soil for good. The only thing that makes me feel like I am an

American is paying my taxes anyway. Maybe a lawsuit would make up for some of the things, but I could never get that time back. I just want off this soil. This shitty city can have this shitty shitizenship. I wouldn't trust any of my ex-employers to give me a good job reference since my first letter, and especially after this letter. I need the red tape cut and my record cleared so that I can have a fresh start in another country like Canada or the Netherlands. And I don't care about paying all of them high taxes in another country. I just care about their human rights and not being targeted. Let me go, it's the right thing to do. I deserve a better life. I only have one life to live, and the American dream is not obtainable, but the American nightmare is. It's almost as though these guys practice witchcraft with their black magic. If I was an ex-American living in Afghanistan with full citizenship and this happened to me over there, people in America would say that's what he gets for moving over there. One question, who's the real enemy? If America found out that another country had done this to one of its citizens, it would impose sanctions on that country. I feel like I am in Nazis Germany, Red China, and the old Soviet Union altogether. This is corruption beyond belief, don't you get that? They have done everything to provoke me into retaliating with violence, but I haven't, and for this alone, I deserve the Nobel Peace Prize, a medal, trophy, and some kind of world PEACE award for keeping the peace and not retaliating. Why should I love and stand for America after I have been treated like this, that wouldn't be intelligent. Now when I see the American flag, I see a cold calculating killer that spits all kinds of "Dark Mind Games" to put you in the ground or prison just for kicks. I need to flee to another country to begin the healing process, no way to do this on American soil. Why would I want to leave my family and go to another country without knowing anyone there? I think that speaks volumes. I am a man who has nothing left but the truth. Put yourself in my shoes. Now they got me living in the ghetto where people have gotten killed at the end of my street and guns have gone off just outside my window and girls have even got shot and killed by my building. Swat has even raided my next-door neighbor's house. I had never lived like this before until I started writing letters. My country has betrayed me, and for me to love this country, would be like me loving my pit bull after it has eaten my children alive. You're heartless, soulless, and mixed with monsters and no better than hunks, chunks, clumps, and lumps floating around in the sewer, you disgust me Nigga!

You can also read all my letters on Myspace under "diddy". Any contribution to help me get off this soil for good will be greatly appreciated, and I will be selling the American flag, my degree, and an apple pie on eBay, so look for it. Thank you.

Roy Snell,

    Rational

    Human

    Expatriate

P.S.

They have a better chance of finding Jimmy Hoffa's body than they do of catching me in a lie.

SUPER TUESDAY

November 2, 2010

The Final Chapter

I Emailed This letter all over Amerikkka on Election Day with the title "9-1-1, I'm under
attack by the local government and I don't know where to turn. Please help"

Bob Duffy, the Lieutenant Governor of New York, is not the Christian you think he is. The city of Rochester is out of control. They're killers, manufacture drugs and are very violent. I have to unscramble their forest of lies, and that takes time. Keep this in mind when you're reading. I have never been caught in a lie. The MRI Lie Detector Test Is My Boss And Will Never Fire Me. I have been in my apartment for like 5 years because of retaliation, and Bob Duffy is the main guy behind it now. Can I please have some help? Can someone check out Jesse Cross, class of 2004, Spencerport High School? This guy grew marijuana for the police and made $143,000 every 3 months. My name is Roy D. Snell, and you can read all my letters at www.blackplanet.com. Search for diddy9470 and look at the pictures I took for proof. Bob Duffy should be yanked out of office, or the integrity of the Governor's office will always be questioned by people who know the truth.

Lieutenant Governor of New York / Former Mayor of Rochester

Bob Duffy is the head of this Institution. In fact, he is the Institution. He must have known about all the retaliation towards me. Did he permit it? If something like this is done for as long as this has been going on, it's done in his name. Let's follow the facts. On February 2nd, 2006, the Mayor wrote me a letter in response to the letter I sent him regarding his police department, and he told me where I could go to take a civil service test and to contact Rochester Works. I just finished writing him a long letter about all the Evil retaliation the college and police departments were doing to me. Two days after I received his letter, I emailed my letters around the country, exposing all the Evil. Everything in my letter checked out, so they came up with lies saying that I was an unlikeable person, even though the police caused me to give up looking for a lawyer to sue the college, I was an unlikeable person, so it doesn't matter that they sent 30 police cruisers after me, pulling out guns on me, and pretending like they were going to run me over, in order to keep me in my place. They did this to deflect blame and justify their racist oppression. Not too long after I had emailed my letters, I met with Internal Affair where I was introduced to Chris Brown, a.k.a. John Pittman look-alike, who was the main guy that told everyone that people hated my guts and that I was an unlikable person. I can't stop them from lying, so I asked Chris Brown, a.k.a. John Dettman look-a-like, was Mayor Bob Duffy going to give me a job with the city, and he had a fit because he didn't want me to mention his name in the interview because I was being recorded. He could have killed me. Listen to the tape. That being said, they're going to hit the roof on what I am about to write. M.C.C. first put the police departments on me, now the Mayor has taken over protecting their racist practices by pulling strings and working quietly like a master card player behind the scenes.

John Reynolds [a high school friend] called me up all excited on a Saturday, the day before Father's Day 2008 practically begging me to come down the street to Maplewood Park because he was a Vendor at the Park for the weekend. He told me that he would give me free food and whatever I wanted to drink, and just come down as soon as possible to keep him company. I think he called me back after 5 minutes just to make sure I was on my way. When I got there, I was bombarded with questions from people I didn't know, and John told me that it was totally cool. One guy who was doing most of the questioning was older, around 60 something, that was head of security somewhere. The other guy was the head of security for the Public Market. Then all of a sudden, someone told me to look over there, and I noticed the Mayor of Rochester talking to other Vendors. I watched him as he made his way around, shaking hands with people in and outside around every single Vendor booth at the Park while talking to them. I also noticed that there weren't any uniformed officers around anywhere. He was just walking around with another African American by his side the whole time. When he arrived at John Reynolds's booth, where I was, he stood back away from the booth, asking John how was business. Remember, when he was talking to the rest of the Vendors, he was up close and personal talking with them while he shook their hands. Then he was looking at John, but was really talking to me when he said; "I grew up around these parts and I have made mistakes in my life when I was growing up, and I could have easily gone down the wrong road, but I turned myself around, and was lucky enough that I didn't get into too much trouble. I understand how it's so easy getting in trouble and so hard getting out of trouble." That's what he said, just about word for word. Who was he talking to? It certainly wasn't John, because he doesn't have a record. At the time, John had told them that I was very popular in school, they had seen me in the yearbooks getting names at the library, and knew they didn't have a chance and that I was going to prove them wrong on their biggest lie, at the time, over the internet. The police had completely demolished my reputation at the time, and I hadn't seen a paycheck in like four months. So I gave the Mayor a look that said, I am going all the way through with this, by writing letters and letting everyone know what you guys did to me. Not a mean dirty look, but a look that said, I am still telling. John Reynolds and the Mayor started talking in code next. John said that he had called his office before because he had problems with some kids hanging out by his place. The Mayor told him to call his office anytime. Why would he say that? Wouldn't you think he would say, call the police? But to call him personally, that doesn't sit right with me. He almost grunted the words, "Call my office to John". He kept interrupting John when John was telling him about the so-called problem by saying, call my office, call my office, call my office in a hurried, almost grunted tone. If the average person went up to the Mayor with some kind of problem, he wouldn't say call my office like that, he would say call the police. And even if he said, call my office, he wouldn't keep saying it, like it's a top priority or something. Call my office was a code word for "this guy isn't going to play ball, can I count on you because I really want to get this guy, can you please help me, for I will return the favor? Whatever that favor was, I don't know, but you best believe there was something in it for John. He never shook John's hand like he did the other Vendors. Like I said, he stood far away the whole time. Then he walked away mad because he had on black shades the whole time and when he left, he looked at me as his eyebrows met. After he left, John looked at me with the guiltiest of eyes and had an overly excited look on his face like he just won the lottery. If they honestly thought I was the person that they're making me out to be, the Mayor wouldn't have been there like that. A person could meet me once and know I would never do them harm. They know this better than anyone, but are really mad at me because I have proven institutionalized racism within the machine shops. I am not the problem; I am only a messenger with bad news about these racist realities.

When I told the people in the Vendor booth how the Mayor shook everyone's hands when he was talking with the rest of the other Vendors, then when he got to the booth where I was, he stood far away talking to John Reynolds but was really talking to me. Everyone had a scared look in their eyes, and ran up to me, trying to convince me otherwise. They were trying to use their best psychological ploy because they knew I knew what was going on. Shortly after the Mayor left, I was asked to go up and get a wooden crate in front of the park that they left on the grass, and then all of a sudden police cruisers came out of nowhere looking at me mean as hell. If I had talked it out with the Mayor, do you think they would have met me there looking mean? I went to the bathroom after that, and an officer was outside the bathroom, in fact, I almost hit him with the bathroom door. Then, when I left the park to go home, I saw police cruisers all along the way looking at me very mean. The police were already in all my business, but after the Mayor gave me a mean look, they really had me surrounded. It was like he said, destroy him by any means necessary. And the police will do anything to please the Prince of Rochester. At all costs, never mind how. At all costs, the Mayor will protect his police department in return, no matter what crimes have been committed. Like the Taliban protecting Bin Laden. The Mayor has greatly contributed to my demise. He got people to do his bidding and dirty work for him, while his hands remained clean. And when everything works out in his favor, he could take the credit because it shows that he is on top of things and a competent Mayor. And when things don't work out in his favor, he could just pluck one of the many scapegoats. That way, his hands always stay clean. It's certainly easier to silence me by sacrificing my future than admitting to all the Evil and massive discrimination. To think the Mayor could be impartial after he was the captain of the police department is hilarious. Aren't those the same people that got him elected? That's a conflict of interest.

The next day, which was Father's Day, John called me and begged me to help him work because he was short-staffed. I also knew this was a setup by the way he pleaded with me over the phone. John was looking at one of the many eyes on me when I was working, then he asked me to wipe the chair his son had just sat in, and I looked up just in time, and John was smiling ear to ear at one of the many eyes that surrounded me. Just imagine how I got treated at work. Why did I subject myself to all this? Because I have Faith built into my DNA, and even though I knew that John was involved, I just knew in my heart that John was on my side even though he told me to leave the college alone, I thought he would tell them the truth about how I really was and that everything would work out without me getting hurt. Then John had the nerve to say to me, "What do you call one white guy and 100 black men in a room together? I said what, and John said a correctional officer and laughed so hard, snot came out his nose. John and I were the closest of friends, and we both had never talked like that to one another before, he didn't think like that. Before all this happened, you could have counted the arguments we had on one hand. Now he is telling me racist cop jokes. Racism is so strong, I didn't even know it was that powerful. How did they get so many people to turn on me so fast that I had strong friendships with? The bottom line is I can't offer anyone anything in my position, and they can offer them everything, or take away everything. Not to mention the cops telling all the lies they want. By law, cops could tell you all the lies they want, and am sure they used that law to their advantage when it comes to demonizing me to people.

Real racism is quiet, and by the Mayor giving me that mean look, and then racist things happening to me afterward is an example of true racism. How can all these people threaten my life with weapons and walk around smiling at me as if they have gotten away with murder? The only thing that makes sense is that the Mayor made sure that nothing happened to them by giving them complete immunity, or something. If that's not racism, there is no such thing as racism. He probably thinks that since he doesn't wear a white sheet over his head and burn crosses, what he did was racist. He has no desire to protect my basic rights and is the main person behind these vicious acts of racism, and I want justice. I don't know how Andrew Cuomo is supposed to clean up Albany when his running mate is a politically evil, polished, professional lying, corrupt demagogue. Look what he did when he double-dipped. That's unethical and drives up the deficit. He knew what he was doing the whole time. A real Christian wouldn't do that, but a fake Christian who deceives and is out for number one will.

From the book, To Kill A Mockingbird and I quote, "As you grow older, you'll see white men cheat black men every day of your life, but let me tell you something and don't you forget it—whenever a white man does that to a black man, no matter who he is, how rich he is, or how fine a family he comes from, that white man is trash. That being said, ask the Mayor under an MRI lie detector test, did he know I was going to be there that day at the

Park, and how did he know, whom idea was it? It shows that he directly conspired to set me up. For a billion dollars, the Mayor could not pass that test. If he were to ever take that test, it probably explodes. And given the choice to choose between a liar and a thief, I would pick the thief, because you can always watch a thief. That being said, he knew I was being set up, and it makes all the sense that the police put pressure on me just after he left and countless savage racist acts happening to me as a result. Can you imagine a black Mayor doing this to someone white, and getting away with it? Rather you like me or not isn't that important because I know I go against a lot of people's value systems by telling the truth. What's relevant is that the Mayor has gotten away with crimes, and is the role model for what people think the law stands for, and should be held accountable for his actions. Perpetrators of wrong should not benefit from their wrongdoing. This is why thieves are not allowed to keep the things they steal. Evil needs to be punished, and not rewarded for crushing people with a job in Albany, so Evil can have ridiculous range practicing their Evil thrill of crushing people.

SOCIAL SERVICES

I went from making 35,000 to 6,000, and I didn't receive a paycheck in 8 months at the time. So I was forced to contact The Dept. of Social Service again because of the position this city put me in. Anyway, the last letter I wrote checks out, so they ran out of options, this time they threw a Hail Mary whopper of a lie. If you knew that someone had their car hit on purpose by the police, been abused by the police, went to prison unjustly because of the police, that your life is in jeopardy, and in poverty out of retaliation, why would you want to be mean and slick-talking and hurry this person out of your office knowing that you have the power to help this person and stop the evil? When I first arrived at my social worker's office, she had ulterior motives / hidden agenda intended to deceive me from the start and was trying to cloud my wits. Some scientists and experts say that multitasking kills your focus and decreases your productivity. That being said, this is something that they would know. The first thing she said was, we have to multitask, do you know what multitasking is, then she tried to explain what multitasking was to me like I was a child. Then she said, I don't have a lot of time, and by the way, why don't you just move? If you move, everything will be better off. I don't think they will follow you across State Lines. While she was talking to me, she was like, fill this out, read this, fill this out, read this, I don't have a lot of time, hurry up, I have people waiting on me, trying to distract me on purpose. Then I asked her did she want me to sign one of the papers here because it didn't have an "X", and I wanted to make sure I was signing in the right location because she gave me orders really fast with lots of papers to sign. Then she snapped at me and said, "This is my second time telling you, to place an "X" here, then sign". All of this was done on purpose. While she was talking to me, I stopped filling out the papers to answer her questions and respond to what she was saying, and she snapped at me and said don't look at me, look at the papers, fill the papers out, can't you multitask, hurry up, I have people waiting on me. Then she knew I didn't have a cent, and tried her hardest not to give me anything by arguing and fighting with me to sell my car. She said that my car was worth more than 500 dollars. How did she know what my car looked like? My car is a beat-up 1992 Cutlass Supreme. You should have seen the anger in her eyes when I tried to justify my car being worth 500. All the while, saying hurry up, fill this out, read this, read that, fill this out and why don't you just leave. After all, I have been through, you mean to tell me that they want to attack my intelligence and slick talk me, rather than getting Satan off my back, so I knew what she was doing and was done playing her little mind games. So I basically didn't answer the last question of the form and stopped filling out the papers, and asked her what I put for an answer here, she told me, and I said can I leave? She said yes, so I left. I simply wasn't sophisticated enough for their tricks and lies. I knew she had me write the wrong answer, but I didn't care. After I left, she told everyone that I could not read. It's like programming a computer with false information, then spamming people to death. She was attacking me the moment I entered her office, with her mean eyes and the way she was talking to me by saying over and over again, just leave. If anything, they should have sorted out the truth, not taken sides.

So, altogether they gave me like $200 for emergency

food stamps, $385 for my rent, and $35 in food stamps a month for a year. Obama increased the food stamps for people, so they sent me a form saying my food stamps would be increased if I signed and returned the form in time, I mailed it back that day, and I have always received $35 in food stamps for one year. If one does the calculations for what I got from unemployment, then, you would see that they gave me below what they gave others. If this isn't retaliation, I don't know what is. Then I had to sign a piece of paper saying that I would pay the Dept. of Social Service back in full. Under the circumstances, I feel that if I had blond hair and blue eyes, and all African American government did what they did to me, I wouldn't be forced to sign Jack. What are they really communicating? Some city agency wrote me a letter, saying that if I didn't attend an appointment, my food stamps would be canceled. I called my caseworker and told her, and she yelled in my ear, what are you calling me for, I told her, and she said to disregard the letter. I asked her what Social Service was going to do about my Landlord breaking into my apartment, and she screamed very loud in my ear again and told me not to call her again, then hung up the phone in my ear. Then a year later, when they found out that I really could read, and trust me, they knew this the whole time but wanted to silence me at the time. They sent me this food stamp form to fill out, with the maximum number of food stamps a single person could get. I never signed the form, or the other form they sent me a year after that.

Question, how often has Social Service done the dirty work for the Mayor, police, and other city agencies? How many lies have they gotten away with, and especially with people who couldn't defend themselves?

What's the difference between the Police and Social Service? I think these are very important questions.

They put a bounty on my head and hired a hitman

Where there is an attempt on one's life, there is an employer. Who do you think the employer is in this case??? About a month after meeting with my caseworker and the lie that made her the toast of Rochester, on my blood and sweat, someone hit my car again. The police hit my car before and left white and blue paint as proof on my car. If one were to take a paint test on my car, the test would come back positive showing they did indeed hit my car, because NO car that I have seen has blue and white paint. Even if it is a car with white and blue paint, since there are lots of different colors of blues and whites, what is the probability that out of all the different whites and blues colors, the same white and blue that they use for their cars, match the white and blue marks on my car? This was in the heat of the moment, I rest my case. This time, someone hit my car with an object of some sort on the passenger side by my rear tire. This was in front of the police camera. Altogether, someone hit my car like 4 times. Then within two months after meeting with my caseworker, I was coming from my sister's house at exactly 12:30 a.m. I was followed by a car from the time I left my sister's house. There wasn't one police cruiser in sight from my sister's house to my apartment, but this car followed me the whole way home. I turned on my street looking for a place to park, and I noticed a white male in a black jeep with tinted windows with his engine running and headlights on looking at me. I immediately knew who it was, because he had his driver-side window down, and I recognized his jeep with the tinted windows, but I wanted to get a better look to make sure. I had to park way down the street and I took my sweet time getting out of my car because the black Jeep was still there with its headlights on and engine running. I finally got out of my car and walked up the sidewalk slow, and as I was walking up the sidewalk coming closer to the jeep, I saw his face looking at me as I was trying to pass the parking lot by my building, the black jeep sprung to life REALLY fast and almost hit me. I jumped out of the way as fast as I could, and still, his right mirror barely just missed hitting me. He just stood there for almost a full minute looking at me through his tinted windows. I didn't go anywhere; I stood there watching him as he was watching me. He drove away slowly, and I went into my apartment building. The most important thing to know is, that there is a state-of-the-art police security camera with a perfect view of the street where I park and have the perfect view from the time I got out of my car until I enter my building. And since police know where I am 24-7, and on rare occasions I am out of my house at that time of night, hands down the police planned everything. As a matter of fact, you can't catch me outside when it's dark out no more than 10 times within a year because of the police, and 10 times is being very generous. If it wasn't for the Holidays and my parents' birthdays, you probably wouldn't catch me outside at night at all. They're the ones who followed me from my sister's house and told that guy my pinpoint locations, or else he wouldn't have had his headlights and engine running on the whole time, ready for me. Bottom line, if I didn't have quick reactions, I would have been hit for sure. Most importantly, he had his driver-side window all the way down, so the police camera had a 100% perfect view of him. They could have even counted the hairs in his ear if they wanted to.

So who was driving that black-tinted Jeep? I don't know his name, but I wrote about him in my last letter. He is a plant manager of some sort in a machine shop that works in Wayne County, and offered me a job one night. He said that he was a biker and went to Michigan University or State. I know his Jeep because we left the same time at 2 a.m. from the Charlotte Tavern when John Reynolds deceptively set me up. That day John called me and begged me to come to his bar early, he told me to come back to the kitchen so he could cook me a steak and gave me drinks after drinks on the house. Shortly after, the biker from Wayne County who tried to run me over with his Jeep, offered me a job like 100 times, then wanted to fight me because I said I wasn't going to work for another machine shop. Could you imagine me getting into a fight with someone who was just offering me a job, and I said no and tried to fight him because I was drunk? That's what the police report would have said. I was in the back of him the whole time when we left the bar that night because I was headed in the same direction as we traveled down Lake Ave to go home. He made a left on Ridge Rd / 104 that night going East.

So the first time I met with Social Service, my caseworker yelled in my ear over the phone and told me to buy a cat for the rats in this one apartment I looked at. Then he gave me the wrong information on purpose that could have put me on the streets, and if it wasn't for this one lawyer coming to my rescue, because he changed the dates leaving me two more days to search for an apartment before the Fire Marshal put me on the street. And the judge gave him an openly nasty, mean look for it too. Then they told me that they were going to pay the security deposit and first month's rent, then at the very last second of the last 2 days I had left, they changed their mind and said they were only going to be giving me first month's rent and that was final. So I sold my 800-dollar toolbox with like $3000 worth of tools that hadn't been used for 300 at the last second, or I would have been on the street. About 3 years later, my caseworker told everyone that I couldn't read. They're supposed to be the referee and not take sides, but they are. Ask Social Service to explain the fact that I filled out one of their lengthy applications a month before I met my caseworker in front of their cameras. Trust me when I tell you, I am followed everywhere, especially in a place like that where they can watch all my movements on the camera with ease to see if I even sneeze. My ex-social worker's definition of multitasking isn't doing one thing as fast as you can, and then doing another really quickly, and so on. Multitasking to her is reading, writing, listening, and answering emotional questions all at the same time. No pause in between. Hurry, hurry, your car isn't worth 500 dollars, hurry, you should just leave, hurry, keep your eyes on the paper, can't you do four mental things at once, hurry up. They're nothing but a bunch of fake friggin humanitarians that dance for the devil. I give up!!!

Interpretation, Social Service has been infiltrated by the police, college, and or the Mayor. They put my caseworker in charge of damage control and with her verbal diarrhea telling everyone that I can't read was like saying "fire at will" and gave Satan a real motive and the green light to do whatever. So anything goes I guess. It's like giving community approval to Evil. It has put my life in danger. There is a law for that, Reckless Endangerment, and that's a felony in the State of New York. Defamation of Character as well. These are new charges. I live in total loss of honor and reputation, and have been sentenced to eternal humiliation and acts of extreme violence and racist cruelty. They have run this slick lie into the ground, saying I can't read. It's such an obvious smear job, so obvious and so nasty. You would think a decent person would throw this silly head game in the gutter, but I had to live with this irrational horror. They're not open to truth or reason. They cannot be reached by rational arguments. Reason has no power over institutionalized racism.

The Police Are Selling Drugs

I quote myself from a letter dated December 29, 2004, to Roland Paul of Rocon Manufacturing. "And speaking of drugs, there are employees who grow marijuana and sell it to people who work there during working hours. One of these employees told me he made over $143,000 last year. I asked him why did he work there...he said, "Dude this job is just a front." Jesse Cross told me that the police approached him, not the other way around. The police told him that his house was the perfect location and that's why they chose him. I downplayed the $143,000 a little; he actually got out a calculator and said this is what I make every 3 months. I looked at the calculator, and it said $143,000. I said $143,000 every 3 months, he said yes. He said the police take care of all his money, and even if someone were to tell, it would be next to impossible to follow because it's so well hidden. He said, these guys know what they're doing, and have every single angle covered. I asked him where did the drugs go, and he said in the city. He said once the marijuana is in duffle bags and off his property, he cleans up so well that no one would ever know that marijuana was grown there. He told me that the police told him that he never had to worry about helicopters ever flying over and that it was taken care of. He also told me that the police asked him to work in some kind of lab where he could make real money. He told me that he said no and that he was happy with what he was making. The police would ask him all the time to work in this lab, and he kept turning them down. I honestly don't know what drugs they had in that lab, it would be a guess.

Crucial questions that need to be answered. Why would they choose this location? If you were a cop, would you pick this spot? How long have they been getting away with this? Are these things going to be going in front of the police cameras on purpose? Since the helicopter crew knows about this, who else is involved, and how high up the ladder does it go? How many more locations are there? Where are the Labs? Why would he turn down working at the Lab after being asked repeatedly? White men used to encourage slaves to run away so that they could catch them, and bring them back to their masters for a reward. The same thing is happening now when the police manufacture drugs and drop them off in the city, so they can work their way in front of the police camera. If people can blame Obama for the oil spill, I think it's fair game to blame the Mayor for having his police department grow, manufacture, and sell drugs on a large scale.

Sean Dukes

This one guy, around 60-something that was an ex-policeman, knew I was good friends with Sean Dukes. He had all the respect in the world for Sean, then looked at me with glossy eyes and said the police killed him. That Bob could never let anything go. I don't know if Bob the killer knew Sean before this or not, but Sean ended up dead as a result. I had no idea that this had happened. I believe what they say on the news like everyone else, so I wouldn't be thinking along these lines. He told me the officer's name was Bob. I told this one girl from Greece Olympia who knew Sean too, that if something was to happen to me, make sure you tell people what I told you about Bob killing Sean. Her name is, Stephanie Speakman and ask her when did I tell her this, and does she remember the cop's name that I said to her.

Why I Have A Canadian Flag On My Car

Tommy, my neighbor who lived across the street, who does things for the police, that has killed lots of people when he was in the Army, threatened me with a 45 two weeks after I moved in, had moved out when I wrote my last letter. The police know what time I come out of my apartment to move my car, and after I wrote my last letter, the police must have told him that I wrote about him, because he was outside looking at me with a crazy grin in front of the police camera when I went outside to move my car. Tommy also visits my one neighbor whom I went to school with. Anyway, lots of people look at me as if I am a weak person now because I never leave my apartment. One day, I was supposed to box one of my other neighbors because of the weak position the police put me in. In the wilderness, when animals see another animal wounded, they attack. There is no difference between living in the ghetto and Hollywood. He never came out of his house that day to box me, even though lots of people were there to see us box. My one neighbor that I went to school with knew everything that was going on with me and the police and knew my biggest fear at the time. Since I am being investigated, I wouldn't want to have the police catching me on tape boxing or anything like that. So he was trying to use my fear against me by acting really funny in front of the police camera, so I took my boxing gloves over to his house and asked him did he wanted to put on the gloves in front of someone he respected. Ask the guy who lives downstairs from him. He backed down hard, then came over to my apartment a few days later at like 2 am with his dog who would bite anyone if he gave the word and wanted to fight me in front of the police camera. Who comes to the door at 2 am with their shoes on, by the way? He knew that I wouldn't do anything, so he tried to advance his position in front of the police camera, as in, am on your side, while smiling and laughing so the camera could see him. Look at the video. He knew that I didn't do anything to the other guy, and knew that I wouldn't do anything in front of the camera. Put yourself in my shoes, if it's true that the police are on me like I write, would you want to fight on camera? Who have you ever heard of that wants to fight in front of the police on purpose, smiling and laughing in front of the camera? By him smiling and laughing towards the camera, wouldn't you say that he was comfortable starting a fight in front of the police? By having all these cops on me, has made me weak, not strong. Everyone can see this. The police have been trying to build a case against me ever since my first letter. So I have become the king of just letting it go. Who in their right mind wants to get in a fight in front of the police? He knows the camera is there, and watches my building like a hawk. He knows everything that's going on and wants in, so he could cash in on my life as well. He was behind in rent like 3 months and had to come up with something. Shortly after, he got a job. I could just about bet my life that the police had something to do with him getting a job too. I have even caught him looking up at the police camera and smiling up at it on occasion when I walk by. The police must have given him permission to drink and drive, because I have seen him back out of his driveway extra hard, then race down the street while his neighbor said "I am surprised he hasn't been pulled over yet, because he always drives drunk and speeds". I have seen this happen twice, and the police camera is on the street 24-7.

For the record, he was a freshman when I went to school, and the only freshmen that I knew were my friend's brothers and sisters. He told everyone on the street that we were friends in high school after he knew I lived here. He knows lots of my friends, but for a billion dollars, he couldn't give you one person's name that could say we even had a conversation before in school. When I was writing down all my friends in one of my letters, he told me to put his name down. He could tell you that I was really popular in school, been in lots of fights and that's all. I can tell you all kinds of stories about the fights I have been in, but nothing is more convincing than me fighting. If given the opportunity to fight him, would I? Hell yeah, but not if it's going to ruin my chances of getting into Canada by getting arrested for fighting. If that's the case, someone could walk up to me and hit me over this letter, and I would turn the other cheek, because I don't want to spend another month in the U.S. The police settle all their scores in the county jail, that being said, that's the last place I want to be. Can you imagine me getting arrested and getting locked up there? Next thing you know I would have a shank in my neck, and the police justifying it, saying that I started something with one of the inmates. Rather, I was in the right or wrong, they just want to get me in the jail cell so they could settle the score.

So why am I putting this section in my letter? In my last letter, I wrote that I have been in like 150 fist fights, and the police have always been trying to get me to fist fight since my first letter so they could show that am out-of-control violent, so they can build a case around it. And when I don't fight by turning the other cheek, they could say I was lying about those 150 fights to prove me wrong on something. Now they can show you proof that I have backed down from a fight because the guy is way bigger than me and since I have lied about that, I have lied about everything else too. Once again, I will fight that guy anytime, any day, if that's what they want, as long as I don't get arrested and mess up my chances to move to Canada. That night, I told him that I would be over to box him in the morning, and he begged me not to come over with the gloves. I didn't want the police looking for us to fight, so I acted friendly to him in front of the camera for like two weeks, and then never talked to him again. This happened like six months after the biker almost ran me over, and since then, the police have always tried to provoke violence with me after I met with Social Service. Can any man be courageous who has the fear of death in him? You can do all kinds of things if you put the fear of death in him. Ask yourself why I would endure such humiliating treatment. And to think the police didn't have anything to do with this in any way is hysterical. I don't know if the police got him to start a fight with me in front of the camera, or told Tommy to tell him to pick a fight with me. But like I said, who wants to fight on camera on purpose, making sure you're smiling, so the camera would see you? Am sorry, but that's not rational to think the police weren't involved. Read this section again, and watch the video. So, altogether, the police got my landlord, my superintendent, my two neighbors that moved out, Tommy the killer, and now my one neighbor I went to school with. That's six people that I know about, and that's just where I live. They were already all over me, but after that, they really increased their violence towards me in the following paragraphs.

Here is a word-for-word letter I left outside police headquarters on 5-23-2009.

Dear Evil,

The only reason I have pepper spray is that something happened when I was jogging. You KNOW what I am talking about!!! Here is the pepper spray back, since you're having a cow. P.S. I don't talk to liars and deceivers. It is beneath me. Stop the violence!!! On 5-22-2009, your Agent was standing too close to me at Family Dollar 352 Driving Park Ave at exactly 7:30 p.m. Look at the video. You could erase it, but it will only prove my point.

Interpretation, I went jogging, and an undercover came out of nowhere looking at me with fire in his eyes like he wanted to tear me to pieces, then he turned away and looked over the railing like he was looking for something then walked away. As he got farther down, he stopped just looking at me very mean. This happened in an area that a car from the road couldn't see, something like a blind spot and the perfect location to ambush someone. I don't know who anyone is anymore, so I went and bought myself some pepper spray to take with me when I jogged, and the police were trying to engage in violence when I went back jogging. The next time I went jogging, the police got out of their car and tried to run up to me across the street to initiate violence, so I kept jogging faster, then another cop with black shades on, timed where I was going to be jogging next, then slowly walked behind me, as in, here I go, come start with me. Knowing damn well that there probably was a riffle pointed at my head the whole time, somewhere across the street in the bushes. Everywhere I went; the police tried to engage in violence, so I dropped off the pepper spray with the letter dated 5-23-2009, at Police Headquarters and stopped jogging.

I have the flag on there because the biker tried to run me over on the sidewalk in front of the police, the police jumped out of the bushes on me when I went jogging, then sent the same guy that destroyed my hard drive back over to my apartment. That was the last straw when they sent him back over to my apartment. Lots of people would hurt someone who has destroyed their hard drive on purpose. How would you feel if someone came over to your house after they had destroyed your hard drive 9 months before? It definitely was the police who sent him to my apartment, because I haven't seen him since, and he knows that there are police cameras outside and inside the building. They wanted me to attack him, so those animals could manhandle me. I remember that day when he came to my apartment to destroy my computer. He rang my doorbell, so I had to go and let him in downstairs, and when I opened the door, he was talking to two police officers. I closed the door back and waited for like 5 minutes because he was still talking with them. He ended up telling me that one of the officers had just come home from Afghanistan. He also kept telling me how the police thought he was very smart. In other words, they were cheering him on. As I said before in my last letter, I knew the guy was a snake, but I didn't think he would destroy my computer on purpose. Why? Because I don't think like that. The next day I went to find someone to fix my computer, and the police followed me and even parked down the street from the house where I was getting my computer looked at. The guy I took it to, said he had never seen anything like it before, and he had 10 years of experience fixing computers. Like I said, they want violence, anyway, they can get it. Not wanting to get sucked into their violent psyche, when the guy came to my door, guess what I said? I said, "If you don't get away from my door, I'll call the police". People with a superego would have responded differently. That was the last straw. Shortly after that, I put all these Canadian flags around my car. They've tried every trick in the book to lure me into violence and attack them, so they could kill me justifiably. I don't want to spend another Thanksgiving or Christmas here, because of my experience with this evil government. I look at Canada as like a three-piece suit, and the U.S. as nothing but a tank top and some dirty drawers, and I don't want to see another Santa Claus.

Police

On September 11th, 2010, the police broke into my apartment. How do I know, because I always leave a small piece of paper in the door jamb when I leave. When one opens the door, the small piece of paper blows out into the hallway, 100 times out of 100 tries. All that being said, when I came home and looked in the door jamb before I unlocked my door, I didn't see the little piece of paper. I unlocked and opened my door slowly, and there was no little piece of paper. But when I looked in the middle of my apartment floor, I saw the exact piece of paper I left in the door jamb when I left. I do this all the time, and especially on September 11th. My landlord is not around on Saturdays, and he knows he isn't supposed to be in my apartment without my permission. And, even if he was around on Saturday, it would have been in the morning. I left my house at 2:30 pm to go to the Public Market. So you see, it was the police because they have a key to the building, and since my landlord would do anything for them, especially since I told on him breaking into my apartment, in my last letter, why wouldn't I believe the police have a key to my place. My neighbors across the street asked me why the police were always in my building, and that they had a key. He would know, because he is always on his porch.

The brakes on my car weren't that great, since I don't drive my car every day, I was prolonging to get them fixed. The police knew this too. One day the light turned yellow, so I sped up fast so it wouldn't turn green, then an undercover came out of nowhere and slammed on their brakes in front of me. I slammed on my brakes as much as I could and came within inches of hitting their car. I didn't have to write this part in here because I know I was in the wrong for not getting my brakes fixed earlier. But can't you see their frame of mind, when it comes to me?

You remember when I said the police were waiting for me outside at night on my last day working at Jasco, and he slammed the door extremely hard? Well, he got out of his car really fast, slammed the door really hard, and went straight into the house of Tommy, who threatened me with his 45. By the way, when I was going to my car about 2 weeks after I moved in, when he approached me, standing sideways, because he had his gun on him right then and there and threatened me with it. Ask the guy how many people he has killed. When someone used to get into a little argument on the street, he would go into his house get his 45, and pace back and forth aggressively. Neighbors on the street used to watch with excitement, just waiting for death to show itself. The neighbors used to get other neighbors and say, "Tommy is at it again, watch, watch". This guy, Tommy, wasn't evolved in anything, he was looking for trouble. I don't think a guy like that belongs with a gun. Then

I wrote about how this guy threatened me with a 45, and what do you know, when I went to get in my car, he was standing by my car, right in front of the police camera, looking at me seriously. You remember when I said it was an empty threat, well it wasn't, I downplayed it a little just in case. Good thing right? If you were to go to his house, you would catch him listening to the police radio. He knows everything that happens, even the police officers' names who've made certain arrests. He could count on them, and they could count on him.

On April 22nd, 2010 at about 6:30 pm, I heard the police outside my window, when I looked out my window, I noticed two policemen standing over a white man unconscious lying on his back. One of them walked a few feet and started urinating on the side of the building, while the other officer spread the unconscious man's arms out like a cross, then bent over, while the guy was still unconscious, then farted in the guy's face. When his partner came back from urinating, the officer that spread the unconscious man's arms out like a cross, farted in the guy's face, and said to his partner, "Look, it's Jesus". Then they both start laughing really hard. I could hear them now, that was a long time ago, let it go.

You can count the times when I am outside when it's dark, and the police go out of their way to let me know that they're watching me. When I go outside at night, it's like I see a thousand tiny red, beady eyes in the darkness looking at me. They would turn their steering wheel violently, rather than in back or in front of me. Police have passed me in their cruisers or unmarked cars and blinked their headlights at me tons of times. Whether they were in their cruiser, pickup, or whatever car they were driving at the time. They would pretend to have a car pulled over by the side of the road at times, and when

I go by, they race behind me as fast as possible. I have passed the Rochester Operating Center tons of times, and tons of times cars were waiting for me to follow and put pressure on me. They follow me for a bit and then turn off somewhere. People have come by to pick me up in their cars, and wherever I went, the police still followed me. One day I would see like 20 cop cars, all of them going out of their way to show me that they were watching me, and they would flash their headlights and as I passed, I would see their back break lights in the mirror, then the next couple of days, or weeks that go by, I barely see any cop cars. It's no set time, it's sporadic and aggressive. It's like sneaky Guerrilla Warfare, which is psychological violence. They would follow me so close with their bumper, it was as if my back bumper was kissing their front bumper. They use the police cameras that surround me to their advantage. It's like shooting fish in a fish tank. I could be driving, then all of a sudden, a police cruiser would speed up behind me with their lights flashing, and I would pull over, and then he would speed past me like he was going to a call. This could be in front of the cameras or not. When I come out of the restaurant or store, they would park their undercover car by mine, or drive away really fast, or let me know that they're there. They enjoy playing with my life like a child plays with food. At the very least, it's like shooting at my boots to make me dance or something.

I would go to McDonald's, Subway, Burger King, and the like, and there would be a girl going out of her way to look at me with bedroom eyes, then when I went out to my car, there would be someone in their car trying to engage conversation with me. Sometimes I would engage, then after a couple of minutes, the same woman that was looking at me with bedroom eyes would be the girlfriend or wife of the person I was talking to. Interpretation, The police followed me there and had their wife or girlfriend in the car with them at the time, and told them to get out and see if they could make me say something to them out of the way, so they could blow it out of proportion and turn it into violence. The only place I go, really, is to get something to eat, and that's because I have to, or I wouldn't even do that. So they have put two and two together, and figure since I don't have a girlfriend, they figure they will tempt me by having girls come around me with short skirts on, or super tight pants on bending over and smiling at me, anything to build a case on me, so their crimes against me will be minimized. I don't know how I can have any kind of life and decent relations with anyone, with Satan on my back like this.

I know it's hard to believe some of the things I have said. Ask someone like a gang member if he has seen something like this before. Ask someone who knows and works with people in the ghetto if they have seen the police put pressure on people like this before. A counselor who works with gang members would probably know. You have got to know someone that went through the pressure "and most likely they're in jail or dead as a result", or know someone that works with people in the ghetto, or thinks like them. And since most people don't think like them....I am screwed!!!! To begin to think like them, think of a Lion in the jungle who hasn't eaten in a month, and then all of a sudden he sees a wild deer. Police are straight-up hunters, and the college threw me to them like I was a piece of meat.

I was driving through the Walmart parking lot when a police cruiser cut me off so badly, that I had to slam on my brakes, or I would have driven right into his car door on the driver's side. I went to the police station to beg them to leave me alone, and one of the officers behind the counter said "Just go and talk with them", as in, if you work this thing out with the college, everything will be fine. I went from the police station directly to the college afterward. As I was leaving the police station, he yelled out, "Don't say anything about what just happened". They even had Bouncers telling me, when I used to go to the dance clubs, to just leave the college alone, they're not racist.

Have you ever seen a dog that won't rest until he finds his bone or toy? Well, that's the hunter psyche they have when it comes to me. They are golden-tongued professional liars with years of experience in the art of lying, with interrogation skills to back up their lies. These guys will lie to your face quicker than a crackhead will lie to a Priest. They could say almost anything convincingly, but I can't. Remorse, empathy, and guilt are something that's not in Satan. They could tell any lie they want to by law, and people would chew on their words like a piece of meat. They know all the double-crosses, booby traps, and angles to put pressure on one's life. Most people don't, you have to think like them to come to an understanding. They have a fiendish, insatiable passion of hate toward me, and always try to set me up because of it. The police's only job in society is to serve and protect, not take sides with the college and pull out their guns on me, demonizing me, faking hard with their cars, trying to run me over, hunting down people that know me so they could set me up over the phone or in person. Well, there's not much you could say about their honesty, besides its good for a couple of laughs.

There have been places that I have gone, and out of the blue, a person with a "City of Rochester" t-shirt on would stop dead in their tracks and stare at me like they were losing their mind. They have talked to my neighbors about me in the apartment I live in, and I would hear my one neighbor run up to his door when someone came to visit me. Sometimes, I would see the shadow of his feet for a long pause, stopping by my door when I had visitors. This guy used to beat up his wife all the time, but the police had bigger fish to fry. They have also told my neighbors about me where I used to live in Gates and in Ogden too. They took 3 of my letters down from the Myspace website and left the rest. They have tried to contact me on Facebook, and have tried to get some of my ex-friends on Facebook to set me up on the site and over the phone. So I never go there, unless someone leaves me a message. I used to hang out with these two girls, we were just sex friends, and one of the detectives slept with her. And since all the cops and every department know me, this just proves their mindset. I had all my fun with her, but that's not the point. I give them as much room as you would a dangerous animal that lives in the jungle. Shop Rite is the cheapest store in Rochester, and I could throw a rock at it from where I live, I have never gone there because police are there 24-7. There are times when I have gone to move my car, or just went to the store, as I would park my car and walk to my apartment, lots of times, a car or truck would be parked on my street and all of a sudden start their car and speed really fast past me. This is not just one incident, it's incident after incident. This all happens in front of the police camera. They have devoted enormous amounts of energy into oppressing me, punishing me over and over again with their vicious minds, and then blaming me, so they could justify their oppressing. They follow me everywhere and act like they're reading the newspaper, playing with some electronic device, standing around looking bored, giving me those I could kill you eyes, or trying to set me up with another person. And by the police putting all kinds of people on me, what they're doing is giving people the opportunity to play police / double agent, and the green light to commit crimes, without punishment. How many people would turn that down? Then they say, "We don't know why he won't come out of his apartment". Even Nazis in Germany said they didn't know anything about the concentration camps at first.

Police Son / Relative, The Smoking Gun

If 100 people got charged with terrorism, and only two were Muslim, when the trial starts, who do you think would be the first two to go to trial? Back in 1991, around 15 people beat up two other persons at the area beach. They convicted me for punching and kicking one of the men at the beach, when I have proven with great certainty that I didn't. Anyway, it was in the paper, on the radio, and in the news every day. They used to even have long deep hateful discussions on the radio every day. The public was screaming for justice, so they even made me go to trial first. Of the 15 people in the group, only two were black. One was the son of a police officer or relative of a police officer who turned himself in first and got complete immunity. Well, it wasn't me, or I wouldn't be writing about it. If you can't get the truth out of a 20-year-old who never read a book, who didn't have "Game" and who had an open heart that Stevie Wonder could see, you're in the wrong field. I talked with the Head Detective, and he knew I didn't do it with great certainty, and shook my hand as he said "I know you didn't do it, but I guarantee you'll hang for it, am sorry I have to do it to you". I told my lawyer about this when I went back to my second trial, so she called that same detective up and asked him did he say that. When she got off the phone with him, she said that she totally believed me. Everything already has been checked out, and trust me, the police believe me, but still won't admit it. I thought about this for a while, and you know why he told me that he was sorry even though he was sending me to prison? Because the other black guy already admitted to him that he had done the crime, but he knew that his father was a police or relative and would be getting complete immunity. And no matter if 1000 men did a crime, and two African Americans were involved to any degree, you can bet your last dollar that both or one of them will be going to trial. Can you imagine the outcry of the public if they knew African Americans were involved and didn't go to trial? There you have it, this explains the reason why he shook my hand and apologized to me. Then a few months later, I told this one hot girl who was looking for the spotlight that I had hit the guy. Without me saying why I told her that in this letter, and trust me, they know why because I have proven that too. So it didn't make a difference what came out of my mouth, because they still would have achieved sending me to prison. Like I said, if you can't get the truth out of a 20-year-old who had never read a book, who didn't have a "Deceptive tactic mindset" and an open heart, you're in the wrong field.

Ego

I sent my letters out, and this one guy read it and said that I had an ego. First of all, look at any good book that was ever written and read a book review of that book. There is always going to be someone who says something bad about the book. And that's just the facts of life. That being said, my letters are negative to the extreme, because these people are racist to the extreme, and get to practice their racism to the extreme on me with immunity. I am just writing about events and facts. Anyone who writes negative truths is bound to get a bad review from somewhere. I would just like to say, that I don't know how anyone can take sides with Satan without reading my letters from start to finish uncovering all their lies, and not just the chapter headings, or the last chapter, but from start to finish. For the record, that guy who gave me a bad review didn't read my letters from start to finish. He only read parts of it. It doesn't take an analytical reader to see this. Don't believe me, read what he wrote again. The guy thought my letters were an internet scam because I asked for money the last time, because this city fights with putting you in poverty, and then demonizes you to death with area Employers. He had a subjective frame of mind and thought I was an internet scam artist when he wrote his review. It was my fault for asking for money from the public. At the time, I couldn't help it, because they put me in a position where I didn't even have food.

If I had an Ego, they put that in check and knocked it off my shoulder, as I divorced it when I went to prison. In fact, they broke my spirit a long time ago when they put me back in prison for 6 months for a speeding ticket, just because this correctional officer was mad at an inmate. At the time, I was taking 15 credit hours in college, when 12 credits were full-time. I was also working 40 hours a week. I had to report in once a week, just to say I was alive, and to sometimes take a urine test. I was working from 6 am to 2:30 p.m. M-F and had to be in class by 3:30 p.m. That only gave me an hour to go from work to school, and I had to report on that day. I did it before without a problem. I was there on time, but when I got there, the officer said that he wasn't going to see anyone because someone made him mad. He made everyone wait, even though people were telling him that they had to be to work, or they would be fired. He couldn't care less and made everyone super late. When I got on the expressway, I was speeding because the officer made everyone late, and I had to take a test that day that I had studied for. I got a speeding ticket in front of the college exit sign. Two days later, I was back in prison for six months. I already was in prison for something I didn't do, now I had to go back when I had my own car, lived by myself, had a girlfriend, worked full-time, went to college more than full-time, and was supposed to be in my sister's wedding that Saturday. If I had an ego like they want me to have, that so-called ego died by the college exit sign that day, and explain why I let that teacher swat his hand in my face 100 times. I am only being real. If you let Satan explain it to you, Satan will say I wasn't supposed to be driving. I was on work release when the courts reversed my conviction, and so I was in society working and going to college for a whole year while I went back to trial, because that's what I wanted. Like I have always said, I didn't do it. So my lawyer punked me and said my best shot was a bench trial, not a jury trial. I told her that there wasn't any way in hell the judge was going to find me innocent by herself on a retrial, and that would mean I could sue the city. She got so mad at me and convinced me that the judge already liked me that the people from Fairport and Penfield were going to be on the jury, and that they hated black people. Go with the judge, she likes you. I did and got convicted in a few days. And when she sentenced me, she was only supposed to give me time served, but at the last second, the media was there, and she sentenced me back to prison. I didn't even look at her as I left the courtroom in custody. I was supposed to go back upstate, and the judge made sure that I just went back on work release. The whole time I was in society I was driving, and my record was clean, and when I got on work release they told me that I couldn't drive unless certain papers were signed. She said any day now, and the papers will be filled out. I couldn't wait, because I had to work full-time and go to school full-time, and needed a car to do so. The papers weren't signed yet, and I had to work and college already started. Then I got a speeding ticket because of that cop, but if you ask Satan, he would say, you should have waited to go to college the next semester, so here are six months in prison.

How can I have a superego, when I let a teacher swat his hand in my face like 100 times? Or being treated like shit at work, as a result of the teacher swatting his hand in my face. If I was a dog and got treated this way, and I finally bit my abuser, people would say, you should have left the dog alone, and that's good for the abuser. Ego is all about winning. Look how many times I have lost. By me leaving this country, I am still losing, because I don't know when I would ever see my family again. No matter if I won a settlement of a billion dollars, I still lose. Because they have stopped me from having a family of my own and denied my parents the opportunity to see me raise children and become grandparents. All that being said, they're not going to stop me from telling the truth about it. Let's say that someone ran over your child in the street, then took off and was at large. Wouldn't you want this person caught? So I let it go a long time ago before these Demons ran over all my children without blinking. And how would you feel if people told you, let it go, you have an ego, all the while a racist Klan put in overtime to make your life miserable? I let what that teacher did to me go a long time ago. I told them that in my letter, I just wanted to learn computers, everything about computers. I had COMPLETELY won my case, but took this cowardly route, because of all the police pressure. Satan brought his funky ass around and destroyed my chances of learning that too. The biggest problem I had with the college mainly was the valuable skills I didn't learn as a result. And because I let that teacher do that to me for so long, the college and the police are like, oh hell no, we can't let people know it was that racist, so we have to show personal responsibility negligence on my side. So people could say, even though that was a bad thing, I could see how that could happen to a guy like that. In other words, they have been trying to justify their racist behavior since the beginning, and can't stop if they wanted to. Like trying to trick me and treating me like shit at every single job. They would say something like what is 2 + 2, 3 right, then on to the next racist tricks. Then they tell other people that I won't let what went on in college go. The same people that are saying I have an ego, are the same people that have a Superman sticker on their police cruisers. I didn't know Superman was in love with cocaine.

Look at Tiger Woods's wife. I am sure she would have stayed with him if it was just one woman, but it was way too many. One can make the argument that his ex-wife has a super ego too, because she wouldn't just let it go. They have been serving me from sun up to sun down, every place I breathe since my first letter, and then have the nerve to say that I just won't let bygones be bygones with my oversized ego, so they could continue to serve me and justify their continued racist oppression and secondary status. Step back and ask yourself, what traps and double-crosses have I tried to set? What traps and double-crosses have they tried to set? By one even setting such traps, shows that they can't let something go. Read all my letters, and please tell me where my lust for power at, because ego is about power too, right? I have even said that I never want to be a supervisor, because I don't want to tell anyone what to do. If I had this ego, one would have seen my claws. When a man attempts to deal with me by force, I used to answer him with force. Now I am the king of just letting it go, as I am skilled in defeat.

My Intelligence

Racism happens all the time and is one of the hardest things to prove. You can go a whole lifetime and only have known a few cases where someone has proven racism. I have proven it with great certainty. That has to count for something when it comes to my intelligence. Look at how I tried to go into a completely different field, which was Computers. Look at how I proved, with great certainty, that one can't pass both parts of the exam without hands-on training. You can pass one part of the exam, but not the other part, because knowledge isn't complete without experience, hands-on experience to pass the second part of the test. Again, they tried to put me in a position where they could say, "He just can't do it". Nice try, you almost had even me fooled until I really thought about it. For someone who could come into a field and not know anything about how it works, and come up with what I came up with, and a very short time, doesn't show that I am a fool, but that of an intellect. And they knew what they were doing the whole time. Ask who benefited from this action.

When I was in prison, I had a calm mind, because I didn't have too many distractions. I think I came into prison with a 3rd-grade reading level but left with my GED and a reading score of 12.9. The highest the test allowed. So how did I get my GED and score 12.9 in front of a class with the prison guard watching? If you think those red-neck prison guards leave prisoners alone to take that test, so they can look good in front of the Parole Board, you know nothing about hate and believe in the Easter Bunny. You indeed have millions of students graduating from high school who can't read, but not one person whom I have met with a GED, especially earned from prison, can't read. I had overwhelming test anxiety when I took my GED, because that test meant everything to me, so I could have done a lot better. But I still passed. Anyway, how did I make the Dean's list in college too, if I can't read? Have Satan explain this. The only thing I never did when reading was read out loud. I hate my voice as is, and for a long time, I could only exhale for 10 seconds, 15 seconds at the most. Would you want to read out loud if you breathed like that, and always gasping for air? I even got anxiety reading to myself, so I would silently read when I read anything. You would think education is something that can't be taken away, but they have even taken that away.

Landlord

My landlord knew about me even before I moved in. When I went to give him my security deposit to move in, he had this look in his eyes I own you, I shouldn't let you move in here, and if you even breathe loud I'll kick you out. He would think of a reason to come to my apartment, and then with a fake smile, ask me all kinds of direct/indirect questions, the whole time I had been living here. Do you love to fight? What do you think of this or what do you think of that, always trying to squeeze info out of me. It's on the same line as an interrogation. If the police offered you to play detective, 9 out of 10 people would accept in a heartbeat. He is a straight-up spy for the Police.

When I first got a lawyer, she asked me did I know why African Americans can never be racist. I never pondered the question before, and I wanted to listen to her since I was paying by the hour, I told her that I didn't know. They now think I don't know what racism is because my landlord asked me word for word about everything that my lawyer and I talked about. I knew I was being recorded the whole time when I met with my lawyer because she was really talking to whoever was listening at the door or in the other room when she was talking to me. Anyway, how can a black person in Rochester not know what racism is? When they're faced with it directly or indirectly throughout their lives in Rochester, every single day. It's true, a lot of people can't give you a technical definition of what racism is like a philosopher can, but that doesn't mean they don't know what racism is. Most of the guys in the machine shops don't know how to explain what they're doing to the machines, and exactly how it works, but they know what's going on at all times. They just know that it works, because they have lots of experience dealing with the machines. In my opinion, every African American knows with great certainty what racism is, because experience is the best teacher you know. So my landlord asked me every single thing we talked about.

About a month after I moved in, I had my music a little loud, not all the way up, just a little loud. My landlord knocked on my door like he was a gorilla and pointed his finger in my face and yelled so loud, the whole building heard it and told me to turn down my music. It was like he wanted to fight me. So I basically listen to music with my earphones the whole time I have lived here. The next time I saw him, he had a big grin on his face. At the time, just about every apartment played their music extremely loud. My next-door neighbor had a top-of-the-line system that was one of the loudest I have heard to date. He always had the volume at its max, and one day, my landlord just knocked on his door and asked him to turn it down, very calmly. This happened lots of times with different neighbors too, because it seemed like everyone had a mean system. And he was always calm and respectful dealing with them. Isn't that a form of discrimination when my landlord pointed his finger all in my face yelling really loud out of his mind at me, when he didn't do the same to the other tenants? Since they told him a teacher at college swatted his hands all in my face, and I didn't do anything about it, it seems like that has excited him because he wants to do the same. He is like the police partner in crime now and could tell you all the details way better than I can. One question, what authority and right does my landlord have to interrogate me? In the end, the local police aren't going to do anything about my landlord, because how could you attack or retaliate on someone when the police gave the orders?

They made him come to my apartment when I was emailing my letters over the internet, and he didn't outright tell me to stop emailing, but he said to take it easy, that we're taking care of things now, be patient there is no reason to freak out, or something to that effect. Roy, let this thing go, drop it. Then I told him that I had killed rats. He saw for himself, that I had rat poison all around and over 10 mousetraps by my front door leading into my kitchen alone. He even stepped in mousetraps in my apartment before. He knew that I was terrified and climbing the walls, but thought it was funny. He told me he would take care of them but didn't, because he wanted to see me suffer first, because of what I wrote in my last letter about him breaking into my apartment. I had killed another rat, and my neighbor came over to my apartment and saw a rat run across my couch. That was the last straw, so I called a city agency, and soon after that, I got served with papers to get out. This was an act of retaliation. I have been here for over 4 years without ever missing a rent payment. September 1st, 2008 was the first time I missed a payment, and on September 17th, 2008, I got served papers to get out. I have paid my landlord 5 days 2 weeks 1 and 2 months rents in advance consistently, and he still tried to kick me out. His lawyer came up to me outside the courtroom laughing and asking me, do I have a place to stay. I told him I wasn't moving anywhere, he looked at me mean-looking then went right up to the Bailiff and said something, and the Bailiff got in back of me and looked at me aggressively the whole time I was in court. Then, when I went up to the bench, I asked the court lady who takes care of papers behind the bench, if she would pass these papers to the Judge, and she screamed at the top of her lungs and said, I am not passing anything. At the top of her voice, because she knew about me before I got there, obviously. I was explaining to the Judge about all the rats in my apartment, and my landlord lawyer was smiling from ear to ear and laughing, right in front of everyone in the court. I had two weeks of unemployment in my account that I couldn't get to because I didn't have a PIN at the time. And they still were going to kick me out on the street, then at the last second, I don't know what happened, but someone made my landlord not kick me out. He came and told me that I didn't have to move and that he would wait until I got caught up with unemployment. He looked at me and said nothing like he wanted me to talk to him. Then I told him about the superintendent threatening me with a gun, and he pointed his finger in my face and said that was a long time ago, and to let it go. I think he had a tape recorder when he came in my apartment, because he said, "Roy, we're friends" and trust me when I tell you, we're not friends, he knows that. As he walked out the door, he jerked his body hard, looked at me really mean, and pointed his index finger at me. He tried to bait me and wanted me to talk about him breaking into my apartment, but I didn't, and that made him mad. Shortly after I needed a Plumber, so Joe the Plumber walked into my apartment with my landlord looked at me with extreme hate, and got into a little argument with my landlord when my landlord had to go and check on something in the building. He told him that he didn't want to be left in the apartment if I was going to be there. He said if you leave this apartment, I'm leaving too. I heard him throwing things all around in the bathroom as he was grunting to himself when my landlord was gone. I never have seen Joe the Plumber before that day ever in my life. And all of this is a result of the Dept. of Social Service lies.

You would think that area landlords would have a bidding war to get immigrants as their main source of tenants. The police probably told my landlord that he would get the contract if he helped them take care of me. I wonder if the people who are responsible for immigrants settling in Rochester know that this building is infested with rats and roaches. The City is supposed to be welcoming immigrants to a better life in America, but instead are welcoming them to rats and roaches. If a black man were to own this building, and this City found out that there were rats and roaches here, there wouldn't be any more immigrants coming here. If one was to come and check behind every single refrigerator in this building, they would find rat poop behind all of them. There were and are so many rats here, that in early August

2010, I killed about 13 rats within 2 weeks, or more like 10 days, and brought them out to the police camera to show them how many I was killing. On August 20th I believe, I killed a rat. This is after I have killed 13 within two weeks. On September 4th, 2010, a rat ran over my foot when I got up to go to the bathroom at about 1 am. My neighbor told me on September 5th that she killed 3 rats on the 4th. Ask the people who put the immigrants here to ask the people that live here, have they seen and killed rats here before. One neighbor has killed like 8, another 5, another like 7, and so on. On September 7th, I killed another one. Me and my one neighbor are the only Americans living in this building, and my landlord raised my rent by $20. I asked my one neighbor, did he raise hers, and she said no. How is that not retaliation all day?

When I first told my landlord that I saw a rat, he said that he would exterminate. Then I told him again and he said the same thing. I told him again, and he told me that it was cold outside and that they were just looking for a warm place. Translation, if you were cold, wouldn't you want to be in a warm place too? Then they said that the basement was built wrong or something and that they had added dirt because it was on an incline or something. They have made every excuse in the book. This one guy told me that works for the owner of this building over a year ago, that they have tried everything to get rid of the rats in this building, but nothing seem to work. What that means to me is, that they can't do anything about the volume of rats coming into the building and that they're trying, but as soon as they give up a little, the building will be overrun with them. I think a very important question to ask my landlord, is how many rats have they killed in the basement. To think he will tell you the truth, though, is hilarious.

Soon after I had killed the 13 rats, I went to move my car, because there is alternating parking on my street, which means that I have to move my car every day, except Sundays. As I was walking to my car, I noticed someone had broken one of the lower windows leading to the basement, by the garbage cans. This site was clear as day, and anyone walking down the street would have noticed this if they looked over in that direction. This was only like this for a day, because I would have noticed this right away. So since I killed 13 rats and brought them to the police camera, to let them know that I was killing a high volume of rats and that I was angry, because of the poverty they had put me in. They put two and two together really fast, and knew that I was going to mention this in my letter as well, so guess what my landlord came up with? And I am saying openly, I am not sure if they are guilty of this crime, but I don't believe in coincidence, especially when dealing with liars. The next day, I heard my landlord outside talking to a small group of people, I guess conveying the building. He probably told them that one of the low-lives from the neighborhood had broken the window to the basement, and that's how so many rats had ended up in the building. Nothing like this had happened before, but you can see how something like this could happen. They lie so much, that I have to predict their lies now.

One night my neighbors were making really loud noises when I was in my bathroom, and no lie, I heard what sounded like 50 rats in the wall trying to get away from the noise that my neighbors were making downstairs. I know what I heard. I even armed myself with whatever objects I could get that were in my bathroom because I thought they were in my apartment.

To this day, I never heard that sound again from my neighbors or the rats.

I have even found rat droppings in my pots and pans under the counter. Not to mention, roaches crawling on my silverware in the kitchen drawer. I had to put a rubber weather strip under my kitchen door to stop them from entering my apartment so easily. That wasn't good enough, so I had to stuff steel wool Brillo pads under my front door because they were coming from the hallway. I have had my refrigerator unplugged for over four months now, because there were roaches all over my food in my refrigerator. And I didn't leave my refrigerator door open either, just so that I could write this because my neighbor had roaches in her refrigerator too. Roaches love my bathroom too, so I keep my toothbrush in a zip-lock bag now. One time I killed like 10 roaches, then put them in the kitchen corner so that I could take a picture of them when I got hold of a camera, and when I went back into the kitchen because I had just killed another, they were all gone and replaced by rat droppings.

My one neighbor used to call them all the time about the rats and roaches. At first, they used to come over and spray her apartment, and say that they were all gone, she would see them all the time and would call after a couple of days had gone by, and they would just ignore all her calls. So she stopped calling because she didn't want to make ways. She couldn't take it anymore and on October 1st, 2010, my Landlord came over to her apartment to see for himself her complaint about rat droppings everywhere. I don't have pictures of this because she doesn't want to get involved. She showed me what my landlord saw, and there were rat droppings all over her kitchen table. There were like 50 to 100 rat droppings on her table. That's just the beginning because there were, it seemed, hundreds of rat droppings in her oversized big box of rice. I asked her was the rice wild rice, and she said it was just plain white rice. Then she took me to her kitchen cupboard to show me all the dead roaches. She told me that she went and made a personal complaint to the office, and they told her that her bed wasn't made or something and that she needed to keep her apartment clean. She told me that the landlord always goes into her apartment when she isn't there, and that's how he knew her apartment wasn't clean. I asked her did the landlord had her permission and did she know he was coming. She said no, that she couldn't stop him, and that she was from a different country and didn't want to make things bad for her. She told me on October 29, 2010, she had seen another rat.

Someone scratched most of my name off my mailbox with some sort of key. The only way to get to my mailbox is you would need a key to the front building door. First, someone just used a key to cross my name out. Can we all agree that whoever crossed out my name on my mailbox, is very comfortable doing it in front of the camera, and not worried about getting caught? Then, after I killed 13 rats and showed them to the police camera, someone tried to rip my name off the mailbox completely. If I had done that to someone's mailbox, they would have charged me with the destruction of government property. And if I wanted to, I could take a plea deal with only two years in prison, or risk spending 10 years in prison.

I have gained tons of weight, because I only eat out, or bring takeout back to my apartment, where the roaches, and sometimes rats, try to get to my food. Or I'll go to the public market and buy mainly fruit and eat it right away and keep the rest outside in my car. I shouldn't even eat takeout here, because the roaches come out of their hiding spot to try to take my food. I have to be on the constant lookout for them. Why would anyone want to cook here? Would you? I haven't moved out of this apartment, because wherever I move it's just going to be a new evil and a different new kind of terror. Most importantly, there are cameras everywhere around my neighborhood, so if the police want to do something to me, they have to do it in front of the cameras and explain why they erased it.

MCC

Proof that MCC sent the police after me. The day after I gave 4 teachers at MCC my first letter, a sheriff came to my Economics class and told the teacher he wanted to see me. He had hot coffee in his hand the whole time, and trust me on this, that wasn't by coincidence. I guess if I had said anything out of the way, he would have thrown that coffee in my face and said it was an accident as he tried to subdue me. During our interview, I told him that I was embarrassed growing up in this one town because I thought they were the most racist police department in Rochester, and one day when I first went back to that town, the police were across the street at a light, then screeched their tires and sped up behind my car as fast as possible. I looked in my rearview mirror and saw that same sheriff in a black pickup truck on his radio as the police cruiser turned off somewhere. Then it was just the black pickup truck behind me. Anyway, this guy used to follow me all over Rochester in his black pickup truck, used to wait outside my apartment, and was the same sheriff who almost shot me outside MCC doors before I went to talk to Mr. Ryther, and was the same sheriff a few weeks after that almost ran me over with his black pickup truck at the entrance of Walmart in Gates, then chased me around Walmart with a gun. Now MCC is saying we didn't put any cops on you; it's in your head.

The sheriff station is next door to the college, and the police used to wait and follow me from college just about all the way to my apartment. Sometimes with their back window down, so don't tell me the college didn't put all the police in Monroe County on me. I have even said to one of the teachers at college "Can you tell them to leave me alone" and he was like who? Like he had no idea, and when I was leaving college that day, there weren't any security or cops to be seen. I remember the first time that I had emailed my letters and the next time I went on campus, I was parking my car and the college alarm system went off. Cops were everywhere, giving me mean looks left and right. When it was time to get back to class I took my sweet time walking slowly, I even went far away to the vending machine and the next building. When I arrived at class, my whole class was standing outside with my teacher. Then the class door opened up, and about 10 security guards came out of the classroom all looking at me, and the leader said, "How are you doing". The whole time, my teacher was extremely nervous and sweating bullets. There would have to be someone who remembers this, the teacher will.

I lost track of what day it was, one time, I went to my teacher's office to get help in math. I got on the elevator to go to her office, and when the elevator got to her floor, the doors never opened, it just went straight back down and when the doors opened, an undercover cop with black shades on looked at me intimidatingly for what seemed like 30 seconds, then the doors closed. I reselected my teacher's floor and this time the doors opened, and I got off and went to her office, it was closed, and I knew right then and there I had the wrong day and why the cop was there. Interpretation, they knew that I went to her office visits to get help and that I had the wrong day, so they controlled the elevator from somewhere to see why I was there, and if I had a problem, they would have blown a hole in my throat right then and there. Ask yourself, how could I possibly know that they could control the elevator like that?

Since my first letter, there were so many security guards and police putting pressure on me just about everywhere in society I went, that it seemed like cops were coming out of the ground. From the start of my first letter, until I graduated. If I went to the bathroom and stayed in there for over 2 minutes, they were in there looking at me with their cold blue reptilian eyes. If I went to the cafeteria to have lunch or just talked with my friends at a table, they would get a table close by and try to listen in on me. I could almost see their ears turning red trying to listen in on me. If my class had a window and was on the first floor, they would casually walk by the window to look in. I could be walking in the hall and someone would say hi to me and I would get a mean, nasty reaction from security guards, staff, or police. One time, I was walking in the hall, and one teacher said hi to me, or I said hi to him first, because this teacher likes me, and one of my ex-teachers looked at him with hate in his eyes. I would leave class and go to my car, and a police cruiser would be by my car in the parking lot, wherever I parked. All of this happened on the main campus. I have gotten the meanest looks from staff, security, and police period. They have stabbed me with their eyes repeatedly. Interpretation, the police didn't know who I was before the college put them all over me to do their dirty work. Before they put them on me, I could have gone anywhere I wanted to. After the college introduced me to them, I couldn't buy a candy bar without them breathing down my throat.

Ask Mr. Brandon, especially under an MRI test, does he know how to crack the Millwright software. Was he the one who initially gave it to Brian so that Brian could crack it and teach him to crack it? Mr. Brandon was in charge of that software because that is his department. If I am wrong, I will do 20 years in prison, if not, I rest my case. Mr. Brandon told me that the Master Task Lathe CD-ROM was easy to crack. Brian used to teach the teachers everything he knew. I bet if one were to walk into Applied Tech and fire their secretary, then tell her that she could get her job back if she told the truth about that MillWright software, the truth would come out. Every single teacher knows about that software, especially the chairperson that's in charge of running the Applied Tech. The thing is, they don't want you to know. I told one teacher on the main campus that I had that software, and she said "fuck you" under her breath. If you were to put 1% of the pressure on them as they have me, you could find out in a day about that Millwright software, because all the teachers, personnel, and secretaries know about it. If these guys are bad enough to break into my apartment, three times that I know about for sure, at two different addresses, why wouldn't they break into my apartment while I am not at home? They have the key and know where I am at all times. Wouldn't you think that I would know how valuable that software was to the case? Why would I just misplace it? Oh, I just lost it!!! I had one copy in my apartment and another in my parent's basement, which got flooded. What really happened to the one I had was they came into my apartment and stole it. I can't prove it but look at all the other things they have done, like stealing my mail for example. If I had that software, for one, M.C.C. would have gotten sued big time by the company, and it would prove lots of things. Ask yourself why I would be still talking about this software if it never happened. If these guys could fill the graveyard and prisons with some he said, she said shit, damn it I want at least one of them teachers to take an M.R.I. lie detector test about that Milwright software because that's where the hate really started.

Ask yourself what does Darwin know that we don't? As in, what was going through his mind when he kept swatting his hands in my face, most people would never do such a thing, but for the people that will, the thing that would be going on in their mind the most is, "I could get fired and lose my house if I get caught. Not Darwin, because he did it 100 times with complete confidence. So what did Darwin know? He knew the inner workings of that college and how they really felt about black people. That being said, Richard Ryther told me when I met with him that the college fired Darwin. This was a lie because Darwin not only works there but has been promoted after all the racist events.

Ask all the teachers at Applied Tech, didn't I use to copy lots of their thick programming and machine operating manuals page by page? Then I used to take them to the library and read them. They all know. When they first got all of these Hass CNC controllers, they came with a very thick manual on how to, they told me that I could come into the CNC lab to learn the controllers on a week that the college was on vacation. It was just me and the manual, teaching myself the controller. Within one week, I read the manual twice and did every exercise in the manual. I even wrote everything down, all the sequences that I did to achieve the results from the manual. This was how I had learned CNC programming, and this was before I had ever had the idea to go on the internet and hunt down CNC instructional videos. It really doesn't matter what it is, if one were to give me a manual, and that manual shows you exactly what to do, how can anyone not learn, unless they're not interested in the subject? Then they had this Func controller in there, it didn't have too many options on it to tell you the truth, and I was able to learn the controller from start to finish and two days flat. Minus the macro programming part. Give me an MRI. This is too important. The controllers are by far the hardest part academically, and the machining is all based on having someone giving you a solid foundation and lots and lots of practice, which equals experience. Getting to practice these skills with raw materials would have been a symbol of my pride and the greatest achievement that would have said, that I can always support myself and my family, with total independence.

Machine Shops and Racism That Just Won't Die

You would think the machine shops would open up their arms to me, but the only thing they have done was try to prove me wrong by putting me in a position where I would be lost and say I can't do it. Most people in the field are one dimension and just do Lathe work their whole career, or just Mill work, or just working with plastics, or just working with sheet metal, or just working with glass. As a matter of fact, most people in the field just know how to work on the CNC Lathe, with a certain Fanuc controller. There are lots of Fanuc controllers that could be used and conjunction with the CNC Lathe, and I am telling you, lots of people just know how to use one series of controllers, to go along with just that one Lathe. I learned tons of controllers, for Lathes, Mills, Conventional, Conversational, and all kinds of different concepts along the way. The problem I had was with learning different skill sets, and you can only get this from someone with tons of experience, they got this experience because they have had a million chances trying, and they just go off of instinct and don't have to think anymore. Similar to tying your own shoes. Look at my adaptability in every single company I worked for and how fast I picked up at all the jobs they had me do. They had me working at this one company working on these big Die Perforating machines that I never knew existed, where people said, you learned that already, because it takes most a hell of a while to be at that stage. Just ask the supervisor.

My supervisor waited until the last minute to teach me this one particular skill that you just can't accomplish doing it once. The next day, when I arrived at the machine, an unmachined workpiece was already clamped down in the vice. My supervisor came up to me and said that he wanted me to repeat this skill on my own and that I was going to be timed because this was a test. He looked at me with anger in his eyes, and said, you better not move this workpiece out of the vice at any time when performing this skill. That he had already tightened the vice, so hurry up, time is ticking. Then a man whom I had never seen before came out of the office, that didn't work there, and stood behind me watching me the whole time performing this skill. The skill was using a machinist indicator to get the circular workpiece perfectly flat. So the indicator would read zero horizontally and zero vertically on the workpiece. Even though he just taught me this skill, I completely understood what needed to be done. I tried and tried, but nothing I did could stop the indicator needle from dancing. People would walk by my machine and smile, as to say, you can't do it, as my supervisor, no lie, was in the best of moods as he started singing. I swear, he started singing. I was spending all day on this and couldn't understand why. Finally, the guy who was standing behind me made small talk with me and left the building. I felt so small and made an excuse that I went out last night and was hung over. I made sure I didn't leave the machine and asked my supervisor to show me how to do the skill again. I watched him closely as he unloosened the workpiece, I said wait a minute, you said not to move the workpiece at all. He gave me one of them stupid looks, as he cleaned away a piece of debris that was under the workpiece the whole time. He knew exactly where to look, too, and then retighten the vice. When he put the indicator back on the workpiece, the indicator wasn't dancing around crazy like it did when I tried. He just looked at me with this stupid grin on his face and didn't respond when I said, you told me not to move the workpiece. Everyone in the building knew, it seemed. The workpiece took like 4 hours to finish, now everyone was in and around the area, it seems, watching from afar to see if I could do it. I was so mad at my racist supervisor, that I performed this skill in recorded time. Then I set up the rest of the tools so that they would know where the workpiece was. I didn't even turn around when I left the machine, as everyone watched my supervisor check my work as I went to the bathroom. You should have seen the hurt in my supervisor's eyes when I came from the bathroom. If this isn't an example of racism that doesn't want to die, what is? Then the Head of Maintenance, a millionaire around 60-something, came up to me and said he had seen everything and that I was doing damn well.

They gave me another test by putting me in the office by myself for 7 hours with a Mastercam programming manual and told me to get as far as I could on the computer writing programs. When they came back, I had about 100 pages or more done and lots of programs on the computer to show all my work. I even made programs that weren't even in the manual. This was all without any help. You should have seen the look in my supervisor's eyes; it was as if I had killed his children. Guess what happened next, he told me not to touch the computer again. Every time I asked, he would give me the runaround and worked me to the bone. Two other black men before me had similar experiences with my supervisor. How would I know that, because other employees told me so? After that, my supervisor kept treating me like shit and working me to death, and it showed up on my face. The owner at AGI is a black belt in Karate and knew that I didn't like the way I was being treated there, so he came up to me in a Karate stance, as if to say, start something, I dare you. Then they called the police on me because the police would be in the parking lot ducked down hiding behind cars and watching me from across the street. Anyway, I learned the concept of machining glass and its inner workings. Not fast, but superfast, where most people they told me couldn't do it at all. I did, and even outdid my supervisor on some things. But it doesn't matter in the machine shops, especially when you're black and the college has a lottery on your head. That is, every single company I have worked for since my first letter, has tried so hard to put me in a situation where I would be clueless, lost, and say I just can't do it, so I wouldn't excel, [so the college would say I told you so] worked me super hard and treated me like shit in front of everybody. I could go on and on. And look at how I adapted to all the things they threw at me and landed on my feet. I have invested all my life into college and work, to only be treated like shit by racist laughing fiends working me to the bone out of retaliation because of some other racist laughing fiends. Sacrifice like this will eventually lead to resentment, even a dog gets tired, I want out.

The heart of my argument is the machine shops are practicing control racism; justified racism and economic racism, which are pieces of institutionalized racism. Their whole philosophy is set up to maintain white supremacy. Every man is free to rise as far as he's able or willing to. If I get a million chances at hitting the ball, I bet I could get a home run. Everyone could get a result after a while. When it comes to African Americans, it's strictly a need-to-know basis, as a result, they learn a few skills a year. It's like chasing leaves in a storm now. The number one reason they're mad at me, they love the way things are. I pointed this out and have been taken to the cleaners ever since. Racism is a big problem in the machine shops because it robs one of opportunity, options, and choices to choose from. People have even said to me in class, why don't black people find something else of their own, this is a white man's field. Why don't you people try Entertainment, and leave the machine shops to us? Screw you and your log cabins chicken-catching pig farmers.

Kodak

I don't know why it's so hard for people to believe that the Machine Shops are that racist. All one has to do is look at the Grandfather of machine shops in Rochester which is Kodak. Kodak is like a big machine shop and was Rochester's #1 employer for years with an advanced high-tech racist practice that has kept African Americans out of the picture for years. This is common knowledge. They had over 60,000 employees at one time back in 1982. Most of the teachers when I went to school at the Applied Tech were from Kodak. My one teacher was a high-ranking Forman at Kodak and I ask him did he think Kodak was racist, and at the time he was working on one of the machines, and he stopped what he was doing, and gave me a really big smile and said: "You bet your ass their racist". He went on to tell me that when they have meetings, even before they have meetings, they make sure who is going to be there with great certainty. If there will be any black man or black woman there. If not, this can be discussed, if so, that can't be discussed. He said a meeting is a meeting, and if they're not racist, why should it matter who is going to be at the meeting? He also said that if they wanted to hire one of their people in the machine shop, where some type of test had to be passed before entry, that they would stand over them and say things like, "Are you sure you want to choose that answer". All of this was a common practice he said. How would I know these things specifically if he didn't tell me? Lots of the people in the machine shops are from Kodak. That's where the college and machine shops probably got most of their slick racist discriminatory tactics from. Kodak has always been the #1 machine shop in Rochester, and sourced out work to most of the machine shops in Rochester. Do you mean to tell me that most of the people in Rochester got their machine shop skills from Kodak, which is a good thing, and not their racist discriminatory practice from Kodak which is a bad thing? That doesn't make sense to me or you. To me, this is like a little terrorist cell that operated for years with the approval of this community. And when one proves racism, the only thing the average person has to say is, so what, everybody is racist. To me that's like saying, so what, everyone kills, so what, everyone steals, so what, everyone is a terrorist. This letter is a result of what happens when hate gets to breed for so long without interference.

Chinese restaurant

They have denied me just about all the pleasures in life. I used to go to the biggest buffet in Rochester, but the only problem with that was it was right down the street from the college. I knew I was in shark-infested waters, but went there anyway. The police followed me everywhere else, so it didn't matter, so I thought. Police used to be waiting at the restaurant for me, and when I got there, the waitress or the hostess used to sit me in their section or place me in the booth in front of them all the time. Or I would get there, and after like 10 minutes they would show up sitting behind me. They had complete control of the place. On one occasion they placed me by this one policeman, and he was talking to a fireman, then the rest of the tables of people started talking to one another like some happy group, then the police with a happy smile started talking to me, trying to get me to join the so-called group talk. I just gave him a short answer and went back to eating. The whole time he had a book with him, and I guess he wanted to get me to open up to him, so I could read him a story. I pride myself on being rational, and even though I know this sounds weird, and not something a rational person would say, but it did indeed happen.

I liked this one girl there because she liked me, so I thought, because she was giving me all kinds of smiles, and when she came to collect the money for the bill, she gave me a sad look because I wasn't responding to her advances. Now all the time that she was giving me these advancing friendly stares, this was out of the view from the cop that was in back of me. I am extremely perceptive, I just don't respond, and people don't think I am on to them. Anyway, I would have responded to her if he wasn't there. As I got home, I said to myself, I should be able to talk to anyone I want to talk to, that wants to talk to me. So the next time I went back there, I tried to make eye contact with her, but she showed no emotion as her face turned into stone the whole time. She kept walking by my table, and I kept trying to make eye contact with her, but her eyes were always straight ahead, like she was in a trance. Then this tall African American walked by my table, then I knew something was up then and there. As I was getting up to leave, Stone Face came over to my table in a submissive way, as 2 African Americans turned hard in their booth to see if I was going to say anything to her, I guess. Interpretation, someone told that girl to show interest in me, and then back off hard, because that's exactly what happened. I went back there a couple of other times, and she wasn't there, but another girl just as pretty as she was doing the same thing with her eyes to me. I didn't want to ruin my chances with Stone Face, so I didn't acknowledge her, and she looked at me with hurt in her eyes like, what's wrong with me? I have always ignored this girl. I was thinking about buying Stone Face some flowers, and then I thought about it. I have concluded that even if Beyoncé wanted to date me, I couldn't date her. For one, where would I go with her? I drive when it's dark at night less than 10 times a year, and don't you think she would get sick of this real soon? I can't have any relations with anyone, because of all the hate towards me the police and college caused. So I came to this realization a while ago, and one day I went back to the restaurant and Stone Face kept walking by my table, then started vacuuming by my table, as slowly as possible behind me. I never turned around, and then she started vacuuming in front of me as slowly as possible, casually looking in my direction and smiling. I never said anything to her, and this was a girl I liked too. She had a pretty face and a nice frame, whereas most Chinese women have a pretty face and no frame, in my opinion.

One time there was an undercover at the restaurant before I got there, I believe. He was really big and tall. This one Chinese girl was out of view from the undercover, and she kept waving at me with her hand as she smiled at me tons of times, trying to get a reaction out of me so that the undercover would see me doing it. Then this same waitress was at my table like 20 times pouring me water every time I took a sip from my glass, smiling sexy from ear to ear when she was at my table. This was again out of the view from the undercover. The only thing that he could see was her back and my face. That is an example of entrapment. She also used to adjust her pants in front of me, like you would do in front of a mirror alone. The police probably said something like, help us out, show him some attention, I'll scratch your back if you scratch mine, let him fall into our trap, and we'll take it from here. Remember, we won't forget. So why did I go back there? Because I loved the food, I said to myself that "I wasn't going anywhere. I want to eat here, and if they start, I am telling." I can't go anywhere as is, and I figured I was safe in front of the cameras. One time I went to the restaurant, and she placed me in a spot facing the wall, and every time she walked by I looked up, and noticed that she looked exactly like the Chinese girl in the movie Kill Bill. The whole time there was an undercover sitting in back of me. Then all of a sudden, she walked by again, and I looked up, and she walked right up to my table and shoved her hands really hard in my face that came within inches of hitting me. Why would you come up to a guy that outweighs you by 150 lbs, and violently shove your hands in his face? Is it customary for a waitress to react this way, to a paying customer, in front of the police? The police probably said to her, do everything you can to get his attention and try your hardest to get him to say something to you out of the way. We're right here, we got your back. Ask me under an MRI, or just look at the video, if they haven't thrown it away, did I say something or do anything out of the way to her like blowing kisses at her or the like? I didn't even wink my eye at her. There are cameras in every inch of the place, prove me wrong. How about if you can prove me wrong on this point, and they have all the cameras on their side, I will plead guilty to whatever felony they want me to. Isn't that what they want, to see me in prison for life, so they can attack me at will? On the flip side of things, by that girl putting her hands in my face, just goes to show that they're teaching people how to treat me. It also shows another hard-proof example of violence they tried to suck me into, and 100% proof that I can't live in this city. If these guys treated me like this in an open restaurant, just imagine how they treated me behind closed doors in the machine shops. So what did I do? Nothing, I just finished my meal, left a tip, and left. They didn't want me going to that particular restaurant, because it was down the street from the college that students and faculty often visit. 99.9% of the population would have taken this incident to the next level, but I just stood right there and took it on the chin.

The next time I went there, Kill Bill went out of her way and even ran up to the front when I came in, asked how I was doing, and seated me. Normally, when they seat you, they leave. This time, she just stood there looking at me, inviting me into a conversation. She didn't care about her duties, she just wanted to talk. We talked for like 5 minutes straight. I asked her did she thought I was greedy because when I eat there, I eat tons of food. Since she was showing me so much attention, I was indirectly asking her why. She didn't know what the word "greedy" was and thought I said something to her out of the way. She asked someone what it was I guess, and have always tried to make conversation with me when I was in the restaurant all the time I was there. Then one day I went up to her when she was up at the buffet with another girl. I told her that this was my last time coming here, and she said why, why? I said that I was going to start back jogging because I had gained so much weight eating there. She said something like we'll be here when you decide to come back or something. Within a week, I went jogging and sort of sprained my ankle, because I was jogging on an uneven grass surface. When I went jogging, the police told the people that are watching out for me, that I was jogging, and it just so happens that I told him what I said to Kill Bill. Again, I told her I wasn't going there anymore because I was gaining so much weight and was planning on jogging soon. Ask that guy, didn't I tell him that? Anyway, I hurt my ankle and went back to the restaurant. When I was going up to the buffet, I saw Kill Bill walking in my direction. As we were passing one another I said "I know last time I said I wasn't coming here anymore, but I hurt my ankle and was hungry". That's it. Then all of a sudden, she looked at me like she was terrified and screamed extra loud at the top of her voice, "What did you say to me". The whole restaurant was looking at me like I did something wrong. I was so embarrassed and should have left then, but I didn't because I wanted to clear myself in front of all the customers. When I came from the buffet with my plate, I said in the softest of voices in front of the other customers to Kill Bill, "I know last time I said I wasn't coming here anymore, but I hurt my ankle when I went jogging and that I hadn't had meat in a while because I was mainly juicing fruits and vegetables and was starving for meat". Can you believe, I said all that to her while she looked at me like, I own you now. If I was a real man, I would have said, Bitch, you know I didn't say anything to your monkey ass out of the way, you know exactly what I said and left the restaurant. They have got me in a very weak state, where I back down from everything under the sun to live to fight another day. If I had this ego that they speak of, I would have reacted differently. Then, when I sat down, this one undercover cop who was sitting in the booth with another cop, turned all the way around and looked at me for what seemed like a minute. There was also this 70-year-old couple that were sitting in the booth together, staring at me the whole time. They didn't too much talk or eat; they would just look at me. On another occasion, I was at the same restaurant when this one African American lady kept asking me all these questions, while one of the waitresses seated this 70-year-old couple right by me, there were other places that they could have sat, but the waitresses sat them by me on purpose, while an undercover cop was in back of me listening the whole time. She asked me questions like what was I doing in my apartment all this time, and I had told her about the police almost running me over in front of the police camera, and how the Internal Affairs ain't shit, how the mayor wasn't shit. The undercover almost blew his cover moving in his seat, while the 70-year-old couple couldn't care less what they were eating and just watched me. They had no idea that I knew they were there for me. Whoever these older people are, they must be very important and are some of the main people behind the scenes, that's against me. My perception is right on time, I just don't respond to situations, but know what's going on all the time. Anyway, they had their entire waitress staff, one by one, come up to me pour me a sip of water, and ask me if they could get me anything. They even had this one waitress pretending like she was washing the table with one foot on the floor, and the other on the booth looking at me, showing me her crotch. All of this because some high-class white trash, wants to protect a bunch of filthy trailer trash that they hated growing up, and have thrown my life to the ground like glass protecting filth. This was all in front of the 70-year-old couple. They even baited me to say something to them. To the 70-year-old couples I have seen, that are pulling the strings behind the scenes, like the man behind the curtain on The Wizard of Oz, isn't 70 years a long time to be white trash. They were there at the restaurant before I was, as well as the two undercover policemen. Either you have one or two waitresses the whole time, not 5 or 6. Then when I left, a clean white undercover car with the spotlight on the side, violently backed up across the street, then as my car faced his from across the street, he crossed the street going like 100 miles an hour passing my car in the Chinese Restaurant parking lot.

There is a way to get down to the bottom of things. Tell Kill Bill that she will be deported if she is lying, and will be rewarded if she is telling the truth, and then explain to her what an MRI Lie Detector Test is. If I am lying, just think of how much time you want to give me, and then add another zero if I am lying. This isn't rocket science. And when you see that I am telling the truth, well that's just one more thing that I have proven. Or ask the rest of them Rent-A-Whore waitresses, have I ever said anything to them out of the way. It just proves that I can't work in this city either, because I wanted to work for the Hospital, and they knew that. I would rather have a lap dance at a restaurant, then at my place of employment. Thanks for giving me the heads-up, Satan, and thank those hoes for the show. By them acting the way they did towards me by trying to get me to say something to them, placing me by people who were there to spy on me, and setting me up as a whole, is racist. I have never had any problems with Asian people in my whole life until Satan brought his funky ass around. Trying to set me up, to cancel and cross out all their Evil, or minimize it as much as possible. A thug is a ruthless brute without a conscience, who will use whatever weapons are available to him and order to beat his victims into submission. In this case, the police used the restaurant to do their thugging, and tried to beat me into submission. And to blame me would be like blaming the victim of a holdup for corrupting the integrity of the thug.

Country Style Buffet

I used to always go there to eat, and the manager used to sit close by with a serious look on his face as he would fold his hands and watch me eat. His eyes barely left my sight, especially on Fridays, when I used to meet my Aunt and Uncle there. I guess to see what was said and how I was interacting with my family. Sometimes I would reverse the game and sit by him on days when my family wasn't there. He would move and sit someplace else, but still keep a close eye on me. At times, I would be there with my family and I guess I was there too long because police went out of their way to show me that they were waiting by my car. I could see them as clear as day out the window, as they waited there looking at me spending time with my family. When I paid my bill and left, the police cruiser was gone. I have even been asked on more than one occasion, "How do you know those people you're with"? One day, the assistant manager looked at me so mean and nasty as I was leaving that he could have killed me. As I was paying my bill on another occasion, the head manager told me that if I filled out this little slip, I would get special promotions sent to me. That was normal, but what wasn't normal was when I put down my email address. He asked me in a prying way like 3 times in a row, "Is this your current email address that you often use, if not, you won't get the special offers sent to you. So you better make sure, do you have any other emails you might want to put down because you won't get these special offers". "Are you sure, are you sure, are you sure", like he was trying to get to the bottom of this once and for all.

Interpretation, the police told the head manager and

assistant manager to keep an eye on me when I went there because I was going there a lot at the time. The police know my Yahoo email username and password because when I was meeting with Internal Affairs they asked me to show them my letters online. So when I went home, I gave my Yahoo account AIDS by signing up to all these "free stuff sites" and changed my email account. The police just had an account that was infested with spam and wanted my new email account.

Aldi

I haven't been to the grocery store in over 8 months, if not a year. I lost track. The security guard there used to look at me aggressively as in, I know everything about you too, start something in here, I dare you. At times, I used to read the labels of the food that I was interested in, and he used to get on his cell phone and smile as his eyes followed me around the store. He saw that I was keeping my distance from him when I was in the store. He must have told someone about this to cover his butt because, at times when I would shop there, they made sure that church people were there. The security guard would ask the cashier for change when I was at the register so that the church people would see that I was keeping my distance from him. So he could say, you saw him, right? He is going out of his way to not be around me, and not make eye contact with me on purpose. He's going to start something here too. I didn't do anything.

Library

Police used to follow me to the library and one time two police officers were outside, and when I walked by they looked at me with their cold blue eyes and followed me into the library. The one officer was so sweet, he made conversation with the librarian behind the desk, while his partner's eyeballs were jumping out of his skull looking at me like he had lost his mind. Then on another occasion, the librarian and I were having a conversation and I asked her how many pages could she read in an hour, or something like that, and this one lady yelled at the top of her voice "What difference does it make" and looked at me with fire in her eyes. I dropped off the book that I was reading a few days later, and haven't been back there since.

Salvation Army

It was my first time downtown after I had emailed letters over the internet, and everywhere I went, undercovers in unmarked cars and cops were everywhere looking at me with their cold blue eyes. I put change into the parking meter and watched the time on my wristwatch to know how much time I had, and went into the Salvation Army and when I came back out to my car to put more change in, there was a ticket on my windshield. At the most, I was a minute or two late. They must have been watching that meter like a hawk. Look at the date on the ticket and the time I emailed my letters, and one will clearly see that that ticket is also an act of retaliation. Haven't I received enough blatant tickets out of retaliation so far? And why was I at the Salvation Army in the first place, because this city put me in poverty.

Eastview Mall

I went Christmas shopping there, and everywhere I went mall security and police would put so much pressure on me, I thought they were waiting for the perfect opportunity to strike me from behind.

Everywhere I went, radios would go off, telephones would ring and cashiers would give me a mean look. I would turn around suddenly, and undercover police/mall security would go the other way or duck down out of my view. I used the pay phone by the bathroom which is right by the security station and the whole time security was looking at me through the big reflection mirror outside their office, looking at me with fire in their eyes the whole time I was on the phone. Then a sheriff came in from outside by the security office doors as I was on the phone, and walked as slowly as possible by me. Every store I went into, security was on point, and I was nothing but a walking GPS. When I got outside, not one but two police cruisers were outside by my car. I had to return something there and haven't been there since. Oh yeah, that mall is like 15 miles away in another county.

Wegmans

When I go in there, security looks at me as if I am an opponent standing in the opposite corner ready to fight me. There were times when I entered, and security wasn't waiting by the door, and then all of a sudden, he would walk hard up front, looking at me, and only me. He would look at me, as if he was saying, "I know all about you, if you start something in here, I'll take you apart". I would be waiting in line, and he never took his eyes off me. This is mainly the Wegmans in Gates.

Tops

I have gone there and the police/security would be at the register before I was and would give me a mean look and make me feel uncomfortable. Obviously, the cashier knew the undercover, because he was standing shoulder to shoulder with her, as he gazed at me with his cold blue eyes. So the only time I would go there is to return bottles, which is very rare, or use their coin machine, which is also rare. One time I was standing in line waiting to return my bottles, and this one guy wearing a City of Rochester shirt just stood there looking at me like he wanted to fight me right there. He didn't care who was looking, and there were cameras everywhere.

Manpower

In my last letter, I said that they would lie, and just like I predicted, they did. The police let them read my last letter, about the part about how they fired me, and as a result, they lied to Unemployment and said they didn't fire me, that my job assignment just ended. This was in October 2008. They almost got away with this slick lie, until I told Unemployment that I wrote a letter explaining in August of 2008 what happened when I worked there and sent it out over the internet and that they had read that letter. She saw right through this lie and granted me unemployment. If I didn't tell her that, trust me, I wouldn't have gotten unemployment. For the record, Jasco, the company that I worked for through Manpower, pays faithful employees' money if they are witnesses and lie to Unemployment and say that they were present when ex-employees quit in front of the Supervisor. As in, I was there when such and such quit. This is a paid lie so, Jasco don't have to pay for their unemployment.

Post Office

I used to live out in Ogden, so since the mail was always getting put in everyone else mailbox at one time, when I ordered a package I used to have them send it to the Ogden address. Sometimes they would send it back, without a word, and I would have to call the company and ask where my order was, and the company would say they sent it back. It turned out that they sent it back because they looked at the name, and knew I didn't live there, and they just sent it back. Plain and simple, they didn't want me getting my mail out there.

The one lady was hitting on me hardcore when I went to get my passport at the counter. After I was done filling out the forum, she told me to come to the side door, so I could take my passport picture. There was this 300 lb officer lady that was in line with black shades on the whole time. I waited what seemed like 5 minutes; when she was supposed to be at the door in a second. When she opened the side door, there was pure hate in her eyes. How could that be, when just 5 minutes ago she was hitting on me? She took my picture and was cold to me the whole time. Just maybe, the lady cop had a little talk with her. The office on Lexington near Mt. Read.

RG&E

Satan follows me just about all the time when I go to RG & E. Since I have been living here, my refrigerator has been turned down as low as it could possibly go without me shutting it off. Within the last year, I have "Gone Green" and have unplugged everything in my apartment if am not using it, and when I use it, I unplug it immediately. So my bill is really low when they come out to read it, and when they estimate my bill, it's like $20 more. So I have complained about my bill to RG & E with the police looking at me, hearing exactly what's going on. Then all of a sudden, the person behind the counter said that I was 100% right and that it was a lot to pay over. I am talking like this, so the police can ease my pain a little, since they want to be in every single thing in my life. I am like; here is something I don't mind you being in. If you let Satan know what you're going to do in the fight, he will know how to dodge your swings so it looks like you're fighting yourself. The police thought I was going to email my letters in September, so they got someone to change my bill really low on the estimate, then high on the actual reading. My bill can't be that high on the actual reading, because I haven't cooked anything in like 9 months, and my refrigerator has been unplugged for like 4 months and I always have my lights off most of the time. I am extra conscious of my usage.

The last time I was at the Dept. of Social Service, I showed my caseworker the summary of what I paid and what I owed, and she immediately noticed something wasn't right, and no lie, yelled out really loud and said "What is this". She probably yelled like that because her Boss was close by, as in, "Look what I have also discovered". She said that she was going to put an investigator on it and everything. I don't know what they did, but they checked it out and nothing came of it. Nothing is probably going to come of it this time either, but I am using the bare minimum. They would love to have me write about something, so they could completely prove me wrong. It hasn't happened yet. I started not to write this part, but I know what I am using. Most of the time my apartment is pitch black while I watch TV, and I use energy-saving light bulbs.

John Reynolds

John Reynolds was selling a ton of drugs in college, and at one point was on Coke so bad, that the Vice principal whom John was tutoring his Autistic child at the time, made sure John didn't get kicked out of college and took him in so that John could get cleaned up. I think John got caught with drugs on him, or he was just so out there on Coke and failing that the Vice principal took him in. It's either one or the other, or both, that prompt the Principal to take him in. If it wasn't the Vice principal, it was the principal or Dean, but whoever it was, their child was Autistic. I know all this because John told me with sincerity himself.

Tears came out of John's eyes one night on the steps of the Tavern when he told me that one of his best friends caught his mother smoking crack. Am not sure if it was inside the Tavern, or next door where she lives, but it was still on the Tavern grounds that it happened. How could you catch someone in their own home smoking crack? His friend doesn't smoke crack, which means that she was smoking crack inside the Tavern. What's so funny about this is, the cops hang out all the time there. I could make the argument that the police hang out in a crack house, especially since his crackhead mother is the bartender. By the way, John's older brother lives there too and is a super crackhead. So, when John's mother and older brother's heads aren't rocking on their shoulders in a deep nod on the couch together, she is serving cops drinks as his older brother walks around the bar geeking talking to police.

This one young girl, "she had to have been underage" called John and told him that she would show him her tits if he gave her a bottle of wine. I was right there at the end of the bar talking to John when she called. John told me as soon as he got off the phone what she said. She must have called John on her cell phone because she came in shortly. She went into the kitchen with Johnny and came out like 5 minutes later. You should have seen her weak eyes as she left the kitchen as our eyes met. It was as if she wanted to cry. She knew I knew what was going on. Less than 5 minutes later, John came from the kitchen laughing so hard, he almost turned as red as a fire truck, laughing so hard you could almost see snot coming from his nose. Question, how would she even know to call John? How would she know that he would go for it? Why didn't she drink it in the bar? Underage, that's why.

Mark

I tried to show them some of my white friends since they told the world that everyone hates me, and just about all of them, the Police have made them schemed on me to their liking. They spit all kinds of mind games on people who know me, making their heads bigger than a pumpkin if they say this or that about me. I used to be friends with this one guy named Mark, and the police have only seen me with him like 3 or 4 times, but that's all it took. I hadn't seen this guy in a while and thought this was the last place the police would look, but they got to him as well. These war strategists tried their hardest to ambush me with this guy. They now know that I had a 12.9 reading level when I was in prison, so if they have found some way of changing it, I have another idea. My conviction was overturned, and when I was meeting with the Judge who sentenced me, I made a point of telling her that I went from a 3-grade reading level to a 12.9 reading level, so if they changed it, you know to look on that transcript. My ex-friend Mark looked at me mean the whole time when he picked me up and took me to this restaurant. His friend told me over and over again to leave the police alone in my letter, and got so mad when he knew that I would write about them. He asked me the same questions the police would have asked me the whole time I was in the restaurant with him. When we arrived back on my street, trust me, he knew the police cameras were there, and he opened the door really hard, and made the meanest look up at the camera. He turned to me with soft eyes next and gave me his card and told me to contact him so he could put me under hypnosis for free. Interpretation, the police wanted him to put me under hypnosis and build something off of it to their liking.

Am I okay mentally after these events?

The police have been in hundreds of thousands of interviews, and know exactly what it takes for someone to snap and kill another human being. You know how you train hard to get into shape, well they're using everything in their arsenal to get me into a mental state so that I would attack them so that they could kill me justifiably. I truly understand what they're doing, and what they want to accomplish. If I didn't have this understanding, it would have driven me insane a while ago. Then they want people to think I am paranoid, but if that was the case, how did I get set up so many times? A person who is really paranoid, or even partly paranoid, is very hard to set up. And they wouldn't trust anyone and let them get too close. There is no difference between placing George Bush in Afghanistan and having the Taliban treating him as they treat me, then having the local Afghanistan government spitting "Game" saying he just imagining it, it's all in his head, he is crazy, no one did anything to him, and if someone did something to him, he brought it on his self. The Taliban put Bush in prison on purpose, always faking hard like they want to hurt him, put him in poverty, and everywhere Bush goes, no matter where Bush goes, the Taliban make sure he gets treated like shit and then deny their involvement. Now, if Bush were to go crazy, whose fault would it be? They have generated much pain, frustration, stress, and anger. What doesn't kill you makes you stronger. That being said I'm still standing and mentally fit. Please tell me where I am irrational and have made a mistake in logic.

Why don't I have a Wife?

The city has declared war on me since my first letter and hasn't let up since. When one is at war, one can't have a normal life. Besides, it's going to be hard enough to say goodbye to my family, let alone my wife and children.

What Does My Family Think?

They don't know how serious it is. They just want me to settle down and get married so they can have some grandchildren with me. People have said to me, why don't I move back home with my parents? Firstly, no matter where I move in Rochester, the police will follow me there too and bring destruction, and I don't want this around my family. My family just don't know what's really going on.

Last Thing

I chose white people basically over my own race for a while, and why, because I was only around white people. One becomes their environment, with the people they surround themselves with. Move to China for 30 years and see how you turn out. When my grandmother died, there were only a couple of tears in my eyes. When one of my white friends died, whom I was really close with, I cried like a baby in front of my two other close white friends. I was as loyal as a puppy dog and after all my faith, service, and loyalty; this is what you do in return? It comes a time that one just can't live with something. I can't live with this, around these people, anymore. If you were to put yourself in my shoes, you wouldn't either, so don't ask me to do what you wouldn't do. Poverty and prison are the same thing, especially if it's done on purpose, out of retaliation. They have convicted me to a lifetime of sweat and misery and make up more shit than Maybelline and have more tricks than clowns have pockets. I don't want to live in a country where they allow this evil to happen, exist, and cover this up at any cost, then have the general public laugh and say, you told him. It is morally as bad not to care whether a thing is true or not, just so long as it makes you feel good. These guys are unfit to call themselves Christians, are more racist than they believe in God, and are really like some stuck-up feces wearing a mink coat. I am in shark-infested waters and am not free to achieve. I don't believe in America, I don't belong here; I want to completely forfeit my citizenship and I don't want to share the same cemetery with these people. I want to live in Canada for the rest of my life.

BOB DUFFY FIRES POLICE
CHIEF AFTER MY EMAIL

Bob Duffy, Rochester's Mayor, fired the Police Chief because of my Super Tuesday email letter dated November 2, 2010, after he came back from Albany. It was on every single News Station and in the Newspaper, then somehow, not another word, it all went away. Below are just a few copy-and-paste articles I found on the internet. Satan has probably scrubbed the internet as much as Satan could.

Quick Departure for Rochester, New York Police Chief CITY HALL: Police Chief David Moore stepping down The Rochester City News by Christine Carrie Fien -- November 5, 2010

Well, something stinks. In a hastily arranged press conference this afternoon, Mayor Bob Duffy announced that Rochester Police Chief David Moore would be stepping down effective Monday. Moore was not present at the press conference. James Sheppard has been named acting chief. Sheppard is director of the city's Office of Public Integrity and is former director of Safety and Security at the Rochester City School District. He is also a former Rochester police officer. Duffy was evasive when repeatedly asked why Moore is leaving or if Moore's departure is voluntary. He said the reasons are personal and
confidential and Moore could answer media questions

if he chose to. Duffy said that as far as he knows, Moore does not have another job lined up. He said that Moore's departure is "our decision," meaning his and Moore's. Duffy said Moore has "done nothing wrong" and has provided "outstanding service" to the city. Also present at the press conference were Council President Lovely Warren and Council member Adam McFadden, who is head of Council's Public Safety Committee. It seems clear that the decision happened quickly, because McFadden said he didn't know beforehand what Duffy's announcement was going to be. Warren said that Duffy called her to tell her about the decision, but would not say when that call took place. Sheppard's appointment as acting chief must be approved by City Council. Sheppard says he will seek the job on a permanent basis. Moore will serve as director of the city's Office of Public Integrity until the end of the year. The OPI is essentially the internal affairs office for the City of Rochester.

****

Rochester police chief quits suddenly

The Associate Press - November 6, 2010

ROCHESTER, N.Y. (AP) — The surprise resignation of the police chief in New York's third-largest city has local officials wondering what precipitated the move. The shake-up at the Rochester police department unfolded Friday afternoon when Police Chief David Moore met with Mayor Robert Duffy and agreed to step down. "Things developed over time," Moore said. "I don't think it would be appropriate to discuss my conversation with the mayor." In a separate news conference, Duffy said Moore "has done nothing wrong" and praised him as "a good man." Neither gave a reason for the sudden resignation, which was reported by the Democrat and Chronicle newspaper. Former Deputy Chief James Sheppard will take over as acting chief. Sheppard currently runs Rochester's Office of Public Integrity. City Councilman Adam McFadden said Saturday that he was puzzled by Moore's ouster, especially since Duffy will leave the city in January to be the state's lieutenant governor. Duffy, a former police chief, ran for lieutenant governor on the winning ticket with Democratic gubernatorial candidate Andrew Cuomo. McFadden said he was surprised that Duffy did not leave key people in place, since a new mayor will likely want his or her own people. With a population of 219,773, Rochester is New York's third most-populous city after New York City and Buffalo.

Posted by Law Enforcement Corruption at 9:01PM

An email from SCLC in Atlanta Georgia

They told me that they were my lawyers and how much money they would sue for. Police would fake really hard with their cars like they wanted to hit me, every single time I left my apartment. They had my phone tapped, and I felt that it was just a matter of time before they killed me, so I dropped all communication with SCLC and hid in my apartment.

Lionel from SCLC in Atlanta Georgia

Please give me your local contacts for the SCLC and NAACP in your area, any churches or religious organizations/ contact them, and please give them my info and set up a phone conference call with all of us please note - I know you don't want everyone in your business, but we must start here, we need a press release, please summarize your letters into one page, we don't want to tell everything at one time and there are something's we do not want the press to know yet so please let's get the ball rolling

My Response

There isn't a SCLC office here, and if it is, I can't find them. The NAACP has an office here, but they don't have a phone number anymore. I even called the Operator, and they said the same thing. They have an email address though, and I could contact them through there. I don't mind anyone being in my business, because the police have allowed everyone already in my business. To be honest, this is just my opinion, but these people are friends with the people in power. And when they sued Kodak, they made a side deal with one of the head Ministers, and he took a large payoff and left town. 100% sale out. The black people of this community have been raped by Kodak since they allow black people to work there. And when it was all said and done, black people got the short end of the stick when the lawsuit was over. I told older black people about my case, and that I wasn't working with the NAACP, and they said: "Good for you". Don't get me wrong, because if it wasn't for them, the police would have probably killed me a long time ago. They have followed me everywhere, and I haven't said too much to them. It was all strategy on my part. I wanted the police to act a fool when people weren't looking, and they have, a million times it seems.

I will contact them through email and give them your info. I don't know whom else to call. Am sorry I took this long to respond, but I don't have the internet anymore. I use a laptop, and when I can get an open connection to the internet, I do. This is the only way to contact you because they have stripped the kid of all my money. If there are any more people you want me to contact, please send me their email. I will be working on a one-page letter to sum everything up.

P.S.

Contact me at jspeace34@gmail anytime. As a matter of fact, I'll create another email to make sure they don't have that one, so we can talk freely. And I'll make a PDF of all my letters, from the first to the last. This way, it will be so much easier to read, because reading them on my Blog is hard.

Dear NAACP Rochester Branch

I am in the process of suing the City of Rochester for all the atrocities they have done to me. I am in contact with The Southern Christian Leadership Conference in Atlanta, Georgia, and they want you to contact them. Actually, he wants to have a phone conference set up so we can ALL talk. I was supposed to do this like two weeks ago but misplaced his number. Anyway, the guy's name is Lionel and his number is 404-839-xxxx. I went to the Dept. of Social Service, and my caseworker told me that she would pay my landlord off so that I could live there. My landlord told me that he didn't receive a call from my worker stating that they would pay. I told my worker this, and she said what is he talking about, your case opens up on the 13th and he will get his money. That's what she kept telling me. I just found out 24 hours ago that they're not going to be paying my rent, and now they're slapping me on my Beak saying I would have 72 hours to leave. The problem with this is that they told me this at the last second. I could have been looking for an apartment all this time. Now I would have to leave my furniture behind. They did this on purpose, and it clearly shows another act of retaliation. I will retaliate by telling 3 more events that I know about. I haven't got caught in a lie yet. They're juicy too.

If I can't find an apartment in 3 days, I would have to be put in a shelter. I have my parent's house keys, and I could go over there or to any of my sister's homes. At any time I choose. Because of all the Police pressure, they wouldn't want me living there. They feel that the police would be in their business too. Not to mention that all my family are very competitive and materialistic, so I can't count on my family at all. Nor should I be put in this position to have to count on them. That being said,

I will walk the streets if I ask my family for anything. They haven't a clue this is even going on, nor do I want them to.

Can you do me another favor? Rochester Works sent me to take a Reading Test. I went there, and they wanted me to take a Reading and Math Test. I haven't done math in a very long time, and haven't a clue what math is going to be asked on the test. I took the Tabe Reading Test back in 1994 and scored a 12.9. The highest score possible. Well, if they won't let me take that test without taking the math part, well I suggest that I take the SAT Critical Reading Test. This is a much higher reading test than the Tabe Test. Just let me know a week in advance, so I can read some books to get the juices flowing because I don't read all the time. And since everything is based on this reading test, the Gate will be wide open for me to sue, and Johnny Cochran, if still alive, couldn't save Satan. Thanks for your time.

Roy Snell

Email to NAACP on the first day that I moved into my new apartment

Today's date is March 15, 2011

I called my caseworker yesterday, which was March 14, 2011, and told her that I found an apartment and that my new landlord would call her with the details. My caseworker and new landlord talked everything over, and I was told to come into Social Service the next day, because it was only five minutes before they closed, to pick up a landlord statement and to have my new landlord fill it out, then return the statement to Social Service that day. I had my landlord fill out a landlord statement today, and he said"She told me over the phone to make sure that I date the landlord statement March 13, 2011". So he did. Firstly, why was he told to date and sign something deliberately on purpose that wasn't true, because today's date is March 15, 2011, and NOT March 13, 2011. Does this make any sense to you?

So why did my Social Service caseworker tell my new landlord to lie on the paperwork? Ever since I first met my caseworker, she has always told me that the dept. of social service would pay my back rent so that I did not have to move. My old landlord told me that no one from social service had promised him any money on my back rent or any kind of money whatsoever. I told my caseworker, and she threw up her hands and said "What is he talking about, he will get his money when your case opens up on March 13, 2011" She kept telling me this, then at the last moment, my old landlord came into my apartment and told me that this was his apartment now, and that the Fire Marshal was on their way and that I would have 72 hours to get out. I called my caseworker and asked her if it was true, and she said that I had 72 hours to leave. I told her that she knew how things were going to play out when I first met her, and that she had led me on the whole time with lies. And that I could have been looking for an apartment the whole time the first day I met her. They wanted the Fire Marshal to put me on the streets so that I would lose ALL of my possessions and be put in a shelter. I told her that her actions were clearly an act of retaliation, and that I would retaliate by telling 3 more secrets about the City of Rochester. They have me on a recorder saying this because I said it on purpose.

When this city first put me in poverty, the dept. of Social Service just about did the same manipulative tactic to me. Just read my past letters. Actions speak louder than words. Now I have to give away most of my possessions because it's too short of time to find a truck. All of this is going on at present. March 15, 2011, 3:17 pm.

Thanks for your time again.

Roy Snell

EVIL LANDLORD

I have told my landlord tons of times that I didn't want him in my apartment without me being present. I had a sign on the door that read, "Dear Landlord, New York State law says you have to give tenants 24 hours' notice before you can enter their apartment unless there is an emergency". I want you to honor this law by not entering my apartment, unless I am here, or you give me 24-hour notice. He broke into my apartment like 5 days later when I wasn't there. Am always home and in my apartment, and someone must have told him I went shopping or something because that is when he entered my apartment. Very sneaky. My lock wasn't working as it should have for at least six months, so he decided to make this an emergency as his excuse to break into my apartment when I wasn't home. He goes into everyone's apartment when he feels like it, but loves my apartment the most. When he confronted me on why I had that statement on my door, he was recording me the whole time and said that he had the right to come into my apartment without me being present, because it was an emergency to change the door lock. I said emergency, but you knew about my lock for like six months. His eyes hit the floor as he changed the subject. I didn't know this then, but he had already changed the door lock when he confronted me about my sign on the door.

My landlord almost got me into a fight with some people who live down the street. He said that a guy saw me punching the hell out of the apartment building with my boxing gloves on. He said that the guy said I was just hammering away on the side of the building. The next time I saw the guy, I just looked straight ahead like he wasn't even there. Then the following time I saw him when I was walking to the store, he had around ten Spanish men with him looking at me confidently as I walked past his house, you could have heard a needle drop as I walked past them. To this day, I don't know what was said, but my landlord is the reason behind what happened. My landlord confronted me about this over the phone while he recorded me the whole time too. I would call him, and he would let the answering machine pick it up all the time, then call me back. He has always tried to trick me on the phone while recording me, so I never call him about anything, no matter what. For the record, I own two pairs of boxing gloves, and none of them have any kind of scratches on them from so-called hitting the apartment building. This was all BS.

My landlord knows that Ms. DeJesus is a Raging Drama Queen. He told her that he was kicking her out because I kept calling him, complaining about her loud music. I told her that I didn't care how loud she played her music, that I was used to an army of children screaming at the last apartment. She kept coming to my apartment and confronting me as to why I would call the landlord about her music when I promised that I wouldn't. I told her that I didn't, and then one day she came over with her cell phone and played me the message of my landlord threatening to kick her out because of all my complaining. To this day, I have never called my landlord once about her music.

There are 5 apartments here altogether, and only 3 Electricity Meters in the Basement. I and Ms. DeJesus don't pay for Electricity or Gas, but my other neighbors sometimes pay 300 dollars a month for Electricity and

Gas. This is fraud. He told my one neighbor not to turn up or down her heat in her own apartment, that if she does, the main heater in the basement will short circuit or something. Question, why would my landlord care how much heat she was using? Shouldn't she control her heat if she truly pays for her own heat? Their bill will be a little more in the future because he is planning to make another apartment out of the tiny Laundry Room. My apartment number is 4, but when he sends someone to my apartment, he tells them to go to number 5. Why, because the apartments aren't numbered correctly as they should be.

Two of my neighbors got into a big argument, and one neighbor called my landlord to tell him about it. My landlord told him to call the police and then texted him with my neighbor's personal information such as his Social Security number and told him to give it to the police when they came. Isn't this against the law? My neighbor told me that he still has the text message saved as proof. He has told me enough times that his best friends since the 3rd grade are policemen who graduated with him at Aquinas. This should prove his motivation and actions towards me. I wish he had the same motivation for getting rid of all the rats the size of squirrels around his apartment building.

Ms. DeJesus blew marijuana in my face about 3 months ago while I was walking past her apartment outside. She was on the porch smoking marijuana while talking to a ten-year-old. There are two surveillance cameras close by that have the perfect view of her actions. I told my landlord about this, and he got mad at me and said that was last year. When I told him that it was, in fact, two months ago, and that my apartment always smells of marijuana because of Ms. DeJesus, he said I don't care who smokes marijuana here. When I was young, I used to smoke it all the time. He has told me that it would be okay for me to smoke marijuana in my apartment about ten times now.

My one neighbor just had a baby 3 months ago and had to buy a $200 dehumidifier or something that purifies the room of smoke, because Ms. DeJesus smokes so much marijuana. Ms. DeJesus was even growing marijuana around the apartment building outside until someone pulled them up and stole them. Ms. DeJesus got into an argument with my other neighbor about stealing her marijuana plants outside because he was the only person that she told about them.

Thank you,

Roy Snell

Tuesday, June 12, 2012,

Dear Chicago Mayor, Police & Media,

There is a guy by the name of John Steward that lives in Rochester, N.Y. that has killed many people on Chicago soil when he lived in Chicago. I have tried and tried to remember when he first came back from Chicago bragging to me how he had killed many people. I am pretty sure he went on his killing spree between the years of 1989 and 1990. I could be wrong, but this is the best that I can come up with. I am pretty sure that there wasn't any snow on the ground here.

He was in a vicious street gang called The Gangster Disciples. I had a hard time trying to remember if he said that he was in The Gangster Disciples or The Vice Lords because he said both gangs were at war with one another. That was until I saw the History Channel's Gang Land season two, episode nine titled "Gangster Inc". John demonstrated the very same gang signs and hand-shaking movements to me. I have watched the Vice Lord's hand shaking and gang signs too, and this wasn't what John showed me. So out of both gangs, The Gangster Disciples are the only ones to touch one another on the shoulder like that when greeting one another. John touched me on my shoulder the same way and did the same exact gang signs as they did on the video. The video that I have of this is 44 minutes and 32 seconds long. Fast-forward and watch this video on YouTube or Google Video somewhere and watch this video from 22: 45 to 23:00 especially. This is exactly what John demonstrated to me when I lived in Greece, N.Y. when I was 19 or 20 years old.

I am just throwing this out there to cover all my bases. Let's just say that he was in fact a member of The Vice Lords, and not The Gangster Disciples, that he showed me both gang's hand shaking and gang signs. What I really remember is the handshaking and gang signs he did to me, which was the same way that The Gangster Disciples did it in the video. But no matter which gang he was in, he was in either The Gangster Disciples or The Vice Lords and killed tons of people. If I had to bet my life, I would say he was in The Gangster Disciples. He told me that he had to leave Chicago in a hurry because too many people were looking for him. I don't know what name he went by when he lived in Chicago, but most people in the Dance Clubs know him by his alias, which is Pit. I guess because he looks like a pit bull and loves the Pittsburgh Steelers.

I guess a lot of people would say, why would you be friends with someone that you knew for certain to be a killer? That assessment would be correct, and I can only say that I did it for selfish reasons. I used to go to a lot of Dance Clubs, and John Steward was the head bouncer at the best Dance Clubs in Rochester. So that means that I never waited in line like everyone else. I just had to say his name at the front door while there were like 100 people waiting in line, to get into most of the Dance Clubs in Rochester right away without even paying. I know this is no excuse, I am just being honest.

I think he deserves the death penalty, especially since he came back to Rochester after his murder spree and hung out with the local police. They even let him sell drugs outside one of Rochester's busiest nightclubs and looked the other way. It was the case of; I do for you if you do for me. While at the same time was allowed to carry a gun on his hip openly. You should have seen how calm, confident, comfortable, and the fearlessness in his eyes and demeanor when he was allowed to carry a gun in public by way of the local police. John has done so many favors for the local police and has been rewarded for it. You would think the last thing in the world is a person that has killed tons of people, would want to be a police officer and hang around police every chance they get. I don't know if he is on good terms with the police after my letters, but he used to hang out with them and did all kinds of favors for them. The police used to even go to his private stripper parties, where sometimes sex was involved. The private stripper parties used to be held all across Rochester at various Dance Clubs and Bars, mainly on a Sunday Night.

So why am I spilling my beans now? Plain and simple, it's just his time. Not to mention that the police hired him to tell people that everyone always hated my guts in a convincing way. A lot of people that I knew would hang out at the same Dance Clubs where John was the head bouncer, and John made sure that they would get VIP if they said this or that about me. It was all lies, but since John sided with the police and started the police's hate campaign against me, it's just his time now.

I quote a part of one of the letters I wrote.

February 9, 2006

Quote:

Speaking of Moe's, I know where and whom the police got their information from when the college said "People don't like you, Mr. Snell". I won't say this Moe's name, Moe doesn't know that I know, but trust me on this; once this letter reaches you, the police will let Moe read my letter. TRUST ME! This Moe has the mentality of kill your parents, screw your friends, and have a nice day just to fulfill Moe's childhood fantasy of becoming a cop. Not to mention that Moe took the police test lots of times and failed. At least that's what Moe told me. This Moe I am talking about is a bouncer at the dance clubs who know most cops around town. Moe hangs in the street more than traffic lights do. Most of Moe's friends that Moe hangs out with are bouncers too. Not to say that they are bad people, but most have King Kong personalities, just like Moe and Moe's around the world. To tell you the truth, I get along with most of them because they know my history and that I am a good boxer. I don't get along with all the Moe's, because Moe is a born manipulator and always looking for an opening, but always respects someone that can fight. Back to the Moe who told police that or the police made him say that. If the police have all their money on this Moe, and think that he's a franchise star quarterback, let him start the game coach! I know something they don't know. Let's just say, if I should die today, I am in good standing with God. God will take no revenge on me whatsoever. As far as "Moe" goes, by God's law, He has to take revenge. Use your imagination. By the way, I haven't got caught in a lie yet, because I speak reality.

End Quote.

February 9, 2006

Quote:

I told "Moe the bouncer" at the bar about all the police and mall security guard pressure, and he said I was just seeing things. I asked him if he could remember a time that I lied to him, he said no, but that I was still seeing things. Then I told him about the part when the cop told me not to email my letters anymore. "Moe the bouncer" got mad and said, what was the officer's name, as in I can't believe the guy slipped like that, he knows better than that, he's messing everything up! It happened exactly like I just wrote it. By the way, did I mention, "Moe the bouncer" has one police sticker on his car and another on his wife's car? Did I mention that "Moe the bouncer" also carries a gun on the side of him when he's working at night outside the dance club? Only if you knew what I knew, laughs out loud. If "Moe the bouncer" had those police stickers on his car before all the police started messing with me, I didn't know about it. I know for a fact he didn't have a gun, at least not a legit one, before police hired him to try to kill my character.

End Quote:

This is the first time I used his real name in my letter, and the last time I spoke about Moe, A.K.A. John Steward.

August 11, 2006

Quote:

John Steward Killing Spree

John Steward came over to my house one day all excited about moving back to Rochester from another state where he had killed lots of people by being in a violent street gang. I don't know how many people he killed before, and I don't think John knows either, or maybe he does. He told me that he shot and killed people all the time in another state. Imagine someone winning the lottery, that was the excitement on his face when he told me all of this. He even tried to explain the gang signs to me and everything. Like some excited professor on speed. I can't believe his deep love for guns and weapons, it's sick! First of all, I haven't got caught in one lie, because I write reality, that's why I am so convincing. Secondly, if I was going to lie, why would I pick this lie? Does that make any sense? MRI lie detector, please! Ask Kevin Roule, what was the name of Danny who had red hair, limped, and looked like Malachai from the movie "The Children of The Corn"? That guy would most certainly know. A guy named Oscar that tried to give his girlfriend an abortion with a coat hanger that was in the paper a long time ago. That was John Steward's best friend. One day I worked in the mall and Mark DiRisio and Rick from Spencerport came and picked me up with my other friends from Spencerport. John Steward was in the back of his pickup truck with all of us and I said out loud, to the rest of the people in the back truck, "John was in a gang and used to shoot and kill people" Ask Mark DiRisio and Rick if they remember that, and how did John react? Ask John Dettman and Matt Cookinham how long ago I told them that John Steward was in a gang killing people. Ask Tory Weaver, John's best man at his wedding, did John used to be in a gang killing people. I have listened to tons of rap music, and don't know how to do one gang sign. John knows how to do them like a pro and hardly listens to rap music. All the police have to do is shove official papers in his face welcoming him into the police dept, but he must pass an MRL lie detector test saying he never killed more than two people. That the test is not 100% accurate and might show a false positive on one, but not the other, and that they allow their men one screw up and the test process because they know the machine sucks, and that this is a one-time offer. Or something like that. I bet he'll run "Game", Jedi mind trick and weasel his way out of it. Isn't this something, this guy went to another state and went on a killing spree then slid back home like he was in the Major Leagues, looking at the police like an Umpire as he slid past home base, "am I safe", "of course we love you". John Steward was even hired by some of the police to spy on their cheating wives, while the police were at work. And he also hangs out with them too. He is a security guard outside the bars who wear a gun openly that the police gave him. He also works security at Rochester only amusement park where lots of families take their kids. I know the name of the gang and the state where he went on his killing spree. I will not talk to the local police about this either. Would you? A message to the police from me, Don't be afraid of people who attack you, be afraid of friends who flatter you!

End Quote

.

I would just like to revise a few things in the above-quoted letter. It took me forever to remember Danny's last name, but then one day it just came to me. His name is Danny Cochran. I think that's how you spell his last name, I could be wrong, but that's how you pronounce it. And to be completely honest, I don't know if John Steward even told him, but they were close friends. I don't know how he could have rushed and told me everything, and not even mention this to Danny Cochran. The same thing goes for Oscar and Tory Weaver. I just think that they would have to know. I can't think of anybody else that would know. The problem is, even though me and John Steward were friends, we hung out with different crowds. John Dettman and Matt Cookinham will 1000% remember me talking about this whenever John Steward was around. In fact, the last time I saw John Dettman he came up to me at a Sports Bar on Exchange Street and said, "I can't believe they gave your friend John Steward a license to carry a gun, if they only knew what he did". I haven't seen Mark DiRisio and Rick in a long time, but at least one of them should recall the incident in the back of the truck that night. There were at least five people in the back of the truck that night, and I can only recall Mark and Rick.

As you can see, I have written about John Steward's killing spree before, but never wrote or told anyone the city where it happened, and what gang he was in until now. The way John was talking, killing 10 people wasn't anything. I have no idea what the total number is, but the body count is high. This Perp must be brought to justice. John also has a brother by the name of Sean who lives in Chicago, at least when these killings took place. He could have a different last name and even another half-brother. I am not positive; I am just covering my bases again. I know that John said that people didn't know who he was, so I am not sure if he left a paper trail when he was in Chicago at the time because he was super confident that he got away with all the killings. I will not cooperate with the local authorities on any level of this letter. Why? They're sabotage artists that speed lie like they have 3 tongues, that have destroyed my life with their demonic lies.

Thank you,

Roy Snell

P.S.
If I have to, I will testify, just as long as it's not in the wintertime in Chicago.

Chicago Mayor, Police & Media,

September 17, 2012

Monday, September 17, 2012

Dear Chicago Mayor, Police & Media,

On Tuesday, June 12, 2012, I wrote you a letter regarding John Steward who lives in Rochester, N.Y., who was in a street gang called The Gangster Disciples that killed tons of people when he lived in Chicago. At the end of my letter, I stated that I would testify to these facts in court. That was then, this is now. I have a change of heart now, and I officially would like to say that I will not testify under any circumstances. I got harassed on Tuesday, June 12, 2012, right after I emailed you about John Steward. I am sick of being sabotaged, bullied and punk'd. The last time I was harassed was on Saturday, September 15, 2012.

The only thing I am interested in at this time concerning John Steward is taking an MRI Lie Detector test about what he has told me in the past. Other than that, this killer could stay on the loose, if it involves me testifying in court, that is. You could blame you know who for my change of heart.

Best regards,

Roy Snell

P.S.
Can you tell the Local Authorities to stop tapping my computer and taking down my letters over the internet? Just asking. Thanks

ANIMAL SERVICES OF ROCHESTER

Thursday, September 27, 2012

Dear Animal Services of Rochester

Ken Torres, street name, K9, has been breeding and selling high-quality dogs out of his apartment since he has lived at 28 Hawkins St, Apt. 1. He has been breeding dogs out of his apartment for over two years now. Ken Torres said on Wednesday, September 26 at 7:35 p.m. that his dog was the real deal and that he would sell one of his puppies to a guy who came to his house for $500 without papers. The guy said that he just had to have it and would come back later that night to give him $50 and the rest of the money on Monday, just so that he wouldn't sell the dog to another person. Look at the surveillance cameras outside the Oaces building, located at 30 Hart Street, Rochester, N.Y. 14605-1122. Watch and see, don't the same guy that came over to his house, come back Monday and buy his dog. They never said what time Monday, which would be on October 1st, 2012. He told the guy that he sells his dogs over the internet and that he takes really good care of them by feeding his puppies, Puppy Chow. He also showed the guy his catfish that he keeps in his fish tank and said that it bites. I think this is also illegal, but I could be wrong.

Isn't he supposed to have papers for the dogs? How would I even know that dogs come with papers, because I have never owned a dog? The reason why I know this is because the only thing Ken talks about is breeding dogs. He said to one of his friends outside that, "there are ways to get around that and if someone asks for papers on a dog when they go to get the dog registered or something like that, to tell them that the dog didn't come with papers, and that's how you get around that". I also overheard him say to one of his friends outside that he purchased something over the internet, to inject the dogs to get them pregnant. He said it took him a long time to get the right kind of breed that he wanted, and now he has finally created the dog that he wanted. I am pretty sure that he said the breed of dog that he has now, was around in the 18TH hundreds. Then he went on to say Jose was the man, and how Jose's dogs are the best. He wishes he could get his dogs to look like Jose. By the way, one of the dogs that he had pregnant was just a puppy.

He was really upset before the dog had her puppies because the dog would just stay in one place all day long. He said that he didn't know what was wrong with it, that she, the dog, should have had her puppies, and that he badly needed the money. He talked about taking the dog to the Veterinarian but didn't have the money. One of his dogs had 8 puppies. He said that he thought that he had to give the dog a C-Section because two of the dogs just wouldn't come out. This he told his mother when she came over.

Ask just about anyone in the neighborhood if he sells dogs because I have seen him ask a lot of people. I overheard him talking with one of the neighbors, saying that all he needed to do was have a good batch so that he could get back up on his feet. He said, "I might be down now, but just wait and see when my dogs have their puppies". The neighbor said that he would ask his sister if she wanted one, and he thanked him.

About two weeks ago, I heard Ken say loudly that he was doing all the work to his girlfriend, and he made her get in the room where he keeps the dogs and made her clean it up, but not before he threatened to hit her. She told him that she didn't even like dogs, but he said that she would benefit from him selling the dogs, and made her clean up whatever the dogs had left behind. I think this was on the day when the main dog had her puppies, or it could have been the final cleanup of what the mother left behind after the birth. Whatever it was, it was a big project, because they threw away rugs after the clean-up. He said that he was the man of the house, and what he said goes. She tried to calm him down by saying not to hit her, that she was his wife. As she went into the room and started cleaning up the mess, he told the nine-year-old to get up off his ass and go help your mother. He bosses his girlfriend's kid around like no tomorrow and makes him always clean the dog droppings outside in the front yard and in the dog cage. He yells at the kid and says that he didn't do a good enough job, and to do it again. While his girlfriend and the nine-year-old were in the room cleaning, one of the dogs did something that he didn't like, I heard him scream at the dog, and then I heard a commotion as the dog started crying. In other words, he either hit or violently shoved the dog into its cage.

More proof that he has been doing this ever since he lived here. When he moved into the apartment that he lives in now, the landlord charged him $400 a month or more, plus he had to pay for Gas, Electric, and Heat. He has told me that his bill was sometimes $300 a month, and he pays my landlord an extra $50 a month for having the dog. Where does he get all this money, when he is on Welfare? He has a girlfriend who lives with him now to share the cost, but when he moved in, he paid for everything himself. So where does he get the extra money from? Breeding dogs and lots of them too. I know all that I know because the only thing that separates our Apartments is one door. If I sneezed, he could hear me loud and clear, as I could hear him loud and clear if he sneezed.

Thank you,

Roy Snell

Enclosed is a copy of a letter from my landlord dated May 8, 2012. There is another letter regarding Ken Torres's Catfish dated May 8, 2012, but that letter was addressed to Ken Torres only.

2024 UPDATE

Interpretation, Ken Torres was my evil landlord's right-hand man who put pressure on me and spied on me in the name of my landlord the whole time. Once he got loud with me outside, while he had his huge vicious pit bull leash in his hand. One word from me, that pit bull would have killed me. Not to mention my landlord breaking into my apartment, and Ken Torres looked the other way, no matter what evil he did, Ken Torres was complicit. My landlord was stealing from him the whole time, and milked hundreds out of him, by stealing his RG&E. I brought everything to fruition but could only prove half of it, wasn't believed entirely until the landlord kept stealing, and I told the new neighbors that won in court behind it. My ex-landlord, Carl Justice, had the outlets Jerry Rigged, so Tenants would pay for half the outlet, and Carl the other half. Not sure if it was the top plug or bottom plug, but the father and son electricians told me that it was done on purpose, that the whole house needed to be rewired, and that whoever did it certainly knew what they were doing. This also included the onsite Washer and Dryer because I could not use my microwave if the Dryer was on, which wasn't even in my apartment, but I would lose power in my apartment if they were on at the same time 100% of the time. He did the same thing to the Gas stove, the front burners Carl paid for, and the back burners Ken Torres paid for, when Carl Justice was supposed to pay the total cost, but is an Animal Cracker Crook. Not sure if Carl removed a heating element from the basement, but the City made Carl put in a furnace or two, hence the reason why Ken Torres's RG&E heating bill was so high. Mr. Torres loved Mr. Justice and would laugh and drink a can of beer with Mr. Justice in his apartment on occasion. Quote: "A pimp is happy when his whores giggle. He knows they are still asleep". End quote, from the book Pimp, The Story Of My Life by Iceberg Slim.

My letter to Animal Control did not have to be written, I get no pleasure in telling on anyone. It's the same as beating up a 100-year-old person, or even a child. I can't get any kind of self-esteem beating up a child or a 100-year-old. I feel the same way when it comes to telling on people that did not do anything to me personally. If something doesn't have anything to do with me, why would I care what they do? One thing I love about myself is that I don't have a jealous bone in my body. Talk to anyone who knows me, and have them give you some examples if Satan convinces them to lie. Look at all these secrets that I know, people don't tell all these secrets to jealous hateful people. That said, every single person that I have told on has directly or indirectly worked with Satan to set me up and destroy me as much as possible, mainly for personal gain, besides one person. Trust me when I tell you, I feel terrible about telling on this person who didn't do anything to me whatsoever. I felt really bad for a long time behind it, but I had to show and prove who Satan truly was. That person would be Jesse Cross, who made $143,000 every 3 months, which is almost $600,000 a year. Ask yourself, what do you think, percentage-wise, was the police cut? First off, the Police don't split anything 50/50, especially since it was their ideal system and operation. Let us say it was 50/50, that's still over a million-dollar operation that Satan had going for a while. Jesse Cross probably got like 5 or 10% of the Money Gross, with Satan keeping 90 to 95%. This is all the small money because the BIG MONEY was in what they were doing in the Drug Labs. I still don't know what drugs Satan was manufacturing in their Drug Labs, but that is where Satan made most of their dirty drug money, which probably helped the 110,000 overdose deaths last year in the United States.

<h1 style="text-align: center">ROCHESTER POLICE</h1>

June 28, 2013

Dear Rochester Police:

On Wednesday, June 26, 2013, at about 9:45 pm I called 911 to report a fugitive who's been on the run for 8 months. The main reason that I called was because every single time the authorities came to my apartment building, they would knock on my door and ask me if I saw the fugitive. As of right now, I haven't gotten caught in a lie yet, and when they asked me about him, I would say "No". Of course, I had seen him, but because of all the sabotaging the police had done to me, I didn't want to cooperate and help my Oppressors. As time went on, I didn't want to be arrested for lying, so I was caught in a catch-22 situation, and I was tired of what was happening upstairs. So I called 9-1-1 at the phone booth around the corner, and when I came back, the following events followed.

Mr. Barksdale came into the apartment right after talking with the police, with a mean look on his face, and said that "I was a paranoid motherfucker". I said I wasn't and that he needed to look in the mirror because he was outside laughing and talking with the police like they were his high school friends. [About a month ago, I told him that I thought David Moore; the ex-police chief, was a good man. I said, when it comes to people, you can never say all of them, maybe 75 or 95 % of them, but not all. He said all the police are a piece of shit, I said you can never say all; he raised his voice and said "All of them are a piece of shit".] So when I confronted him on being a hypocrite, just after he came from outside with a mean look on his face, saying I was a paranoid motherfucker, he got really angry and said "fuck you, you fat piece of shit". I said fuck you too and called him an ugly motherfucker. Mr. Barksdale then went to the door, where they were tons of police on the porch and all around the apartment building, and said to the police "I have to close this door now because I have to handle this motherfucker". He then closed the door, so the police couldn't enter, aggressively approached me and asked me what I wanted to do. I told him to get out of my face so he wouldn't come any closer, and he yelled at me and made sure he said "am on parole and am not trying to go back to prison", all the while still being aggressive to me. I said "I have treated you really well", and he said, "I don't give a fuck" and kept calling me a fat fuck and a paranoid motherfucker, etc. I said, as loud as I could, that I did not care how many people he had shot or killed in the past, and that if he didn't get out of my face that I would beat his ass into the carpet, or something like that. He backed away from me and opened the door and said yeah, yeah, or something like that. My whole thought process at the time was, that if I backed down from a killer once, I could expect to back down from him every single day, especially when you share the same kitchen with this killer. He got out of my face when I said that. That's all I wanted. He then went outside and told the police that the argument was about me hating the police and that I was drunk. For the record, I just started back drinking and only had two beers.

In short, one of the officers must have said something to Mr. Barksdale about me outside, because we never had a problem before until that night. I wanted to show them that I get along with my other neighbors, so I went outside, and all the police were on guard watching me. I went to my neighbor's apartment and told her what happened. As I left her apartment an officer said "Watch your back" to another officer who didn't see me coming, and I said, "I wasn't going to do anything to anyone". Then one of the officers on the porch said "I want to see you guys do it, my money is on Barksdale". I said, "This happened because of you guys". There was dead silence when I said this, and tons of police were around.

Mr. Barksdale not too long ago has been released from prison, altogether serving 20 years of his life behind bars. He has shot and killed people in the past, and the police think that I am supposed to take his aggressiveness lightly. Police don't take anything lightly themselves, but expect me to take angry killer words lightly. I outweigh the guy by 100 lbs., and he is 51 or 52, and do you think I want to be beating up my elders? And after the police left and, in the morning, Mr. Barksdale threatened me with a gun. He said that he was going to hit me with the 4-5 if I got out of line. He said this, knowing that I could hear him through the door. People even gave this killer a platform to speak about his gun experience. If this killer had shot and killed white people, he would not have a platform to stand on period. I don't plan on getting into another fight again in life, and haven't gotten into one since 2003 I think. So don't worry about me getting into a fight, unless I 100% have to. The police have sabotaged me and put me in situations where I must fight, because someone had their hands on me, and I still haven't gotten into a fight since 2003.

The problem is not me getting along with other people etc, the problem is White Supremacy. I have spoken truth to Power in past letters, and ever since then, this Power has hired the police force to destroy me. Since 2004 you guys have sent over 1000 women after me, trying to set me up in a sexual nature.

Trying to make me out to be a Monster, when in truth Monsters sent them my way. You guys have aggressively faked really hard like you wanted to hit me with your undercover / police cars about 10 to 15 times. Had civilians threaten me with guns. Had civilians put their hands all over me. Gave civilians the incentive to sabotage me at work, all the places that I have lived, and nearly all the places I have visited. If this is true, how can one say I am paranoid? If anything, being paranoid is smart while being constantly sabotaged. And if all of this is true, how can one possibly like and love the people who are responsible for these events? You guys made sure I got treated like dirt everywhere in society and showed me nothing but violence at first. This lasted for a long time, but now you guys have switched gears, and sabotage me every chance you get, because you know sabotaging is hard to prove. I could still prove a lot of it, but not all.

If this sabotaging continues, I will have no other choice but to tell some Really Big Secrets. Trust me; you would not want these secrets getting out. Trust me when I tell you, I don't want to spill the beans, but enough is enough. And another thing, how can one person know so many secrets, if that person is so-called not liked by most people? Do you actually think that all these truths that I know come from one source? People only tell secrets to people that they like. Enough is enough. The ball is in your court.

Roy Snell

P.S. Can you please stop tapping my computer?

SOCIAL SERVICES, MARCH 14, 2014

March 14, 2014

Dear Social Service

I just received a letter from your office, saying that I have to take an Assessment Test on March 25th, 2014 at Work Now Assessment. One, I haven't done any kind of math for almost two years. In my last letter, I said that I would be more than happy to show whomever that I know Trigonometry. I basically said that I wanted a financial incentive if you wanted me to take that Math Word Problems Test / Math Test. It would work out in your favor too, because you can always say, we offered him $20,000 and he still didn't take the test. I am not the one who has to prove these lies, I have my GED and a Degree, remember? As for the Reading Test, I haven't read a book in a month or longer, but since I have astigmatism, I need two full weeks to train my eyes by focusing my eyes on a spot on the wall and or paper for some time and focus my attention on the little red hand of a clock. I also need to be almost out of breath before taking the test by exercising just before. This is, of course, if you want me to score 12.9. By the way, why does it seem like I am always being deceived? Most people are told that they would have to take these kinds of tests 2,3 and 4 months in advance. So why do I get a 13-day notice? The only thing I could think up, is you're trying to catch me slipping, so you can say, see see see see. Then again, you have caught me slipping, I guess, because I was under tons of stress in my last letter, and now am under enormous stress. So, I'll be working on my astigmatism under extreme stress, but there is no way that I can take that math test. No more tricks, let's come up with a figure and I will study as hard as I can for that Math Test. Remember, in all the tests that I took in college / GED, I was in academic shape. So are you saying that once someone gets in shape, they stay in shape? Are you saying that I have never been in shape? Oh, I get it, you're saying that I can't read at all. At least you did say this. Now you're saying 12.9? Are you aware that I took that test over 20 years ago? Hasn't the difficulty level been raised since then? I don't have the books that you're teaching students out of, I am mainly talking about the test format. Send me a letter in the mail letting me know what you want to do. If not, I'll show up, but I will not be taking the Math Test.

The police have invited aggression towards me; it's like waving a red flag in front of a bull. In this case, this bull was high on Crack, had a temper tantrum, and tried to fight me in front of Parole and the Police on June 26, 2013, and they sided with him. One would do just about anything if they knew they wouldn't be prosecuted. Without fear of prosecution, anything is fair game. People would run red lights if they knew they wouldn't get in trouble.

On November 7, 2013, Barksdale checked into Rehab to clean out his system from going on a Crack binge. He was on this smoking binge for at least six months, but if you were to ask him, he would tell you that he started smoking Crack because his nephew passed away. Fact, I called Parole on Thursday, June 27, 2013, to report that Barksdale had threatened me with a gun while he was in the kitchen, knowing that I could hear everything he said. Fact, I called Parole a week later, which would have been on July 3rd or July 5th to report that Barksdale had gotten into a huge argument over some drugs. A guy came to

Barksdale's door and after a few seconds yelled out "You Got Me Carrying This Shit, And You Don't Even Have My Money". Barksdale tried to quiet the man down by telling him that I could be listening, and the man said "I DON'T GIVE A FUCK ABOUT THAT, WHERE IS MY MONEY". After hearing that conversation, I knew it was about drugs, I just didn't know what kind of drugs. So I went straight to the pay phone and called Parole. I even told Parole to look at the security cameras across the street at the Family Learning Center, because the cameras have the perfect view of Barksdale's front door.

I don't know how detailed Parole was when they talked to Barksdale after I called, but I had to endure constant pressure from Barksdale while he was on Crack the whole time. We were supposed to share the kitchen and living room, but Barksdale moved my stuff out of the way and had 85% of the kitchen and living room. I didn't even go into my own refrigerator unless I knew that he had left the house. Weeks later I decided to go into my refrigerator, knowing for certain that Barksdale was in his room with the door closed, and just about all the time he would come into the kitchen to get one sip of water, looking at me with a hard face. He has even given me a couple of sharp jerks with his body, like I was going to jump out of my socks. Then he would go over to my neighbor's apartment and tell them that I was terrified of him. I am terrified of the Police's powerful discretion that they have because if anything happens, they're just going to decide it was my entire fault. There was nothing I could do except try to ignore him and boil with rage.

He left a big gas can in the living room that we were supposed to share for about a week. I didn't say a word about it, for fear that he would have one of his "Crack Rages"and the Police taking his side. I would go to the store, and when I got back, he would be on the porch looking at me with Crazy Cracked Out Eyes. Drama makes him feel alive, especially while on Crack. I don't think he is on Crack now, but I still have to deal with the residue left over from this Drama King.

Twice someone was dropping me off and wanted to see my apartment, and Barksdale came out of his apartment, while on Crack, looking at me and the person I was with very aggressive and intimidating. He had the look that said, if you brought someone for me, bring it on because my family is just a phone call away.

On December 1st, 2013, I overheard Barksdale tell his brother Patrick that he was going to kill me. So I called my landlord and told him that I was under serious pressure from Barksdale the whole time after he tried to fight me in front of the police, which was about 3 to 4 months. I also told him that Barksdale had just come home from Rehab.

On March 11th, 2014, I came back after being away for a whole week. I went into the kitchen and living room and noticed Barksdale had 95% of the apartment that we were supposed to share under his control. I kindly asked him to move his things, and he exploded on me and said "I don't have time for this fucking shit, one of my relatives down south just died, leave me the fuck alone". He said this extremely loud, and I said, "Watch who the fuck you're talking to". He said that he had something for me, and then he yelled into the phone all these names and told them to come over to his apartment now, that they had to help him beat me down. They called back within seconds and said that all of them were coming over. As I was leaving my apartment to call 9-1-1, Barksdale said "he doesn't want it, I don't think you have to come over, he knows what's up". So I called 9-1-1-around 7:30 just to get this incident on record, and the Operator said the only way that she could report anything, was if I wanted a cop car to come by, I told her that Barksdale was friends with most cops, and not to send a cop car. I just went back to my apartment.

On March 13, 2014, at around 11: am, I called Parole to report about Barksdale. I completely explained the situation and told him that I wanted to make sure that I talked with someone who didn't have ties to Barksdale at Parole. Not only does Barksdale know the Police, but he also knows the people at Parole very well. He even has a relative who works there, and was a Pallbearer at one of his relative's funerals. Barksdale said he looks white but is mixed.

On March 13, 2014, Barksdale said "I should put a contract out on that fat fucker, I know the people that would do it too". I have to get out of this house because he is going to make me kill him". Shortly after that, he went to the store to get some cigarettes. This was around 2:10. Check the cameras outside across the street.

On March 13, 2014, Barksdale helped my neighbor shovel his driveway for a quick buck. While shoveling, Barksdale kept telling my neighbor that he was going to kill me, that he had to move, and that I had called Parole on him. He kept saying, over and over again, how he was going to kill that motherfucker.

On March 13th, 2014, Barksdale said, "I don't know why he even called down there to Parole, doesn't he know that I know all of them down there? Then he said if he was anyone else, he would have gone back to prison that day. "I can't wait for Patrick and Jesse to come back to town, because there's going to be a Black Panther party up in here. Then he went on to say, I got something for that motherfucker on my last day here, no matter what. Then his female relative said, "I know what you can do to him". She then walked over to him and whispered in his ear, which I couldn't hear, and Barksdale said, "I got some other things too. All the events that happened on March 13, 2014, I heard very clearly on my bed, and when Barksdale was talking to the neighbor next door, I was standing in the kitchen, and all that I heard is here.

On March 2, 2014, Barksdale was arguing all day on the phone with one of his family members about getting into a car accident. He is on parole and doesn't have a driver's license, and hit another car from behind with the truck he was driving. Barksdale was driving for months and commented that he wasn't worried about getting pulled over by the police.

Barksdale's family got together with bats and brass knuckles and went out and beat someone up badly. Barksdale saw that I was in the kitchen preparing my meal, called one of his relatives on the phone, and made sure that he played it on a loudspeaker so that I could hear how they had thrashed the guy, all the while Barksdale looked at me. Then Barksdale said, "It's a good thing y'all didn't call me because they wouldn't have found the body. Barksdale and his brother Patrick were mad at one another and started shooting at each other. Barksdale said he was trying to shoot me, so I went shooting at him. I can't make this stuff up. Barksdale has even said, if he goes back to prison, it might as well be for killing someone, because I'm just going to get life. I have been in and out of institutions since I was 15, and have spent 20 years of my life behind bars.

All of these events happened, not because of my character, not because I did anything to Barksdale, but because of the weak position this City has put me in, and the Police giving Barksdale the green light to do whatever without fear of prosecution. Anybody that's been in prison for 20 years could smell fear. If this guy had a fear of prosecution and didn't have such a big family, he would be terrified of me. Proof, he tried to get in a fight with me in front of the police, knowing that they have to break it up, and calling his family on me. He might as well have a rape whistle around his neck. Fox News summed up some of my mean points every night when they were talking about Putin and Obama. "When you back down to people, other people get funny ideas in their heads". The Police have put me in this situation since my first letter and is one of the reasons why I am neutralized and isolated from society. I am a disgrace to the word freedom.

SOCIAL SERVICES, MAY 30, 2014

May 30, 2014

Dear Social Service:

"I will finish this letter over the weekend. So just think of this letter as incomplete with spelling errors. Sorry about this."

Parole Is the Root Cause, Not My Character.

The last time that I wrote I said that I would take that reading test, even though I was under a great deal of pressure, I said that I would still take that test. A day after writing that letter, Barksdale sucker-punched me in front of his female relative while I was in the kitchen, and I had no other choice but to defend myself. Barksdale cowardly crawled up in a little ball and hid his head so tight that no light or air could possibly enter, as he said, "If you don't stop hitting me, I am going to cut you with my knife when I get up". 9-1-1 was called and Barksdale went away in the Ambulance with bruised ribs and was on crutches for a week. From the time Barksdale entered the door coming from the Hospital, he talked nonstop about shooting me. He even said that he should shoot me through the door and then call the police on himself and say that he did it. The next day, I overheard one of his male family members say in a mean, loud voice, "What is all this really about". Barksdale said that his parole officer said that I called Parole complaining that he was selling drugs back in July 2013. That his parole officer hates me and that he should just move out. Firstly, how does his parole officer know me or anything about me in a personal way? I called Parole back on July the 5th, 2013, not the 3rd as I said in my last letter, because I remember it was on a Friday and not on a Wednesday. Barksdale had gotten into an argument over drugs that day, and I thought he was on cocaine or marijuana, since cocaine stays in your system for three days, I immediately called Parole before he could get it out of his system. So when I called Parole, I told them that I wanted the conversation to be recorded, that Barksdale had drugs in his system at present, and that it was an emergency that someone tests him instantly. The secretary was excited and stayed on the phone with me for a while because Barksdale's parole officer was out of the office. I completely explained what happened to another parole officer who was in charge and knew Barksdale. He said that they would be on top of it. Really? The only time that I knew Barksdale's parole officer came over to the apartment was when his parole officer wanted to question one of Barksdale's female relatives about a murder. Barksdale tracked her down and made her go and talk with someone, he said that they hadn't checked up on him once the entire time since being released from prison, which was seven months ago at the time he said it. My point, Barksdale was on Crack for at least six months, and one day he went to Parole and said he needed to check into rehab because Crack had taken him over. He said when he told his parole officer this, his parole officer said, I knew you were on Crack for a while, just look at all the weight you lost, I was waiting for you to come to me. I guess after this meeting took place, I am just assuming, because Barksdale kept offering me marijuana, and about a week later, he told me that he was going to rehab for a week and to watch his apartment. My reason for explaining these events was to prove that Barksdale and his parole officer had an unusual relationship that could have put me in the cemetery. Even if I did say that Barksdale was selling drugs, Parole had no right to reveal the source. It's much worse than that, though, because I

NEVER NEVER NEVER said he was selling drugs. I said that he had drugs in his system, and they knew that. They didn't just lie to someone like Pee Wee Herman. " Roy said that you're selling drugs". The character Pee Wee Herman would have laughed. They knew what they were doing when they told Barksdale, who has been in prison for 20 years and has tried to even shoot his own brother in the street, when they said "Roy said you're selling drugs". Am sorry, but to me, it's not only endangering my life, it's attempted murder on my life, and it 100% explains why Barksdale put all kinds of pressure on me pretty much the whole time after I called Parole on July the 5th, 2013. When I speak of sabotage in my letters, this is exactly what I am referring to too. It's very hard to prove, but I wouldn't have connected the dots unless I overheard Barksdale's relative say loudly "What is all this really about". If I wasn't at home at the time, I would have missed out on this key information. Barksdale confronted me about this back in 2013, but I thought he had made it up on the spot. So that makes it twice that Barksdale has spoken about me calling Parole and saying that he was selling drugs. Can you imagine me saying something similar or the same thing to a bunch of gang members about a parole officer that would have compromised his life like my life has been compromised? No doubt I would have been sentenced to life in prison. Just let it go, Mr. Snell you might say, but why should I have to keep putting these kinds of events in the back of my mind? I want Justice, not someone to talk to so that I can suffer in peace. If it wasn't for Barksdale's female relative telling the rest of Barksdale's family that Barksdale sucker-punched me and that Barksdale was the aggressor, I could have easily been shot by one of his close family members. She told them how Barksdale had complete control of the apartment that we were supposed to share over the phone with Barksdale relatives. She told them everything.

On May 18, 2014, I called 9-1-1, because Barksdale came over to my apartment when I wasn't at home, and told my neighbor that he had to get the rest of his belongings. My neighbor told him that he couldn't let him take anything without me being present, and that he could only move his belongings in my neighbor's bedroom until I got home. Barksdale physically moved my belongings into my neighbor's bedroom and told him to tell me that he would be back to get his things, but not before bad-mouthing me. For one, Barksdale took all his possessions when his Lease was up on May 1st, 2014. I guess now I have to look over my shoulder for him too on the street.

I have been threatened 1000 times with a gun by Barksdale because Parole lied to Barksdale, and you know what the police are saying? The only people who get into these types of situations are those who put themselves in that situation. As in, "Hey, you over there, Have you ever been threatened with a gun? No. Well, do you know anyone that has? No. I rest my case". They think up some good ones, I mean, what do you say to that? Anyway, I didn't get arrested, obviously the police had read my letter and knew what was going on, but they started this ordeal and Parole created the lie that could have put me in the ground. I still appreciate that I didn't get arrested, even though they started this mess. I do have to address what the officer said before he left. He said that they understand this time that it wasn't my fault, but I just can't seem to get along with the neighbors that live in this building and pretty much anywhere I go. I told him that people don't want me to come around because everywhere that I go, the police follow me there. This is only true when speaking of a few people, but most people are like, so what, we're not doing anything wrong, at least most white people feel this way. I have been letting Satan say whatever, now it's my turn to tell the truth about my neighbor's past and present.

My Neighbors Past and Present

Three families have lived upstairs since I have lived here. Two African American Men, one moved out not too long after I moved in that I got along with, then the other African American moved in that I got along with very well. After that, a Caucasian lady moved in with her daughters and mixed live-in boyfriend. My landlord Carl told her to watch out for me, you have to keep your eye on him. She later told me that my landlord said I was a child molester. I told Barksdale what she said when she said it, and after we got into a fight, he kept repeating that I was a child molester and shouldn't be living across the street from a school. Please don't believe me, ask Barksdale. They totaled the apartment moments before they moved out because they hated my landlord for a lot of things.

The apartment that I live in now belonged to Ms. DeJesus, and she lived here when I first moved here. We got along well, well until my landlord kept calling her telling her that he was going to kick her out because I kept complaining about her loud music. I told her that I didn't call, and Carl the landlord kept calling her, and one day she came to my apartment and let me listen to my landlord telling her that I had just called complaining about her loud music. To this day, I have never called my landlord complaining about her music. So obviously we couldn't stay friends. And about the same time, my landlord told one of the neighbors down the street some lies that almost got me into a huge fight. They moved out a while ago.

Three families have lived in the front apartment since I have lived here. The first Renter lived here before I moved in and goes by the name of Ken Torres. He was my landlord's right-hand man and enjoyed a couple of beers with him on occasion. He used to breed lots of pit bulls by injecting them with something in his apartment, and when it came down to it, my landlord said that he didn't know. Anyway, he was my landlord's spy and was always in everyone's business, and I did an experiment on him. I would burn incense and cough like I was smoking marijuana, and my landlord would come over to my apartment at really odd times. He has even come over at like 10 p.m. saying that he had to work just right outside my door, in the dark too. Ken Torres was pretending to be cool with me, but was only out to spy on me. So I wrote a letter to Animal Control about all his illegal pit bulls that he made tons of money on.

Next, a Spanish young man by the name of Dave and his girlfriend moved in. We got along and one day when he was in the process of suing my landlord, my landlord called him up and said "Roy just called me and told me that he heard you and your girlfriend plotting against me, I know all about it". I heard this extra clearly because when he got off the phone, he slammed it across the room and told his girlfriend word for word what I just wrote. I immediately banged on the door to get his attention and told him that I hadn't even seen the landlord for nearly three months at the time. He sued my landlord and won.

The next person who moved in was Ken Barksdale, and you already know how that worked out.

New neighbors moved in on either May 16th or May 17th, 2014. My one neighbor told me that she and her boyfriend used to do Heroin. They were happy that I didn't do any drugs, and sometimes when her boyfriend drinks, he might be a little rude to me, just ignore him and don't take anything too seriously when he gets like that. I wanted to protect myself because I just got out of a terrible situation with Barksdale. So on May 24, 2014, my landlord came inside the apartment and slid some papers under my neighbor's bedroom door and I told him what the lady told me. I don't care what anyone does, as long as it doesn't affect me, so I wasn't trying to gain favor, I just wanted to protect myself so no one could say, "He doesn't get along with these neighbors either". That same day, May 24, 2014, probably right after my landlord got in his car, called and texted my neighbor saying that one of the neighbors called him complaining about them being on Heroin, that now it might not be okay for them to stay. It's only three apartments in use right now, which means there could only be two people who called. Like I said, they just moved in, and my landlord doesn't even know if my neighbor even had a conversation with my other neighbor that lives in the back named Marry. Fact, he knew that I would be telling them that he came over because he opened the front door of the apartment and slid papers under their bedroom door. My neighbors confronted me as soon as they came home. The lady immediately knew it was me, she just told me about her Heroin past but really liked me as a person so she didn't want to believe it. Am a terrible liar, most Crackheads and Heroin junkies are excellent liars, and she believed me because she likes me and wants to believe. Just like most people don't want to believe the City of Rochester is capable of most things that I write about in my letters, they don't want to believe in Evil. It's human nature. The lady that lives in the back has lived here before I moved here. I get along with her and her granddaughter quite well.

Work Now College St

On March 25, 2014, I went to my scheduled appointment on College St, and the night before and ever since Barksdale and I got into a fistfight, he was disgruntled about losing that fight to me. He repeatedly spoke of shooting me through the door etc. etc. I didn't do any kind of studying, and watched as many comedy movies as I could to get Barksdale off my mind. When I declined to take the test, the people there got angry with me. I tried to explain a little what was going on, but was talked down to. The lady that was talking down to me, was the same lady the year before that screamed at me for not doing so hot on the Math Test. She yelled at me in a room full of people, and I did nothing but walk away. I did great on the test, but time ran out, and I didn't get around to 22 of the questions. She was commenting on this, and I told her that I wasn't in academic shape when I took that test and that I had no idea that I would be taking a test on that day. So since they were angry with me for not taking that test, I was a little firm in explaining, and that's all it took for these sympathizers, that buy into silly lies this city has been hammering into people's minds about me, called someone to make sure they were present the next time I would be in the office, which was about two hours from then.

Two hours later, I met with Pat Hicks and like I said, they were mad at me since I didn't take the test. She tried to get me excited, just so she could write it down. People in the end would think I was out of control that day, all this in the name of creating reasonable doubt, when the only thing that happened was Satan's lies manifested into a situation. For instance, I tried to explain how Satan was sabotaging me just about everywhere in society, including my last WEP Assignment at Hope Initiative. She said basically I was paranoid. I said the police had run me off the sidewalks with their cars. She said that I was a liar. I told her that I hadn't gotten caught in a lie yet. She said that I was a liar. I said something like these people are responsible for thousands of events and I don't have to lie, the truth is bad enough. She told me to leave Rochester then, and I said I would like to leave the country, but not before I have Satan pay for their crimes in court. She asked me what my short-term goal was. I said suing Satan in court for all the atrocities he is responsible for. She asked me what my long-term goal was. I said suing Satan in court for all the atrocities he is responsible for. I wanted to do anything to persuade Satan from sabotaging me, so I said to write that part down. Remember when I said they called people to make sure they were there the next time I would be in the office? Well, there were two African-American Males there the whole time. If I knew they were there, so did Pat Hicks. Guess what she wrote down on the paper that day for comments? Roy said he wants to leave this country; he even made sure I wrote that part in here. She is what, I like to call, one of Satan's sympathizers, because no matter what evil events take place, Satan can always count on his sympathizers for support. It's the American way. On a side note, I ended up taking a reading test that I wasn't expecting until the last second. My eyes were trained, and the teacher made everyone always feel very relaxed in his Resume class. I didn't have time to panic and took the test. Am pretty sure I scored 100%. Everyone there has been completely professional, I don't have any complaints, and there's nothing one can do about a sympathizer. This is the perfect example of Satan's conditioning people to lose compassion for me because of all their deceptive lies and tricks, that if someone does harm me, people would look the other way.

People Do Like Me

If one were to read a book on racist strategies that are effective, one would find a character strategy that true Racists have used over and over to justify a racist incident. I don't know when Racists first used this strategy, but it had to have been in the 70s. This is how it works. You can be as racist as you want, just make sure there are no video or audio recording devices around, and remember to never use the "N" word. If you follow this advice, you can always say "I don't know what it was, but we never liked the guy". Oh no, I am not racist because I didn't like the guy, that's just silly. These lies would have never worked in the 60s, but are working now. A tyrant will always find an excuse for his tyranny. It's almost impossible to get anything across to an animal, this is how Evil continues.

I have yet to see anyone or even hear of anyone who has always been popular since I basically entered the school system in the late 70s be so unpopular. Unless that person killed someone or was on drugs so bad that people couldn't take them anymore. I guess. I could see if a person was popular in High School with a population of twenty, and that person had such a bad character that no one liked him in the real world. I have posted the people that I was friends with to eight large different area High Schools. In fact, my closest friends were the in-crowd to most of the large schools. Since I proved systematic racism, Satan jumped the gun and took "People don't like my character" right out of the racist strategy book, and when Satan found out how popular I was, Satan created all kinds of sabotaging deceptive situations that made their sympathizers say see see see. They have destroyed just about all my environments by lying on me and telling everybody they laid eyes on that people hate my guts. You only get one first impression, and Satan makes sure that he gets my impressions.

Firstly, this City has run me into my apartment with violence, lies, violence, sabotaging, which led to more violence. I can't really go anywhere, I haven't worked in a while, am in conflict with my family as a result, my father gives me these puppy dog eyes, which is a deep hurt because I live in the ghetto, I don't work, I don't have any grandchildren to give him and I see nothing but pain in him. Do you think I want to be around him or anyone in my family when I am living in disgrace? All because of Satan's lies. I avoid the pain as much as possible, and Satan will use anything he can get, so Satan is saying I don't go around my family too often because they don't want me around. Everyone just hates my guts. Fact, my whole family loves me, and I can go to any of their houses anytime I choose. The reason why some people can't come around their own family is because they did something so terrible, that their own family doesn't trust them anymore and don't want them to come around. Not one single person in my family not trust me, they all trust me. I haven't done anything to them. The pain and the hurt in my father's eyes are unbearable, and I avoid this pain as much as possible. Do you know how many funerals I have missed out on because I am living in disgrace and avoiding pain?

I proved that Satan put me in prison for something that I didn't do, and wrote in my letter how an inmate threw bleach in my eyes and face, rather than Satan taking responsibility for putting me in prison for something I didn't do, Satan said, see, people hate him enough to throw bleach in his face. I told you about this guy. Fact, the guy who threw bleach in my face was 100% crazy and shouldn't have had the clearance to work around knives in the kitchen where we worked washing dishes. The prison knew this better than me, so they put me in solitary confinement for 30 days and would throw out my mail when I tried to sue. When I found out what they were doing, it was too late for me to sue. I had just about 20/20 vision, now I have to wear contacts and glasses for the rest of my life.

I don't go around my best friend Matt or his family, because they are happy people and I don't want to rain on their parade. Satan is a master at turning people against each other, and if they were to convince Matt to turn against me, that would crush me. So I would like to keep all the pleasant memories I have of him and his entire family. His mother is my new mom ever since my mother died and by right I should have been at his brother's wedding, but I haven't even attempted to contact them. It's safer for me to remember the wonderful memories of all my friends, it keeps me sane and gives me hope. No matter what Satan does to me, no matter what I have to endure, I can always think back to how it was, that's how I have been able to tolerate all these grizzly hate crimes.

Joe Alberti, a really good friend of mine from high school who is a Doctor now, has been trying to get a hold of me on Facebook. He cares a lot about me and would be extremely happy if I wrote to him and told him I was alive. He wrote, where are you? It's like you dropped off the face of the world, please contact me. Joe has always been in the in-crowd, and I am good friends with his brother and sister too. I could go on and on about the close relationships that I have formed, but my letter with all my friends should have been enough. Lies, shame, and pain have me completely out of society, not my character.

Hope Initiative

Someone elected Hope to stand before me as a friend, posing to be a child of God, at the same time working to protect white supremacy, designed exclusively for my demise. They have walked all over my rights like Christ did water. Ron, who was in prison for 19 years for killing someone, their top welder, had to have a hernia operation that would put him out of work for a month. So I told Hope that I was a great welder, and they laughed and asked why I didn't have a welder's job. I told them I was an excellent welder, that I learned the skill in prison, and no one hired me when I was released. I explained to them in detail how I would weld this, or that, etc. So they gave me a shot the day Ron left. Ron and I used to ride the bus together every day and would have conversations every day. So we were friends before. Before Ron left, he was welding 10 to 15 chairs a day at max. Two days after he left, I was welding 25 chairs. They took my chairs and banged them on the wall, and none of them broke. I personally took their chairs and banged them on the wall, and all of them broke. They had the welding heat too low, the ground was across the room, this was wrong, that was wrong, etc. etc. In short, I personally changed a lot of things and personally taught Ron's welding assistant how to weld. I totally taught him my process and Hope excitement was through the roof. Everybody in the company came back to marvel at what I was doing, and the machine I was using was a piece of crap.

A month later, Ron came back and thought he was coming into open arms, but the second guy in charge of the company immediately went to town on Ron. He told him all the things that I had done, and now the company wanted 25 chairs from him a day, and if he did 15 chairs for that day, he would have to make them up somehow. Ron would work on his break but couldn't keep up, and the second guy in charge used to scream at Ron loudly, in front of me, and when he knew I could hear. He would say, "Do you want me to get Roy in here to show you how to do it". Very, Very loud. Then, when I would come around, he would be extremely kind to me in front of Ron, but still mean to Ron. They treated me favorably, gave me praises in front of Ron, then treated Ron unfavorably, but still left Ron with power over me. When you're on WEP every single company employee has power over you. What do you think happened when no one was looking? They created a ticking time bomb and stepped off so they couldn't be implicated in the crime. I thought they had my best interest, treating me nice and hugging me when my mother died, but were really accommodating snakes that always had something else in mind.

I hurt my back from all the welding that I did, and they put me in this room across from the welding room, assembling the welded material. This even hurt my back more, that I was walking bent over. I was in tons of pain, and everyone saw this. So Hope Initiative walked around looking at me aggressively and called the police on me, because everywhere I went, cops would be like, your back doesn't hurt, you're trying to pull a fast one on us. They were so aggressive that I went to the number one guy in charge and told him that I would sign whatever paper he needed me to sign, and just call off the cops. My back is really hurting me. I said I would say I hurt my back at the playground or whatever you want, just call off the cops. He said that wasn't necessary, and they didn't call the cops on me. The second guy in charge of the company came up to me and said I know exactly where you're having your pain, and pressed his thumb in my lower spine, which brought tears to my eyes. So they knew I wasn't faking it. I started drinking tons of water and rather than riding the bus, I walked really fast to work and lost 70lbs and my back pain, and the cops stopped messing with me, at least for a second.

I was still in the welding room assembling welded material, and bending over to assemble frames, which was hard on everyone's backs. People would have back problems all the time, and when it got bad enough, the company would lay them off. People right and left were having back problems, so I got to thinking, and came up with a workstation that left 100% of the people with zero back pain, easy, and made the job at least three times faster to get the workout. I was supposed to get a personal check for saving the company tons of money on future Workmen Comp Claims and making the job three times faster. Because of me, they now had inventory, before people would assemble these frames when needed. Anyway, I never got a dime, it went to the so-called Christian girl who thought I had it out for the company, even though I was making and saving the company money hand over fist. This nice Christian girl knew that I would be coming up the long stairway, so as I was going up the stairs, she stood there like she was superwoman with her extra tight spandex pulled just about up to her chest, and I looked down for a second, and she went and told management that I had checked her out. When it came time to give me a personal check, at the last minute they gave the check to Ms. Christian and told me that they weren't going to be handing out any checks, ever. To this day, they're still using the workstation that I built, along with the same exact process I used to make the assembly faster.

I ran out of time writing about all the events that happened at Hope Initiative. I will finish my letter over the weekend. So just think of this letter as incomplete. Sorry about this.

Rochester Works

On April 23, 2014, I thought I was filling out a complaint, because I wanted people to know Parole had put my life in danger. If this city did that to me, how far will they go next time? This is extremely serious, and I feel like I am in a war without a gun. Your only response to the violent injustice was "You checked that you're crazy on the form, we have just the spot for you". When I wrote that complaint, it said nothing about mental health. Obviously, I wanted Justice, not another attack. I hold no ill towards the gentlemen who witnessed me write that statement. I want Justice.

Truth about Instructional Videos

If I could learn from a video, like Satan wants people to believe, by right I should be a 10th Degree Black Belt, a Doctor, and a Mathematician within a year. Satan said I can't read, I can't learn by doing, and that I can only learn from a video. They even believe their own lies so much, that now they have even squeezed instructional videos into their courses at the college. I don't understand these videos any better than anyone else does. The only reason why I had a hunger for CNC videos, I wasn't being taught at The Applied Tech, so I figured I would compensate with the videos so that I could compete in the workforce.

In the book Mastery by Robert Green, which was published in 2012, he proves that it takes at least 10,000 hours of practice to be hard-wired in your mind in any field that you choose. 20,000 hours of practice and your mind would have an intuitive grasp of your craft. That being said, I basically wrote about this in 2004 when the college wanted to know why I was so mad at the college and machine shops. So now I got this $25,000 student loan, which I would have never had if I rightfully sued the college, but the college sent the police after me with guns, and I was close to being hit with their cars about 10 to 15 times. How do you think I feel, because as soon as I receive a paycheck, the student loan will be in my account? How many hours of machining training do you think I received at The Applied Tech? I never learned manual machines, I taught myself mostly everything out of a book and the videos helped. So I have to be indebted for 30 years because a bunch of Racists happily took the student loan money, without teaching me the main ingredient, then sent the police to quiet me so thoroughly that I have been out of society ever since. Paying this debt is like surrendering to slavery.

Last Thing

So why all the sabotaging? What do they want? They want to take away the truth by using violent deceptive sabotaging events, so they can have Reasonable Doubt. In the end, they will have successfully masked all their crimes, racist crimes that is. This is a lesson for most evil people in the world. If you don't have something on that person, lie your ass off, when that falls through, create situations that make your enemy look like a Beast, all the while saying they're crazy, and getting as many people, companies, offices, agencies, and businesses as it takes to participate in the fun. Did I just explain systematic racism? I don't have to lie, this City has caused irreversible damage to my life, and the truth is bad enough.

Sincerely,
Roy Snell

P.S.

I will finish my letter over the weekend. So just think of this letter as incomplete. Sorry about this.

SOCIAL SERVICES, JULY, 11, 2014

July 11, 2014

Dear Social Service:

Thursday, June 19, 2014, my landlord called me up and told me that Social Service contacted him, and told him that starting July 1, 2014, they would not be paying him rent for my apartment, because I had failed to give them some paperwork. So on Friday, June 20, 2014, I went to Social Service to inquire about what they wanted. I was told that I had to give them either a Psychological Assessment, ask for an extension regarding the Psychological Assessment, or a Statement regarding the Psychological Assessment. They also wanted me to prove my most recent expenses. This was late in the day and I did not have a clue where to go and get a Psychological Assessment.

On Monday, June 23, 2014, I went all over Rochester looking for Doctors who could give me this Assessment. I went to Anthony Jordan Health Center and two different Mental Health facilities on Alexander Street before I ended up at the Catholic Family Center. All the places I went to said I could not get an appointment then, that it would take like three months, besides The Catholic Family Center. On Tuesday, June 24, 2014, The Catholic Family Center wrote me a statement, and I quote, "Roy Snell was seen here today to complete intake paperwork and has been scheduled for an appointment with Letitcia Alston on Thursday, June 26th. If you have any questions or concerns, feel free to contact the clinic at the number listed below. Sincerely, Catholic Family Center, Mental Health Clinic 546-7220" end quote. On Monday, June 30, 2014, I went to Social Service and gave you everything that you asked for. One, a Statement regarding the Psychological Assessment with two appointments as proof of the Psychological Assessment, and two, a landlord statement. They made copies of everything and I have my receipt as proof.

On July 4, 2014, my landlord gave me a 3-Day Notice to pay or vacate. How could this be, when I handed in my paperwork on time? I could see if you asked me for two statements, but you only asked me for one. I could see if you asked me for the full Psychological Assessment, without an extension, but you did not. You asked me for either a Psychological Assessment, an extension regarding the Psychological Assessment, or a Statement regarding the Psychological Assessment. I held up my end of the deal by supplying you with a Statement regarding the Psychological Assessment and a Landlord statement on June 30, 2014. Now, can you hold up your end of the deal by reinstating me and contacting my landlord with this month's rent?

On July 10, 2014, Letitcia Alston of the Catholic Family Center completed the Psychological Assessment of me. By the time you receive this letter; you should or soon will have the results of the Assessment.

Sincerely,

Roy Snell

P.S.

You can disregard the statement that the teller wrote

today, which was written today July 11, 2014, that asked for an extension. If I asked for an extension this late in the game, that would mean that I would be admitting that I handed in the paperwork late, which you know I didn't.

SOCIAL SERVICES, AUGUST 4, 2015

August 4, 2015

Dear Social Service:

I quote myself from my November 2nd, 2010 letter. Quote: I haven't moved out of this apartment, because wherever I move it's just going to be a new evil and a different new kind of terror. End Quote. I have lived here since March 13th, 2011, and my landlord Carl Justice is in fact the New Evil / New Terror I wrote about before I even met him. I am not psychic, either; I just know how this City operates. People might say just move, I say that would only solve the immediate problem, not the bigger issue, the bigger issue being systematic terrorism, that has turned my environment into a dangerous minefield / Combat zone. This isn't a fixable problem. I can't live anywhere in Rochester, and this City has proven that. I haven't had a cell phone in 9 years, to this day I have never sent one text message and my computer is still being tapped. This is my last letter to this City. The next letter will be over the internet, and I will over prove systematic terrorism, that's motivated by racism.

Satan has made the story about me. Satan figures that by telling lie after lie, no matter how hurtful the lie, the point is that no one will remember what Satan did, they will only remember the lies, making it all about me. My landlord used to be a drug counselor. So that means he was Dope Fiend conscious and rented the apartment to a Crackhead coming from prison, a Stone Cold Junky that snorted Heroin for 31 years, that overdosed in the apartment coming from jail and stole from me all the time. He has put me at great risk. Now he rents to an ex-correctional officer who I believe is a Mole planted here on purpose. I have no control over who lives here.

Recent Landlord Issue

I called my landlord on July 10th to complain about my neighbor intentionally taking over 95% of the apartment that we were supposed to share. They moved my things and threw away my TV box that is under warranty, and I would probably pay $50 if I had to get my TV repaired. Tenants can't take 95% of the space of an apartment that they are supposed to share with another tenant unless they get permission from the landlord. This was done intentionally and what really happened was my landlord told her to just move his things, and if anything happens, call. She definitely got the okay to move and throw my things away. He wanted to see the situation that he created percolate into a violent food fight because it wasn't until July 29th that I spoke with him. He lied and said that he called Mary, the neighbor in the back, and told her to tell me this or that. I said that was also a lie because I was expecting your call, and that I had asked Mary many times had the landlord called, and she always told me no.

On July 29, 2015, the landlord told me and my neighbor were in a dispute, and it didn't have anything to do with him. He said that my neighbor told him that she has 95% of the apartment because we agreed that she would have 95% of the apartment before we had a disagreement, and now I am backing out of the deal that we agreed to. He said I couldn't do that. I said that was a lie, there was never an agreement and I didn't even know she was buying furniture. I said my TV was under warranty, and she threw out my TV box, that if something went wrong, I would probably pay $50 for another box. The landlord said the neighbor told him that the TV was not under warranty. I said that was a lie, and why would I have had that TV box? The landlord said Judy said you said some inappropriate things to a six-year-old, Mary said the same thing when you first moved in here. He said that I had to watch what I say, I said Mary couldn't have told you that because it's a lie. He said, no, Roy, it's true. The last time he knocked on my door to have a meeting with Judy and Me, I declined because I didn't want to get hammered with lies while being recorded. Am good at explaining myself in a letter, but the average person could beat me in a stand-up argument. So I declined to get slobbered by motivated liars. While at the door, he again said I said some inappropriate things to a six-year-old, Judy said something, and he said I had said something inappropriate to a sixteen-year-old. She must be talking about her son, whom I never to this day said anything inappropriate to. Judy heard me talking to the police outside about her son on July 20th, 2015, so I don't know what lie is being told. Since I declined to have a face-to-face meeting with Judy and my landlord, he is kicking me out for something that he created. As you read, you will know why I declined to talk to her.

First Week of Meeting Judy

When Judy first moved in, if someone knocked on my door 100 times, she would come out of her room 100 times and listen to what was said. She didn't know the location of the squeaks on the floor yet, so I heard her all the time by my door. She kept trying to start conversations with me, but I would always be kind with as few words as possible. I told her that I really kept to myself and that it wasn't anything against her personally. Anytime she saw me, she tried starting a conversation with me. Since I am quiet and in my room most of the time, her brother was uncomfortable being in the kitchen while I was there, so I had to talk with them to mainly ease her brother's nerves. He has been in prison, and when a person is as quiet as me in their room 24-7, you have to know how that person is thinking to be at ease in a small kitchen. So I had to talk with him. I told him that I was doing everything possible to stay out of trouble, and that's the real reason why I was in my room like that. He said everything was all cool with him and his sister, that he was the First Crown of The Latin Kings, as he flashed his gang signs. So I thought the landlord would be completely out of the picture this time, wrong.

I said, okay, if we're going to be on speaking terms, these are the rules. I know how that sounds, too. I said I don't care what happens in your apartment, ever. I don't care if you're on Crack, Heroine, Meth, play your music extra loud, fight, stab, or even shoot someone, as long as what you're doing doesn't affect me, I don't care. In return, I said, if there comes a day that we disagree on something, let's handle it without ever involving the landlord. The landlord has it out for me badly. I said this because the last guy used to be on Heroine stealing from me right and left, and when I told the landlord he told him that I was not to be trusted and that I was listening to everything that they did and writing it down. Anyway, my neighbors and I started talking, and watching movies, and I would let them use whatever pots and pans I had. I even hooked up my personal Media Player to their T.V. so they could watch over 100 movies, all for free. Past sabotaging events had me on my best behavior.

One day the neighbors were gone, so I got down on my hands and knees and scrubbed the extra caked-up dirty floor with tons of bleach and water. Judy came home and a six-year-old or something tried to run into the kitchen, I just said you can't come in here now because there was tons of bleach on the floor. Judy said you can't tell him what to do and walked right into the back of the kitchen, then back onto the carpet. I just went inside my apartment, and when things were calm the next day, I told Judy as calmly as possible, if the carpet changes colors, it's on you. She said it wasn't because I shouldn't have been mopping the floor. She had tears in her eyes, as she said they just wanted to come and visit their Aunt and wanted something from the kitchen. I guess she is in a weak state when it comes to kids because hers got taken away.

In April 2015, Judy and I were talking and watching movies in her room one day. I said could I ask you a question, and please please please don't take offense to this. I said I don't know why I feel that I have to ask Spanish people this one question, that I have asked lots of Spanish people this question, and they didn't take offense, but I could see how some could. She said to ask her anything. I said for every ten Spanish men, at least five of them are in gangs, why? She said it was just a family thing, and I told her I think something more is going on, and Spanish people won't tell me. She knew I knew about her brother, and I couldn't get much more out of her.

On April 11th, 2015, Judy knocked on my door and told me she wanted me to meet her older brother. He was going through a rough time with tons of issues. We talked all over the apartment for a very long time. He kept telling his sister over and over again, how cool he thought I was and wanted to hang out with me. While we were in the kitchen talking, he told me that he is currently seeing a therapist. He told me that he was in a gang while he served 15 years in prison, and had tons of nightmares because of all the things his gang made him do. How he thinks cops will come out of nowhere and arrest him for it. He is dealing with heavy things by being in a gang. He said his therapist helps, but it's not enough.

On April 12th, 2015 Me and Judy were talking about her brother's problems from the previous day. I said one of the problems was that he was in a gang and had a tough time dealing with some of the things they made him do. She said my brother wasn't in any gang, I said yes he was, he told me himself. She said something, which I can't recall, then said my brother wasn't in any fucking gang. I said in a general way, without malice or being loud about it, your brother was in a fucking gang. She immediately said, get out of my room, I tried to tell her exactly what her brother said, and she again said, get out of my room. I immediately left her room and turned to look at her when I got to my door. As the little woman inside me said, am so sorry for offending you, that's the last thing that I wanted to do. I am so sorry. Two days later, her brother, the first crown of the Latin Kings, knocked on my door and asked me what happened, and I told him. He said that's how she is. I told him that his sister had too many mood swings and I wouldn't be talking to his sister again. Not too long after, they had a very loud argument about it, and he kept saying he was the only one in the family that didn't turn his back on her. The next day, when I was in the kitchen, he asked me did I hear him defending me last night. I said yes, and we continued speaking when she wasn't around. I completely avoided Judy for a whole month and didn't speak a single word to her until May 15th, 2015. During that time, I could have spoken with her at any moment.

On May 14th, 2015, I was in the kitchen cooking and her son came in, and I left so he could get what he had to get, but he started washing dishes while I was cooking. He kept looking back to see where I was, as in, if you try to sneak up on me, I'll see it coming. Her son and I got along well, he used to ask his mother about me when he called to check up on his mother. He even knows my niece and nephew who go to Gates High. There wasn't any reason for him to act like this. So I said, I don't have a problem with you, your mother, or anyone in your family. I said I stopped talking to your mother because she has too many mood swings, and if I wasn't in the position I was in with this City, it wouldn't be a problem, but I have to keep my nose clean. He didn't like it, but he respected it. That's all I said, in a gentle, sincere way.

May 15th, 2015, Judy had a mental break meltdown when I was in the kitchen, with tears in her eyes she said my son told me what you said. I don't have mood swings. This is all about what you did. You pointed your finger in my face and said your fucking brother, your fucking brother, I have never been talked to like that before, you said your fucking brother, your fucking brother. I have never been talked to like that before. You said your fucking bother, you said your fucking bother. I am going to tell my brother, I am going to tell my brother. Do you hit woman, do you hit woman? I had to tell you to leave my room four times, four times. I said you only told me to leave twice, she screamed and said I told you four times, four times. She said I am going to call the landlord. I was terrified and gave her every cent I had, which was $25. My landlord told the last neighbors that I was writing down every word that they said, writing letters about them, and I was not to be trusted. Her eyes told me she wanted more as she took it, I said that's all the money that I have. I am teaching people that I can be black-mailed, but her eyes dried a little. She said, why did you tell my son that, why? I told her how her son reacted in the kitchen while I was in there, she denied that her son would react like that, and when she believed me, screamed at me and said, why were you in the kitchen anyway when you're in your room all the time. As she spoke, I felt like a deer caught in front of the headlights, I just froze up. Some people operate better in chaos, not me, because all I can think about is how Satan will use this as leverage, and their sympathizers backing them up. So I didn't get the words out of my stomach and say because I was in the kitchen cooking first. I only go into the kitchen most times when they're not home, or when I have heard complete silence in the kitchen for a long period.

About two months ago, after being in Judy's room watching movies and talking for a while, I went back to my room. Let's just say, violence was going on at the time, I knocked on her door softly, so the people who were doing the violence wouldn't hear me. Judy came to the door and said I didn't know you were there, I thought I heard a knock on the front door. I told her about the violence that was going on and how serious it was. She said she knew, and that's all that happened. End of story. When Judy had her meltdown on May 15th, she brought this up and said this incident happened three times on three different occasions. I said it happened once, and you know why, because of the fight that was happening. She said it happened three times, three times, three times loudly. I said when you came to the door, you even thought someone was at the front door because it was me knocking softly. She said that's a lie, that's a lie, it happens three times, three times three times. If a woman thought a man was, or if you caught a man waiting by your door sneaking in a sexual nature three times, why would you ever let him back into your apartment many times after the fact? Why would you introduce him to your family members, watch movies with him, and talk about personal things in general? That's not rational, and if this lie was true, wouldn't it be just a little crazy? When we first started talking, I told her that if I wasn't cooking anything in the kitchen, I would give her and her relatives/visitors complete privacy by not coming out of my apartment until they left. I said this out of respect because this is something that I would like in return, not that she had to do what I do, but I treat people like I would like to get treated, nothing more. On May 15th when she had her meltdown, she brought this fact up and said I was trying to control her by worrying about who she brought over and that she had tons of male friends and I shouldn't be worried about her or what she did. She said loudly, stop trying to control me. She either felt this way when I told her I would give her privacy when someone came over a month before, or said this while she was recording our conversation and anyone that was listening to the recording, would think I was automatically guilty. Ask past neighbors who lived here, didn't I say and show them the same respect?

You know how I got her to shut up about this? I said Judy can I please be honest with you. Please, Please Please, I'll get down on my knees if I have to, please don't get offended, I beg beg beg you, Please don't get offended. She said okay what, just say it. I said I am not attracted to, nor did I want a woman with three children. I had to say all of this because I am more afraid of a lie than I am of a gun. I believe she said all of this while she was recording me, creating evidence. She was overpowering. If this happened anywhere else, I would have just walked away, but this was in the kitchen. This is just about word for word what happened, and you can listen to the recording I think she made.

This was either a great performance or a complete meltdown. Either way, I got swindled out of $25, and she tried to extort me again. I felt if I continued speaking with her, she would have milked me for what she could. I didn't want to ever have an experience with her like that, so I gave her and her family as much room as possible. There have been days that I haven't gone in the other room, which means that I didn't go in my refrigerator because my refrigerator is in the kitchen. When I told her how her son reacted in the kitchen, she yelled and said you have a problem with my son too. I said I don't have a problem with you, your son, or anybody in your family. I told her that she was the boss, and if she didn't want me to speak to anyone in her family again, I wouldn't. She said that she didn't want me to talk to her son again, and especially talk to her son about her. I said I would never talk to him again, I promise. Not one word. The only time, and I mean the only time, I have said a word to him after she told me to never talk to him again was in the kitchen one day because I had to. I was unloading tons of groceries from the car without my neighbor Judy being home, then she dropped her son off and left. He went into his room and shut the door. Like I said, I was unloading tons of groceries, so I put one full bag of groceries in the sink and went back out to the car. I wasn't gone a minute, and when I came back, he was washing dishes in the sink where my bag was. He took his sweet time and when he was done, the sink was filled with water and so was my bag. The little coward came out of me as I said to her son,

I would have moved it for you. He gave me a mean face and went back to his room. It was Father's Day, so I spent the night at my father's, and the next day, which was more than 24 hours that I was away from my apartment, two 9 lbs packs of meat were on the counter completely hot from the sun. Judy came out of her room and said your freezer door was open for a very long time, I wasn't here, but my son said it was open when you left. I closed the freezer door, I put the meats on the counter, and you better be happy I did that in that kind of voice. This was the first time I had spoken to her since May 15th. I said thank you so very much, I appreciate it, how about I give you a movie for your troubles. Only a coward rewards people for violating them. A few hours later, I left a really good movie that everyone wanted to see on her side of the counter and went back to my room. She came out, took the movie, and went back into her apartment. 24 hours later, the same movie was on my side of the counter with a note that read. Roy, I didn't watch this movie, I want another one. I left the movie where it was, later she took the movie and note. She tried to make small talk with me a few times, but I didn't respond to anything, and I haven't said a word to her since.

After her meltdown back on May 15th, I don't ever plan to talk to her again in life. If everything that I have written is true, can you blame me for not talking to her? That's what all the tension is about, I won't talk to her when she comes, I leave, and won't go into the kitchen if anyone is in there, no matter what. When I looked into my refrigerator, everything was ruined and almost hot to the touch. Isn't this salmonella? My water jug was even hot, so they must have closed the freezer door just when I arrived. I don't know if her son peeked into the freezer to see what I had bought, then something came loose, or if the door opened up on its own. Am not sure, they're not thieves, and accidents do happen, but her son walked over the meats for hours. Shortly after, I was in the kitchen and her son came in and just watched me prepare my food. Not a mean look, he was just standing on the side watching me. I don't want to fight anyone, especially a woman and her 16-year-old. Wouldn't that be a felony for me to hit a 16-year-old minor? I have gone to washing most of my dishes in the bathroom sink. I never got bullied my whole life until 2001 at MCC. Now I have to be bullied by a 16-year-old because I am more afraid of Satan's lie than I am of a gun.

More Mood Swings

Mad one minute, nice the next. She had been showing this symptom ever since she moved in, but I figured since her brother was the First Crown of the Latin Kings that she wasn't a Mole and everything would be alright while she worked things out in her head. She told me, when she first moved in, that she had to work things out in her head. She would say things like, my therapist said this, my therapist said that. That car came from nowhere, why did it have to hit me, I just can't get over it. We were talking one time in her room, and she came from left field and said I better not ever catch you in my food. The problem with that is we were talking about Sports or something. Another time we were talking about Resumes, Jobs, and Degrees. I showed her my Resume and told her what my degree was in, then I explained to her what a machinist was, she still didn't understand my degree or what I did, so I said the next degree in my field was Mechanical Engineering. The next day when talking about my field, she screamed at me and said you were an Engineer, you said you were an Engineer.

Clues Why I Think She Is A Mole

When she and her brother first moved in, I asked her what the landlord said about me. She evaded the question at first, then she said he said nothing, I said nothing, she repeated nothing and said I didn't even know who lived here. I said didn't you ask? She said no. This doesn't make much sense to me at all. She later went on to say that the landlord said the woman who lives in the back was nice. Most people who evade a question are usually lying. Every single person who has ever lived here has said terrible things about the landlord, besides my current neighbor, Judy. Every single time I told her the crimes he did to me and other tenants, she either said they were lies or justified his crimes. The first week, while on talking terms, I asked her how the church was and what church they go to. She snapped at me and said, how did you know we were at church, how did you know? Her brother who was on the floor nursing his bad back said I told him we went to church. She went back to being nice again. So my landlord must have told her that I had written about past neighbors and what they said. I told myself, now that I have spoken with them, I have to get along with them, not the other way around. Judy's ex-neighbor and her had some words, not sure what happened, but Judy said she had to show the whole street that she was the law, she kept saying that she was the law, and had her son beat up her ex-neighbor's son with everyone in the street watching. She said they know what the law is now, and she couldn't have anyone disrespecting the law, I am the law. Even if she isn't a Mole, she saw an opportunity and tried to cash in on it. I also told her how the landlord put a 24-hour notice on the tenant's doors, then he would come back in 24 hours and do a check, then come back in another 24 hours when the neighbors weren't home. She screamed and said the landlord has 48 hours, am the law. Then she went back to being nice again. Judy said that I was trying to listen to them, so I would always turn up my TV, and one time I was watching the UFC on high volume, and I heard her yell at her son and say he is doing that because of you, do you hear that? The very next time I was in the kitchen, her son would just stand there seriously watching me. So she sent her son to fight me because I had completely stopped talking to her. Not too long after that, they took 95% of the apartment and wanted me to say something about it. She even made fake laughing sounds when I was in the kitchen. Her taking 95% of the apartment, was an extension of the original extortion. She goes to church all the time and has police and judges in her family, with other city officials that she could call and know. This is what Judy told me.

The landlord is not only a liar and a cheat, but also a thief.

My landlord knew the Heroine Junky was either in jail or rehab and wasn't coming back for his things. Since he is a Representative for the Police Dept. he knew what happened to him. When someone moves out, he takes their name off the mailbox, changes the lock, and especially since Junkies have Junky friends that might want to crash. He told me that he had no idea where he was, and put a note on his bedroom door that said to call Carl as soon as possible. This was all deception, he wanted access to my apartment when I wasn't here, so he could say, are you sure it wasn't his girlfriend, brother, or other relatives that might have had a key, all to create reasonable doubt.

My landlord opened my TV box which was sealed with tons of heavy staples when I was away from my apartment for like a week. The TV had been repaired in a cardboard box without a picture, so no one knew what was in there unless you opened the box up. When I arrived back at my apartment after being gone for a week, I thought no one had been inside the other apartment because I would have seen footprints on the extra-high snow on the front porch. So my landlord was slick because he got in through the side door where there was no evidence. I went up to the box and noticed it had been opened, but like a dumb ass, I kept asking myself did I open that box up? I was going to call the landlord, but that would make me seem crazy. He would have said, somebody opened your TV box and didn't take the TV. No one has been there besides you, Roy, are you going crazy? So I didn't call, and since I didn't call, he thought for sure I did something illegal with the TV. Why would I open the box up when I promised to sell it to my niece for $50 on New Year's Eve? It was a cheap Walmart 32 Christmas piece of junk that I got as a present that lasted only 10 months before it died. It takes a lot of effort to remove lots of heavy staples, I would have remembered this.

Feb 12th, 2015 I was in my bathroom and noticed someone was in the other room. I saw the bright light under the door in the reflection of my bathroom mirror. About three minutes later, my landlord knocked on my door to ask me about the garbage cans outside. I told him about rats in the kitchen and moved the refrigerator back to show him all the rat pebbles, there was a dead rat under the refrigerator that he removed from the house for me. When he came back in, he asked me about some boxes on one side of the wall, but not the other side of the wall, where there was one empty TV box and the other box was open with a TV inside. He didn't ask me about these boxes. He said see you later and for some reason, I went over to check on the box that had the TV inside. It was gone with snow on the box that was kissing the box he took. I opened the front door and said give me back my TV, he kept saying over and over I don't have your TV, I have to go pick my daughter up, call me. I called him twice, and he lied and lied, so I called 9-1-1. The police came over and the first thing he asked me was why I had two TVs. I said the TV had recently died only after having it for 10 months, that I recently got it fixed, and I showed him the warranty that lasts until 2017. I told the police to check the security cameras as proof, and the following day my landlord returned my TV to me. On February 13th my landlord said let me see the receipt, I showed him, and he gave me back my TV. Listen to his complicated lie, which I am sure he had help with. He said the reason why he took the TV and lied to me was because the Heroine Junky's girlfriend's daughter email him a picture of the TV, and said it was hers, he said he wanted to get down to the bottom of things once and for all. Since you have the receipt, Roy, here is your TV back. Before my landlord would lie for the sake of lying without much thought. Now his lies are more complex, lying to create an alibi, so he could hide his crimes. He was trying to cover his tracks on the tape recorder when he first asked me about the boxes, not the TV boxes, but some other boxes on the opposite wall. If anyone that didn't know this was listening to the recording, they would think he was talking to me about the TV boxes. Recording devices is a great mousetrap, but in the hands of devils, abuse and deception are always at play. Just imagine all the crimes one could get away with if the right things are said on a recording device. Deception is fake evidence, but apparently, it's working. So not only did my landlord open the box, he completely took the TV out of the box, went into the Heroine Junky's room, took pictures of the TV in that room, and told me the reason why he took the TV was that the Heroine Junky's girlfriend's daughter email him a picture of the TV, and said it was hers. He took my TV because he thought he was on to something. I was watching one TV, while I had another one in a sealed-up box. So he figured I had something illegal, and wanted to capitalize off of it. He staged a crime scene, made a deceptive alibi while recording me, and created that lie about the Heroine Junky's girlfriend's daughter. There are lots of layers to this devil's lies. He was a terrible liar, so he had the help of a Good Liar, or maybe even a Great Liar, in all of this deviltry. When I talked with the police on February 12, or anytime some situation that was created, putting me face to face with them, I always have tons of emotions, and expected them to slick talk to me, so I was far from being at ease. Funny how I never feel this emotion when I am talking to people that I know have killed someone before. Anyway, would you feel comfortable talking with the very same people who have destroyed your entire life? I didn't even tell him the important fact that someone opened my TV box a few weeks before. So when I was talking to the police, he asked me why my landlord knocked on my door. At the time, I was nervous talking to him and upset about my TV. I said I couldn't remember what he wanted, so on February 20th the police told my landlord to come to my apartment, and he pretended to get into an argument over the phone and asked me, what was the last date he was over here, I said February 13th. When I do talk to the police or my landlord, they play these little tricks with me all the time. So, I guess if I can't remember something while being recorded, whether I am nervous or not, Satan will use this to justify and say I am going crazy, so when I write about the Systematic Terrorism that has me in my apartment in future letters, Satan can call into question my memory, which is reasonable doubt to Satan Sympathizers. As soon as the police left, I remembered that my landlord asked me about the garbage cans outside, that the city was behind on picking up. Nothing against the police officer, but he was recording audio and video the whole time, when I moved my refrigerator back so he could see hundreds of rat pebbles, he backed far away so it wouldn't be on video and said, I saw it. Ask yourself, who does this benefit? My landlord is a Representative of the police, because everything he does to me, the police benefit from it, and are blameless at the same time. I hadn't seen my landlord for months, and when he committed crimes against me, I was away from my apartment for about five days watching a friend's cat. Someone is telling him that the coast is clear. Feb 13th, 2015 when my landlord brought my TV back, I said you knew what side is mine and what side is the ex-neighbor, the one on heroin. So you knew that the story about the girlfriend's daughter was a lie. He said he didn't, that we were to share the whole space. I said that's not true, and you know it, he kept getting mad and saying it was, and moved my boxes to one side of the room. The best way to get along with liars is to let them have their way, especially with this devil, anything other than that would cause war. I wanted the sabotaging and tricks to stop, so I gave in. Ask the two neighbors that I had to share the kitchen with, did we have different sides. As a matter of fact, the last neighbor wanted to put something on my side, but since he was on Heroin so badly, I told him I didn't want to share anything with him. He told the landlord, and the landlord said that was Roy's side, and that you have to talk with Roy about that. So suppose my TV was illegal, and I denied that it was my TV, he would have said, that's your TV because it's on your side of the room, and you know it. Now I have a side, but when things don't go right when this devil is trying to set you up, this isn't your side.

More Landlord Issues

About a month after I moved to this building in 2011, someone violently stole my bike on my porch just outside my door, removing about four railings from the porch. I told my landlord what happened and told him to check the security cameras across the street to see who did it. He said Roy, it's only a bike, let it go. I said that was an expensive bike, and they damaged your property, again, he said to let it go and that I should buy another bike. Months later, someone put a bike in my neighbor's backyard and left. My neighbor told my landlord, and he immediately called the police, and they checked the video within minutes.

The building was crawling with rats and roaches, and my landlord told me that he would be dropping off rat poison. He said that he would leave the poison inside my door. I said I don't want you in my apartment when I am not home. He knew I wasn't going to be home and left the rat poison perfectly in the middle of my unmade bed. He left my neighbor rat poison outside her door, at the time he would always just walk inside her apartment when she wasn't at home. He always tries to rouse me up as much as possible on many occasions like this, so he could record me over the phone. I knew he was trying to excite me, but I had to call him on it. As relaxed as I could, I called him, and he said, am sorry, I thought you wanted it there, blah blah blah.

My one neighbor who moved out a while ago made a deal with my landlord. He would give him money if my landlord would let him still use the mailbox. He was getting some kind of cash check and felt if he changed the mailing address he wouldn't get any more cash checks. My landlord said he paid him well. My landlord told me this a while ago, and this is all that I know about it. I only want my landlord to get in trouble, not the other guy, so I didn't write his name.

My landlord called me extremely angry and asked me why I didn't let the maintenance guy in, and when I finally let him in, I bad-mouthed him the whole time. I was so rude, that the maintenance guy was afraid and left without finishing. This was all completely made up. I think I have a recording of this too. About two years later, my neighbor knew one of the maintenance men and told her that he didn't come over because of me. He said I wouldn't let him in and tried to fight him or something. Again, all made-up lies. If you throw enough tricks, schemes, and sabotage at a situation, something is going to stick.

I was gone from my apartment for like a week, watching my friend's cats in Ogden. When I came back, I noticed all the secret traps I had around my apartment were all walked over. I also noticed that I was missing a little over a hundred dollars in Tokens from the Public Market. I immediately blamed my neighbor who was on Heroin's girlfriend, because she left me a letter on my floor about her boyfriend stealing, and she knew I had the tokens. So you would think she stole them, but I had lots of quarters lying around, and not one was touched. She was the kind of person when she gets 50 cents, she's straight out the door looking to buy a cigarette. And they never had toilet tissue, so they would take showers all the time instead, and I had tons of tissues in the bathroom, not one roll was missing. So I blamed my landlord. To this day I am not sure who took my tokens, but I have the letter that she wrote me still.

My landlord is like the gift that keeps on giving to the police. I have lived here for four years, and the first month that I moved in, my landlord kept sabotaging me with my neighbor, telling her that he was going to kick her out for her playing loud music. He said I would call him all the time complaining. He hasn't stopped sabotaging me since the first month I moved in. I say again, who has benefited the most from this? The police, that's who.

About the Heat

I think it was Barksdale that complained about the heat, and people came out here to fix it. They were in the basement for a while, one guy came up to see if all the vents in my apartment worked right. They had all the vents screaming heat when he left, a day or two later, my landlord came to my apartment to replace the batteries in the thermostat. As soon as he left, I never felt or heard heat coming from the vents again. My toilet tissue stand is right by the vent and my tissue rolls used to always dance, after he left that day, my tissue rolls never moved. What he really did was put some fake batteries into the thermostat. So whatever residue heat came from the front apartment was all mine, which wasn't much, but I never complained.

On October 9th, 2014, my landlord knocked on my door and told me to tell my neighbor something. He already knew he was home, but told me to tell him something. I said I don't talk to him anymore, he is on Heroin and steals my food. My landlord went over to him and told him that I was not to be trusted and that I write down everything that was said in his apartment. So my neighbor knew when it was cool outside, and he wasn't going to be home, he would shut off the heat and I would freeze. After I told Social Service and called the Net Office and said my landlord turned off my heat, having no heat in my apartment for a long time, with a wind chill of like -25, I called my landlord, and he came out here and put some batteries in the thermostat, and ten minutes after he left, pipes busted in the basement. Why would I say he turned off my heat when it could be easily proven? When he was in the basement, I overheard my landlord through the heating vent asking my neighbor if I got along with her, she said yes and that she didn't have a problem with me. So the only thing that I have ever been wrong is when I said he turned off my heat, but as I said, he put fake batteries in the thermostat a long time ago, and I have always been without heat during that time.

Sanchez Upstairs Neighbor

Ms. Sanchez and I were always on talking terms. As in hi, bye, and small talk in general. The landlord put a 24-hour notice on everyone's door and said he was going to inspect their apartment. He inspected everyone's apartment and two days later, I saw him going into my neighbor's apartment when she wasn't at home. I don't know if he just knocked on her door and left, but I was coming from the bus stop and hid just out of his view. She told me to tell her if I saw anyone go into her apartment, to make sure that I told her. I did, and I said it's on the security cameras too. I even told her the exact time to check. She had an issue with the landlord going into her apartment before. I don't know what came of it, but the landlord came over super mad at me, and the next time I saw Sanchez, she was super mad at me and told me that she didn't want to talk anymore. I don't know what was said, but I completely left her alone. The last time I saw her here, she stopped at her door to talk with me, as I was coming from Mary's apartment, her eyes said am sorry for yelling at you, I just said a quick hi and went inside my apartment. That was my last encounter with her at this building. I was told by my neighbors that she moved out when I was away babysitting my friend's cats. I had to take the bus to Social Service for an appointment, as I was waiting I saw Sanchez crossing the street to wait for the bus too. She told me about a month after she moved in that she was going to tell me something about the landlord, but didn't know me well enough yet, so this was the perfect time to ask her about it. I said I heard you moved out when I was away, she was completely nasty to me the whole time. I said I helped you out before and was always kind to you. She said she didn't want to hear about the landlord, he did what he did. I said I was going to Social

Service right now because he turned off the heat on me. I turned away from her and didn't say another word.

They staged that scene, while Sanchez was being nasty to me, recording it, or rather creating evidence again. I knew a cop was there because he snapped his eyes at me, but thought I didn't see it. His face told everything. Sanchez said the only thing she didn't like about me or had a problem with was my negativity. What a coincidence. I told her Parole had a Crackhead put pressure on me, and we got into a fight because of it. I told her about the Heroine Junky that had stolen from me, and that the landlord wouldn't do anything about it. So in that sense, I am negative because people don't want to hear bad news all the time, and Satan worked overtime to get as many negative experiences as he could out of me with my past neighbors. This also proves that Satan was hunting me down that day because he knew about what time I would be at the bus stop.

Someone came to my apartment one day just after Ms Sanchez moved and asked me in so many words, did Sanchez move because of you? The first or second month after she moved in, she had eviction notices on her door. Social Service, Law Office employees, etc have come by with papers asking about her. So the whole time she lived here, she had problems paying the rent. I don't know what was said to her about me, but she was angry or pretended to be angry while Satan was recording.

When Satan Says People Hate Me

It's like gouging my eyes out, it's like using the N-word without using the N-word. Every time they try to set me up with women in a sexual nature, they call me the N-word. When they say I can't read, they're calling me the N-word. It's irrational propaganda, racist, abuse, and any abuse is a crime. It's only a cover-up to be racist, by a network of devilish cutthroats. This letter is far from finished. I can't live anywhere in this City, I can't work anywhere in this City, and I could barely go anywhere in this City. As I said, I will prove systematic terrorism. I don't know what to do about an apartment when I can't live anywhere in this City.

The End, for now.

I AM MOVING OUT

March 21, 2016

Emails to my past landlord who was sabotaging me with my violent roommate. I found out at the last minute that my landlord told my roommate Ed that I was stealing his mail. Ed threatened to shoot me over and over, and I immediately moved out after living there for only six months. I had to borrow money for moving expenses and the first month's rent. Social Service even tried to retaliate against me for moving out so quickly, too.

On March 16th, 2016, Ed shut off all the electricity in the house with the Main Breaker in the basement and then left the house. I didn't want to get into a cycle of this pattern, so I removed all my food from the Refrigerator and went looking for another apartment. I took a landlord statement to Westfall Road on Friday, which means I would be moving as soon as they approve it.

Out of the six months that I have lived there, for five months, I have had to wear sneakers whenever I leave my room, including to and from the shower, because Ed is a coward as he tried to fight me when I had my glasses and slippers on, with a house full of his family members watching. This happened within a month of me moving in. He was expecting a package, and when that package didn't arrive, he thought I had stolen it. The package came the next day, remember? I haven't heard a word from Ed when I am wearing my sneakers, though.

For six months, I have had to listen to Ed threaten and extort Kevin for Kevin's food stamps, as Ed would say, "I'll jump on you, don't make me jump on you". Kevin had to go to the Open-Door Mission just to eat on many occasions. When he would come home after eating at the Open-Door Mission, Ed's Crackhead brother would tease Kevin by saying, "How was Church". I had to smell crack smoke from Ed's Crackhead brother for five months until you just kicked him out for stealing. And speaking of stealing, my food here and there would show up missing, but I never said a word because that would put me into a conversation with Ed, and I have gone out of my way not to say a word to him. My food hasn't been missing since Ed's brother got kicked out.

Ed is just as guilty as his Crackhead brother because his brother has smoked crack for 25 years, and it wasn't a problem until Ed's marijuana got stolen from his room. Now the tenants have to pick up the slack after Ed lets him smoke crack every single day in the living room on the couch, filling the whole house with crack smoke. The liability should be on Ed because he has not only given his brother money for Crack but has taken him to get Crack. Ed knew where to go because Ed used to smoke Crack with him and his older brother all the time. Ed also brags about how he used to stick up and rob people all the time, and started selling drugs at the age of 11. This is the guy you have running things.

Why should the RG&E be split down the middle, when Ed has his family bring over a closet full of clothes just about every week? He has his children stay here Friday, Saturday, and Sunday running wild leaving the lights and TV on, while Ed is at work and his children use up the whole house most of the time. Three days a week for 52 weeks is a lot of electricity in a year, and that doesn't include all their clothes. Most of the time, Ed leaves his TV or light on in his room all day while he is at work. He is riding on the backs of tenants, and it's not fair that I have to pay for his family usage too. Not to mention how Ed took money from other tenants for RG&E, without paying the bill for like four months, then having RG&E turn off the service. Under the new RG&E account, he isn't current, but still collects money from tenants, and wants to collect payment two whole weeks before the bill is even due. He is the reason why I am moving out, and I will be using the $60 that I would have given Ed towards my moving expenses instead. I don't want to live under these conditions any longer.

Thank you.

Roy,

Today is March 14, 2016, and I have yet to pay Ed my share of the RG&E bill. I have had money in hand since March 7, 2016, and still do, but because of his note dated March 11, 2016, and knowing the real reason he wants the money, I have not paid him as yet.

Ed talks extremely loud, and I kept overhearing him over the phone asking people how much they need. Then he said he was out of money and was waiting for me to pay him now. Since I have lived here, I have heard Ed bragging about being a loan shark. He calls it slow money, and people know not to mess with his money. This explains where the tenant's money goes that he gets from them early to pay the RG&E bill. Also explains why he hasn't shown anyone, including his brother who used to live here, the RG&E bill. When RG&E came here to shut off the service, I had only lived here for 8 nights, the guy said the bill was over four thousand, and not a penny had been paid in four months. A day before, Ed got angry with me for not giving him money towards the bill, I told him I had only lived here eight nights, and he said we were all in this together. Not in a gentle kind of way, though. The RG&E bill I saw lying in the garbage said the bill was over five thousand back then.

My question is, do I pay Ed as soon as possible, and pay him on the 13th as I have been, or do I pay Ed closer to the end of the month, because the bill isn't due until the 28th I believe? Also, Ed had his kids stay the weekend, and his children's eyes said, "If you don't pay my father, you're going to get it".

Roy

I went into the bathroom today, and Ed left a note that read," Time To Pay RG&E Bill ". Today is March 11, 2016, and I have always paid him on the 13th, without ever being late once. This note must be for me, because even though he barely talks to Kevin, Ed and I don't speak. Ever. I would have just ignored the note, but I need to cover myself, especially since Ed is such a hothead. Another thing, you asked me to ask Ed for a receipt from now on, and I said no because I would be the only one doing this, and when you kick Ed out for cheating people, the first person Ed will look to is me. He will think I initiated everything. This email is only me protecting myself, and Ed will get his money on the 13th, no later. I hope Ed doesn't think he will extort me like he does Kevin.

P.S.

Notice how Ed traced the letters in his note in the photo attached to this email? I will be at the library until 4:30 today.

Roy

December 21, 2016
Department of Social Services
The Conciliation Team
111 Westfall Road

Dear Ms. Lobiondo:

I got physically assaulted at Hope Initiative twice. Once when the second guy in command of the company, Jim Fox, pressed his thumb into my lower back with great force, bringing tears to my eyes. The second time an ex-employee named Dee would visit work twice a week, even though he did not work there anymore, and would show up drunk harassing me. He would stand in the back or on the side of me, in a gangster intimidating way, while I worked at my station. Employees saw this, especially the third guy in command named Bob. Bob would have this euphoric life feeling when Dee came around, laughing, shaking Dee's hand hard, as he would look at me with warm confident eyes. Bob never treated Dee like this when he was employed there. As soon as Dee put pressure on me, Bob fell in love with Dee. Surprisingly the number one guy in command William Daubney had this euphoria too. One day after we had a pizza party, Daubney said to Dee while shaking Dee's hand hard, you are welcome here anytime, as Dee's eyes searched for mine a crossed the room. One day I went up to the second guy in command and told him that I wanted to talk to him privately because I had had enough of Dee and some of the other sabotaging that was going on. He was slick about it, told me he had to finish something, and like 15 minutes later, recorded our conversation in the office. How do I know, when I tried to tell him that Dee was stealing from them left and right he was calm about it, but when I described to him in detail how William Daubney's excitement towards Dee with me around, Jim Fox had a silent break down and tried to stop me from continuing. Why would he act this way if he was not recording me? One day Dee came up to me unemployed and drunk, jabbed his fingers on my glasses and said, "If I wanted to get you, I would have gotten you by now". That is an assault by someone who did not even work there. Jim Fox saw this across the room, Dee's back was facing him and I could clearly see Jim Fox watching Dee and Me, as my head went back, Jim didn't take his eyes off of us. Another person saw this and asked why didn't I say or do anything, I said because of all the violence in and outside of work, that I was a target. About three months after I left Hope Initiative, I ran into people who work there and asked them about Dee, if Dee still came around, and three people said yes. Dee and I never had any issues when Dee was an employee there, so I do not know what was said to him, but the Management at Hope Initiative was his partner in crime. That is all I want to say at this time about what happened at Hope Initiative, to be continued at a later date.

The first week at Food Link, I had to go to the Emergency because I hurt my back lifting boxes, but my back was already tender from moving. So I made sure I told the doctor that my back was already tender before I started working, and made sure it was in the report. I could have taken the cowardly way out by saying I hurt my back at Food Link, but I said I hurt it elsewhere, basically. I originally hurt my back at Hope Initiative and reinsured it at Food Link. Check all my medical records, and you will not see one thing on me injuring my back. Now I have recurring back pain because Hope Initiative sent the Police after me and left me nothing to stand on.

About a month into working at Food Link, I ripped my extra cheap gloves breaking down tough caked-on food boxes, when I went and got another pair of gloves, one of the supervisors told me and another worker we needed to make our gloves last. So I was tearing down boxes with food on my hands when they had tons of gloves. After lunch that same day, I was finishing up a small apple that I had left over for lunch, and the group leader came up to me forcefully and told me to throw the apple away that second. I had just got to the work area like everyone else, so I said not too loud at all, "Freeze, Put The Apple Down". A co-worker and spy by the name of Willie came over and slapped me on the shoulder with all his weight in front of everyone, which caused instant pain to my back. That is physical assault in front of the cameras, in front of an undercover cop, coworkers, and the group leader. I said "Freeze, Put The Apple Down" because I thought it was extra petty of the supervisor to complain about a cheap pair of gloves, knowing that breaking down just one box could ruin them, so I had to have food and god knows what on my hands. Then, the group leader approached me in his manner about biting into my apple, that is why I said what I said. Willie assaulted me because he knew he could get away with it, and all of Satan's lies, whether it was through another African American or Satan himself, all had to do with Satan's lies manifesting. Fact, people say things all the time around there and at every company without being assaulted, so why do I have the privilege of being assaulted? Satan, that is why. All this happened while working hard with half of a broken back. I could not have done jack about it anyway with my back out of whack. Why would a person who was in the WEP Program care what comes out of my mouth? If you knew you had four dollars under your bed, four under your shoes, four under your TV, and four in your red jacket and someone you never met told you all the places where you had four dollars stashed, you would think this person been in your house right? Willie has said things to me that he could not have possibly known. Just like Satan has eyes all over me in society, they had eyes all over me at Food Link. It is an invasion of my life once again. At times, I felt like I was a sitting duck, while Satan gathered intelligence and tried to build a case against me. Willie told someone who was doing community service that people hated and did not like me. The guy kept saying to Willie, "I don't think so man, I don't think so man". I do not know if Willie knew him before they worked there, but they were sort of close. Willie always tried to analyze my character too. When Satan whispers in people's ears about you, it makes it that much harder for people not to pay close attention and target you in a negative light. I do not care who or what organization sent Willie. I belong to no one in Rochester, N.Y. I belong to only the truth.

I told the undercover cop Kevin, I think, who disguised himself as owning his own painting business, who bought hot food for the rest of the employees on his last day, why I said what I said. He understood and asked did anyone said anything to me afterward. No one said anything, but a lot of people knew, as some tried to avoid eye contact, while others looked at me with confidence. I tested the waters with him and told him that I had not smoked pot since September 2011, and his facial expression said that he was disappointed and hurt by it. Only a cop and or someone who wants something on you would react like this. I told him some of the events that the Police did to me personally, to gauge his reaction, and before I even started he was displeased. So I left it alone. He told me that his wife was on the jury in the Boys & Girl Geneses Street murder trial, and how one of the girlfriends turned on her boyfriend because she was facing stealing charges to save herself. I would think this is something a cop would know, not someone on the jury. I could be wrong. If this guy was not a cop, someone still sent him on my account.

I was one of, if not the hardest worker at Food Link. People would comment all the time on how hard I worked. I do not want to say a bad word about them, but their system is human beings using other human beings, with every single paid employee being the boss. That said, a lot of the paid employees would come and barrow me for whatever assignment since they knew I was strong and a great worker. One day after I came back from lifting tons of boxes, my group leader yelled at me in front of everyone, which made people laugh. Shortly after, he beeped his horn on his forklift for me to come over and move one box, he was letting me know that he was the boss. So the next day I went to the supervisor and asked to work in another location. No arguments. They knew what happened and moved me to another area. My new boss was new from a temporary agency, and he would have me do all these personal assignments for him like getting him coffee and going to the employee locker room to get his jacket. Be quick about it, am cold, he would say. It was also my job to put heavy boxes up from the customer's cart and place them on the scale so he could input their weight into the computer. He kept changing his mind when it came to placing the boxes on the scale. Imagine lifting an 80-pound box on the scale, then having someone say, no not that one, that one, when you go to put it back, never mind you could put it up here. This happened all the time. When I would slow down and make him point to the boxes that he wanted next, he would yell and say that one, quick. This happened all the time. On Monday, November 14th, he yelled at me in front of other employees about which boxes to pick up next and soon changed his mind again. I had enough at that point and went up to my supervisor and told him the next day would be my last. No arguments, no nothing. In fact, the temporary agency boss did not even know I was leaving because of him. He wanted to talk and eat lunch with me all the time, as he thought I was his personal pet. Rick, a paid employee that worked with us, went to the supervisor and said he would leave the company if the temporary agency boss kept talking to him disrespectfully.

An old Nun is a regular customer there, and one day they told her that she could not shop there any longer until she paid her balance off. My temporary agency boss said they're no better than anybody else, and when I went out to put her groceries in her car, he came to the door and said we need you in here over and over. He tried to make it seem like the Nun was trying to cheat Food Link and rushed her along. This lady's arthritis was so bad, that she could barely hold an apple without dropping it. She had a lot of items that she could not pick up and made us uncomfortable rushing. When I was done, I went back inside, and there was nothing to do.

Crime should be about intent, and Food Link never had evil intentions. They did not try to hurt me like Hope Initiative and did not try to set me up in a sexual nature either, but they knew I was being betrayed and lied to, while Satan gathered as much intelligence on me as possible. If I owned a company and I knowingly knew these events were taking place, the D.A. would say something like "They had advanced knowledge, which makes them just as guilty". I worked like an animal for those people, got assaulted, and continued to work like an animal, only to be treated like a slave. How could I work anywhere in this city with these kinds of events going on?

Sincerely,

Roy Snell

LOVELY WARREN

November 29, 2017

Lovely Warren
Mayor's Office, City Hall
30 Church St.
Rochester, NY 14614

Dear Mrs. Warren:

Before people heard the words "Fake News", I wrote "Fake Evidence" in my letter, describing deception tactics that were used to terrify me. Within the last 15 years, this City has committed thousands of felonies on my person, and to balance the scales, they've muddied the waters by creating as much fake evidence as possible. At the end of the day, they have created Reasonable Doubt and justification in the eyes of people who don't understand what went on, and to their loyal sympathizers. This multiple creation of evidence, sabotage, and violent sabotage has been going on for 15 years and has completely left me out of society and in my apartment for around 13 years. The Police went from sabotaging and hitting me in society to sabotaging and hitting me at work. Work is supposed to be a hitting-free zone and not a place to gather as much intelligence as you can on your enemy.

The Department of Social Services has created an emergency, not me, that I do not know how to fix. I have taken Social Service to a Fair Fearing in the past, but they usually did not say too much in the Fair Hearing. This time they had 19 pages of things to say. I got blindsided with lies, and rather than addressing the lies, I froze up. I had to write a short explanation to Albany on why I wanted a Fair Hearing but tipped off Social Service with that short explanation. I was just following directions. I did not talk about the police once or the real reasons why I was on welfare. The police bothered me just after 8/16/2017, because of Social Service, and that was still fresh in my mind. I learned on 11/18/17 that I could be out on the streets because of lies.

Fair Hearing Page # 9

Quote: Mr. Snell was very confrontational and refused to accept the assignment given, stating that he refused to work for the city as he has exposed multiple things wrong over the past 15 years. End Quote.

Am not a confrontational kind of person, I lose an easy debate in front of Alpha males and females. They're super confident and talk a hundred times faster than me. Tammy Perkins is the Alpha in this case. After I declined to work at the Cemetery, Mrs. Perkins told me that one day the Cemetery could hire me directly, and that I would be working for the City of Rochester. I calmly told her that this city has committed thousands of felonies on me over the last 15 years, that I would never work for this city, as in, I would never work for the City of Rochester, and not that I would not work in Rochester or in the city of Rochester. So Tammy Perkins lied on purpose. A room full of people heard every word we said.

Quote: Mr. Snell accused us of being part of a conspiracy against him, in which I tried multiple times to explain the process and reasons for placing him in the assignment given. End Quote.

Not counting Social Service, Rochester Works protected me against the Police at one point and knew about my complete situation since 2004 I believe. I only had one bad experience with them, and that was because of the police. I haven't even written about it, and appreciate it when someone sticks their neck out for me. I never had any bad feelings towards Rochester Works, ever, even after one bad incident. She tried to make it seem like something was wrong with me.

Quote: He did not want to listen to any of the reasons and just demanded a new assignment in which again I explained that we had offered multiple other choices, and he refused all of them, end quote.

This is an outright lie. On 7/31/17 I calmly explained that out of the two prior WEP Assignments that I enrolled in, I got assaulted twice and sabotaged by the first, second, and third guy in command at Hope Initiative. I got assaulted once in front of the police on my second WEP Assignment at Food Link. So I told them I wanted to work in a good environment, around good people, where I won't be getting assaulted. The Rochester Works associate lady went and got her boss or supervisor, and I repeated the very same words to her. Her boss/supervisor told me she had a place in mind that would be a five-minute walk. I said sign me up, and she called the company and the main lady was on vacation that day. They told me to come back on 8/10/17, and when I did, a new face was in front of me saying that I accepted a job to work at the Cemetery and to sign at the bottom. It's like bait and switch that turned into a food fight. I said, I never accepted to work at the Cemetery, and that it was the first time hearing of it. The associate young man went and got Tammy Perkins and

Mrs. Perkins had a cow when I didn't sign the papers to work at the Cemetery, then had another one when I said I could not work at Hope Initiative. So this so-called we offered Roy multiple other choices is an outright lie. I am surprised they didn't give me the option to work in the sewer, and then kick me off because I declined. We looked at a job description at some church on 7-31-17, but if these people are hitting me at work, can you imagine me getting hit in a church, that would be too much.

Quote: Mr. Snell stated that he would just call for a fair hearing and left the building, End Quote.

I was getting super bullied, and she gave me her ultimatum, either work at the Cemetery or Hope Initiative. People are given the option to choose between tons of jobs. So I said, not in a confident condescending tone, that I would ask for a fair hearing because I knew what she was doing was wrong. Security was waiting for me and was on high alert as I exited the building. It was like an escort because security held the doors open for me. I didn't raise my voice once during the whole encounter in the building.

Working at Hope Initiative will put me at great risk, especially since Hope Initiative knows that I plan to write about them in the future. I started to write about them in a letter I gave to Social Service on 5/30/2014, and the Police put so much pressure on me everywhere I went, that I went to Social Service first thing that Monday and told them that I would not be writing any more letters about Hope Initiative. As a matter of fact, I wrote, "Because of you know who", and told them a specific time to check the Police cameras on North Clinton Ave to prove that the Police were terrorizing me on camera as I was walking home from Rite Aid on North Clinton Ave. What do you think happened off-camera? I also wrote in a letter dated 12/21/2016 that I plan to write about them in the future.

Fair Hearing Page #19

Quote: Roy responded to the conciliation notice for failure to accept a WEP assignment on 8/10/17 at RW WEP orientation by phone stating he refused WEP placement because he is not doing any work for "the City" he states he did not want to do work at the Cemetery because he did not want to think about death. He states he did not want WEP at any of the places because he had been assaulted at all the places after he made them thousands and thousands of dollars. Per notes from RW client was offered multiple sites for placement but refused them all. Phone messages from the client indicate an MH evaluation might be needed. The client was sent to IMA in Feb and found to be able to participate for 40 hr but could benefit from MH treatment due to delusional thinking. The client was sent notice for work limited status but took the agency to FH to dispute, stating he has no limitations mentally or physically and was recorded 20. Per SUP must impose sanctions. No SNAP job search form was returned. Imposed WE1 sanction to both TA/ SNAP effective 10/1/17 as 192 with CNS#U26B015016. Ended all pay lines and added MA extension End Quote.

So if I really told her that I did not want to work in the city, or anywhere in Rochester, why would I ask her for another job? By Mrs. Perkins' own admission, she declined me.

This is my main point. The comment "he makes them thousands and thousands of dollars" was taken out of context on purpose, which is a lie / a little bit of deception. I was talking about Hope Initiative, and how I trained their part-time welder to weld better than their head welder. Everything he welded, before I taught him, fell apart 100% of the time. They wanted me to train other people, including their head welder, and I said no. I saved the company thousands and thousands of dollars by creating a workstation that I used to save employees lower back pain 100%. Before that, lots of people were hurting their backs, and Hope Initiative would soon lay them off. This workstation also allowed one to assemble bed frames at least three times faster. Overall, I changed the way they did a lot of things. I would cut raw metal that took the head welder like 8 hours to cut, but took me two hours. After a week, they had an inventory of precisely cut material and an inventory of assembled bed frames, etc., etc. The new problem was where to put all the assembled bed frames. They knew exactly what I was talking about the whole time, but used "he makes them thousands and thousands of dollars" out of context to generate enough emotion so the Fair Hearing judge would come back with a guilty verdict. Put yourself in the shoes of the examiner at the Fair Hearing, when you hear that someone doesn't want to work in Rochester, how would you respond? If you had the best interest of the State in mind, you would rule the way he did, too. You can't un-ring a bell.

Social Service has tried repeatedly to legally silence me, so no one has to account for systematic terrorism on my person for the last 15 years. I went to IMA in Feb like she said, and they asked me why I did not want to work, I told him that I was physically assaulted three times at two different jobs. I left the office soon afterward. So, I think they're lying about IMA saying that I have "delusional thinking" because if it's true, it's not delusional. I doubt very seriously if they said that. Since I am a whistleblower, this city has destroyed everything in my life tons of times and left me to pick up the pieces. Roy Snell can be destroyed, but I can never be defeated, because I wasn't made to be defeated.

At the last fair hearing, I really spilled my beans. I needed to get my last landlord incident on record, that's why I took them to a fair hearing last time. DSS over the phone sort of tricked me into dropping a fair hearing I asked for before I worked at Food Link, because I told them that my landlord sabotaged me with my neighbor violently, that my neighbor kept repeating that he would shoot me. So I moved out immediately, and they tried to blame me. I wanted to prove that I couldn't live in this city, because since my first letter, the police have always gotten my landlords to sabotage and commit crimes against me. I have lucked out with where I live now because I knew the landlord's family before I moved in.

Social Service and Police Partnership

The very last time that the Police came after me was a couple of days after August 16, 2017. On August 16, 2017, I went to Social Service on St. Paul Street about an hour before they were open. I was required to go to the Job Fair at MCC on the same day at 9:30 but told them that I did not feel safe at MCC. I also told them that I would go to any Job Fair in Monroe County, but not MCC. I wrote all of this down and signed it. What I didn't write down is that I got threatened with a gun twice at MCC in the past. A sheriff pulled a rifle out on me outside MCC doors, I was shaken and moments later I told MCC what happened, all they said was, are you mentally okay, knowing exactly what happened, made me get a mental health evaluation when I complained about it.

Social Service and the Police share a super tight relationship, and someone told the Police that I did not feel safe. Since the Police were not bothering me at the time before August 16, they probably thought I was intentionally saying I did not feel safe because the Police are bothering me right now. Or they bothered me because the lady at Rochester Works lied and said that I would not work in Rochester, basically that I just want to be on Welfare for the rest of my life. I don't know what was in their head, but they made sure they got my attention as I was walking home from Aldi on Lake Ave. Social Service wrote me a letter and said I had to explain myself over the phone. I did, and the Police have not bothered me since. So first Social Service sent Security after me, and then they sent the Police after me.

Last Thing

They created Reasonable Doubt where none existed. Well if it's not the Police then who is responsible for creating evidence? Who benefits? At the end of the day, they're going to have a book the size of an encyclopedia of created evidence, and if we go to court, they can sway their loyal sympathizers with Reasonable Doubt. As soon as I write a letter complaining about the latest abuse/assault, it's all hands-on deck, and they go out of their way to muddy the waters by creating evidence. Predators do things over and over, this is who they are. It's their signature, their fingerprint, and their DNA. I have never been threatened with a gun before, and once the Police entered my life 15 years ago, I was threatened lots of times with guns, all my apartments were broken into and evidence missing, they have tried to entrap me with women in a sexual nature so many times, that am paralyzed with terror to work in the Hospital around women for fear that one day they will make the lie stick. They have poisoned the soil of my entire environment so thoroughly, that it's impossible to grow any flowers on this soil. There is no reason why I have to live in fear of advanced lies. This is not even 1% of the events within the last 15 years that took place.

REQUEST FOR A TEMPORARY FAIR HEARING OVERTURN DECISION

December 12, 2017,

The Office of Administrative Hearings
New York State Office of Temporary and Disability Assistance
P.O. Box 1930
Albany, New York, 12201

The Department of Social Service won a Fear Hearing case against me recently, and I received notice of the news in the mail on 11/18/2017. They took advantage of me, by blindsiding me at the Fear Hearing with 19 pages of lies. Enclosed is a letter explaining the blatant lies I wrote to the Mayor of Rochester dated 11/29/2017. I am asking for an immediate reversal, so my landlord can get paid. I tried getting a lawyer to fight this, but all wanted money that I did not have, or could not take any more clients. I have been on a few job interviews, filled out a lot of online applications, and sent out a few hundred Resumes. My bus pass ends on the 21st of December, so how can I even look for employment in a foot of snow? Social Service made this horror a reality by outright lying, and liars should never have the last laugh. Can you please do what is right and reinstate my benefits until I have my day in court, or until I gain full employment? Thank You for your time and patience.

Roy Snell
District No: 26
Notice No: U26B015016

Case Number: BA0497772

P.S.

I have never been caught in a lie.

AFTERWORD

This book is a testament to resilience in the face of seemingly insurmountable adversity. The experiences documented here reveal a "In your face" world of prejudices and systemic failure, confronting readers with the realities that persist for many. My hope is that these stories, painful as they are, will foster greater understanding and spark conversations that lead to change. I believe that through shared understanding, we can work toward a society where such realities can become the past, replaced by a more just and compassionate world.

ACKNOWLEDGMENTS

This book would not have been possible without the support and encouragement of my friends, family, and all those who refused to ignore the harsh realities of injustice. That would be the mature thing to write, but it would be a lie. Satan has scorched my earth, with heavy sabotage that there isn't anyone left really, scientist couldn't even grow flowers here if they wanted too. With strong support, most people could get through any hardships, but with the overt community terrorism I had to endure for 22 years straight, most healthy strong-minded people with support could not have dealt with this community terrorism for this long. 22 years, not counting the whole year I had to deal with terrorism in college before writing my first letter in 2002. That brings this to 23 straight years of terrorism. And let's not forget about all that time I waited to go to Trial, to my last day on Parole. That brings the terrorism to a little over 30 years, with Satan's claws all over my body. I just turned 54 in September of 2024. On a more positive tone. Thank you to everyone who has stood by me and helped me find the strength to continue telling my story. I am especially grateful for the readers who have taken the time to understand my experiences and the broader implications of systemic oppression. Your support fuels my journey and reinforces the power of resilience and hope.

AUTHOR BIO

Roy Snell is a first-time author and advocate who has spent over two decades documenting his experiences and fighting against systemic injustices. His writing delves into deeply personal and painful episodes, drawing attention to the challenges of navigating a world marked by savage discrimination, bloodthirsty racism, and cold-blooded intimidation. Through his work, Roy invites readers to witness the harsh realities he's faced, and the backbone required to persevere. He is committed to exposing hard truths and inspiring change, while being locked up, isolated from the world in his apartment, with nowhere to turn.

CALL TO ACTION

If you have been moved by the journey within these pages, consider taking action in your own communities. Advocate for accountability, support anti-racism efforts, and engage in conversations that challenge callous prejudiced thinking. Together, we can make strides toward equality and create a society that values justice, respect, and dignity for all. I cannot, under any circumstances, live in this country ever again, even if given a Mansion and Ferrari. You can support me by buying my next book, that will be called something like "Racist Animal Crackers on Steroids, 22 Plus Years of Terrorism Book 2". All the money will be for another life on the other side of the world. Wait till you read what Satan has been up to, you won't believe what he did. Always remember, I haven't gotten caught in one lie, the truth is bad enough.